Cisco BGP-4 Command and Configuration Handbook

William R. Parkhurst, Ph.D., CCIE #2969

Cisco Press

Cisco Press
201 West 103rd Street
Indianapolis, IN 46290 USA

Cisco BGP-4 Command and Configuration Handbook

William R. Parkhurst, Ph.D., CCIE #2969

Copyright © 2001 Cisco Press

Cisco Press logo is a trademark of Cisco Systems, Inc.

Published by:
Cisco Press
201 West 103rd Street
Indianapolis, IN 46290 USA

Printed in the United States of America 2 3 4 5 6 7 8 9 0

Library of Congress Cataloging-in-Publication Number: 2001086613

ISBN: 1-58705-017-X

Warning and Disclaimer

This book is designed to provide information about Cisco IOS Software commands for Border Gateway Protocol Version 4 (BGP-4). Every effort has been made to make this book as complete and as accurate as possible, but no warranty or fitness is implied.

The information is provided on an "as is" basis. The author, Cisco Press, and Cisco Systems, Inc. shall have neither liability nor responsibility to any person or entity with respect to any loss or damages arising from the information contained in this book or from the use of the discs or programs that may accompany it.

The opinions expressed in this book belong to the author and are not necessarily those of Cisco Systems, Inc.

Trademark Acknowledgments

All terms mentioned in this book that are known to be trademarks or service marks have been appropriately capitalized. Cisco Press or Cisco Systems, Inc. cannot attest to the accuracy of this information. Use of a term in this book should not be regarded as affecting the validity of any trademark or service mark.

Feedback Information

At Cisco Press, our goal is to create in-depth technical books of the highest quality and value. Each book is crafted with care and precision, undergoing rigorous development that involves the unique expertise of members from the professional technical community.

Readers' feedback is a natural continuation of this process. If you have any comments regarding how we could improve the quality of this book, or otherwise alter it to better suit your needs, you can contact us through e-mail at feedback@ciscopress.com. Please make sure to include the book title and ISBN in your message.

We greatly appreciate your assistance.

Publisher	John Wait
Editor-In-Chief	John Kane
Cisco Systems Program Management	Michael Hakkert
	Tom Geiter
	William Warren
Production Manager	Patrick Kanouse
Development Editor	Christopher Cleveland
Production Editor	Marc Fowler
Copy Editor	Gayle Johnson
Technical Editors	Bill Wagner and Steve Wisniewski
Team Coordinator	Tammi Ross
Book Designer	Gina Rexrode
Cover Designer	Louisa Klucznik
Production Team	Publication Services
Indexer	Tim Wright
Proofreader	Bob LaRoche

CISCO SYSTEMS

Corporate Headquarters
Cisco Systems, Inc.
170 West Tasman Drive
San Jose, CA 95134-1706
USA
http://www.cisco.com
Tel: 408 526-4000
       800 553-NETS (6387)
Fax: 408 526-4100

European Headquarters
Cisco Systems Europe s.a.r.l.
Parc Evolic, Batiment L1/L2
16 Avenue du Quebec
Villebon, BP 706
91961 Courtaboeuf Cedex
France
http://www-europe.cisco.com
Tel: 33 1 69 18 61 00
Fax: 33 1 69 28 83 26

**American
Headquarters**
Cisco Systems, Inc.
170 West Tasman Drive
San Jose, CA 95134-1706
USA
http://www.cisco.com
Tel: 408 526-7660
Fax: 408 527-0883

Asia Headquarters
Nihon Cisco Systems K.K.
Fuji Building, 9th Floor
3-2-3 Marunouchi
Chiyoda-ku, Tokyo 100
Japan
http://www.cisco.com
Tel: 81 3 5219 6250
Fax: 81 3 5219 6001

Cisco Systems has more than 200 offices in the following countries. Addresses, phone numbers, and fax numbers are listed on
the Cisco Connection Online Web site at http://www.cisco.com/offices.

Argentina • Australia • Austria • Belgium • Brazil • Canada • Chile • China • Colombia • Costa Rica • Croatia • Czech Republic
• Denmark • Dubai, UAE Finland • France • Germany • Greece • Hong Kong • Hungary • India • Indonesia • Ireland • Israel
• Italy • Japan • Korea • Luxembourg • Malaysia • Mexico • The Netherlands • New Zealand • Norway • Peru • Philippines •
Poland • Portugal • Puerto Rico • Romania • Russia • Saudi Arabia • Singapore • Slovakia • Slovenia • South Africa • Spain •
Sweden • Switzerland • Taiwan • Thailand • Turkey • Ukraine • United Kingdom • United States • Venezuela

About the Author

William R. Parkhurst, Ph.D., CCIE #2969, is the manager of the CCIE Development group at Cisco Systems. The CCIE Development group is responsible for all new CCIE written qualification and laboratory exams. Prior to joining the CCIE team, Bill was a Consulting Systems Engineer supporting the Sprint Operation. Bill first became associated with Cisco Systems while he was a Professor of Electrical and Computer Engineering at Wichita State University. In conjunction with Cisco Systems, WSU established the first CCIE Preparation Laboratory.

About the Technical Reviewers

Bill Wagner works as a Cisco Certified Systems Instructor for Mentor Technologies. He has 22 years of computer programming and data communication experience. He has worked for corporations and companies such as Independent Computer Consultants, Numerax, McGraw-Hill, and Standard and Poors. His teaching experience started with the Chubb Institute, Protocol Interface, Inc., and Geotrain. Currently he teaches at Mentor Technologies.

Steve Wisniewski is a Systems Engineer for Fujitsu Network Communications. Steve has authored a book titled Network Administration from Prentice Hall and has edited several other Cisco Press books. Steve resides with his wife Ellen in East Brunswick, New Jersey.

Dedication

I would like to dedicate this book to all those who have been instrumental in my professional development and success. Without their help, guidance, and friendship my life would have taken a less rewarding path. There have been many individuals who have had a profound affect on my professional career but two stand out in my mind. I want to thank Dr. Everett L. Johnson, Chairman and Professor of Electrical and Computer Engineering at Wichita State University for being my mentor, teacher, and friend. Dr. "J" made my twelve years at Wichita State University rewarding and most importantly, fun. Finally, I want to thank Dr. Roy H. Norris, Professor and Chair Emeritus of Wichita State University for opening the door and letting me in.

Acknowledgments

Writing a book is never an easy endeavor. Without the help and guidance of John Kane, Editor-In-Chief, and Christopher Cleveland, Development Editor, of Cisco Press the task of writing this book would have been less enjoyable. John and Chris may have cracked the whip occasionally but it was always done with diplomacy and humor. I want to especially acknowledge my wife Debbie for her constant encouragement and for the wonderful job she did in proofreading the manuscript. The number of required corrections was minimal thanks to her efforts and attention to detail. Debbie made me look good in the eyes of my editor and for that I am thankful.

Contents at a Glance

Contents

Introduction

I have been involved with the world of networking from many directions. My experiences in education, network consulting, service provider support, and certification have shown me that there is a common thread that frustrates people in all of these arenas. That common thread is documentation. There are many factors that cause documentation to be frustrating but the most common are amount, clarity, and completeness. The amount of documentation available, especially in regards to BGP, can be overwhelming. For a person who is beginning to learn BGP, the question is "where do I begin"? There are very good books, RFCs, white papers, and command references available, but it is difficult to know where to start. The clarity of documentation depends on your personal situation. For a seasoned BGP designer the documentation may be clear and concise. To an individual preparing for a professional certification such as the CCIE the same documentation may be confusing. Even if the documentation is clear it is sometimes not complete. You may understand the words but be confused on the application. The purpose of this book is to provide a BGP handbook that is clear, concise, and complete. This book is not meant to be read from cover to cover. The way you use this book will depend on your objectives. If you are preparing for the CCIE written and lab exams then this book can be used as a laboratory guide to learn the purpose and proper use of every BGP command. If you are a network designer then this book can be used as a ready reference for any BGP command. In order to satisfy these varying audiences the structure of this book is reasonably simple. Each BGP command is illustrated using the following structure:

- Listing of the command structure and syntax
- Syntax description for the command with an explanation of all command parameters
- The purpose of the command and the situation where the command is used
- The first release of the IOS in which the command appeared
- One or more configuration examples to demonstrate the proper use of the command
- Procedures and examples to verify that the command is working properly
- How to troubleshoot the command when things are not working as intended.

The example scenarios that demonstrate the proper use of the BGP commands can be implemented on a minimum number of routers. This will allow you to learn each command without requiring an extensive and expensive lab configuration. The scenarios are presented so that the purpose and use of each command can be presented without clouding the issue. Some of the examples lead you into common non-working situations in order to reinforce the understanding of the operation of the particular BGP command.

For those of you who will use this book as a tool for preparing for the BGP component of the CCIE exam I would suggest that you read Appendix A, B, and C before diving into the various command examples. Appendix A is an overview of BGP operation and concepts. Appendix B is a review of regular expressions and their use with BGP. Appendix C covers the structure, logic, and use of route maps. Regular expressions and route maps tend to be areas where candidates typically run into trouble on the CCIE lab exam. My hope is that this handbook will help you prepare for the CCIE exam, allow you to properly use BGP in your network, or both.

Icons Used in This Book

Throughout the book, you will see the following icons used for networking devices:

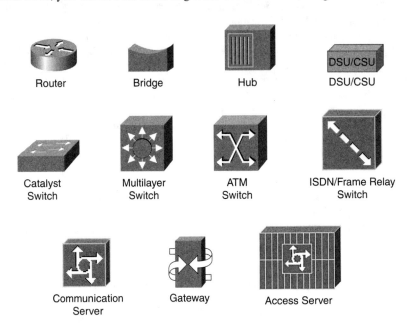

Throughout the book, you will see the following icons used for peripherals and other devices.

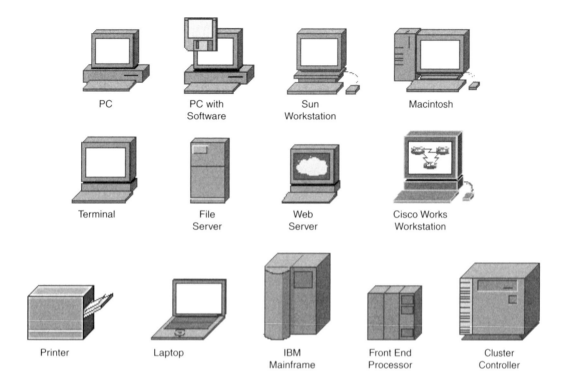

Throughout the book, you will see the following icons used for networks and network connections.

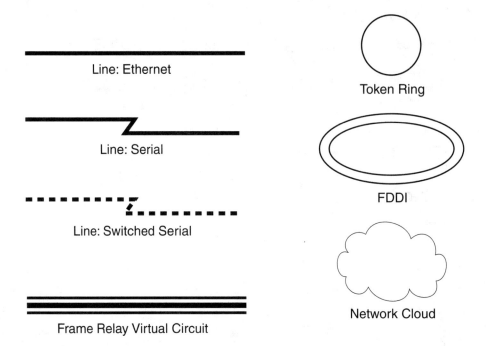

Command Syntax Conventions

The conventions used to present command syntax in this book are the same conventoins used in the IOS Command Reference. The Command Reference describes these conventions as follows:

- Vertical bars (|) separate alternative, mutually exclusive elements.
- Square brackets [ ] indicate optional elements.
- Braces { } indicate a required choice.
- Braces within brackets [{ }] indicate a required choice within an optional element.
- **Boldface** indicates commands and keywords that are entered literally as shown. In actual configuration examples and output (not general command syntax), boldface indicates commands that are manually input by the user (such as a **show** command).
- *Italics* indicate arguments for which you supply actual values.

CHAPTER 1

Route Aggregation

1-1: aggregate-address *address mask*

Syntax Description:

- *address*—Aggregate IP address.

- *mask*—Aggregate mask.

Purpose: To create an aggregate entry in the BGP table. An aggregate is created only if a more-specific route of the aggregate exists in the BGP table. This form of the **aggregate-address** command advertises the aggregate and all the more-specific routes that are part of the aggregate.

Cisco IOS Software Release: 10.0

Configuration Example 1: Aggregating Local Routes

For this example, we will aggregate locally sourced routes. In Figure 1-1, Router B aggregates the four networks 172.16.0.x through 172.16.3.x.

Figure 1-1   *Aggregating Locally Sourced Routes*

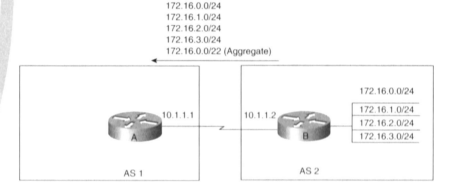

```
Router A
router bgp 1
neighbor 10.1.1.2 remote-as 2
```
```
Router B
interface loopback 0
 ip address 172.16.0.1 255.255.255.0
!
interface loopback 1
 ip address 172.16.1.1 255.255.255.0
!
interface loopback 2
 ip address 172.16.2.1 255.255.255.0
!
interface loopback 3
 ip address 172.16.3.1 255.255.255.0
!
router bgp 2
network 172.16.0.0 mask 255.255.255.0
network 172.16.1.0 mask 255.255.255.0
network 172.16.2.0 mask 255.255.255.0
network 172.16.3.0 mask 255.255.255.0
neighbor 10.1.1.1 remote-as 1
!
```

Four loopbacks have been created on Router B to simulate the locally sourced routes that will be aggregated. A BGP router can advertise an aggregate only if at least one specific route of the aggregate is in the BGP table. The BGP network commands are necessary on Router B in order to place more-specific routes of the aggregate into the BGP table. Before aggregating the loopback prefixes, verify that the specific routes are in the BGP tables on Routers A and B:

```
rtrA#show ip bgp
BGP table version is 16, local router ID is 172.17.1.1
Status codes: s suppressed, d damped, h history, * valid, > best, i - internal
Origin codes: i - IGP, e - EGP, ? - incomplete

   Network          Next Hop            Metric LocPrf Weight Path
*> 172.16.0.0/24    10.1.1.2                 0             0 2 i
*> 172.16.1.0/24    10.1.1.2                 0             0 2 i
*> 172.16.2.0/24    10.1.1.2                 0             0 2 i
*> 172.16.3.0/24    10.1.1.2                 0             0 2 i
```
```
rtrB#show ip  bgp
BGP table version is 6, local router ID is 172.16.3.1
Status codes: s suppressed, d damped, h history, * valid, > best, i - internal
Origin codes: i - IGP, e - EGP, ? - incomplete

   Network          Next Hop            Metric LocPrf Weight Path
*> 172.16.0.0/24    0.0.0.0                  0         32768 i
*> 172.16.1.0/24    0.0.0.0                  0         32768 i
*> 172.16.2.0/24    0.0.0.0                  0         32768 i
*> 172.16.3.0/24    0.0.0.0                  0         32768 i
```

Now modify the BGP configuration on Router B to enable the advertisement of the aggregate:

```
Router B
router bgp 2
 network 172.16.0.0 mask 255.255.255.0
 network 172.16.1.0 mask 255.255.255.0
 network 172.16.2.0 mask 255.255.255.0
 network 172.16.3.0 mask 255.255.255.0
 aggregate-address 172.16.0.0 255.255.252.0
 neighbor 10.1.1.1 remote-as 1
```

The configuration for Router B contains a **network** command for every prefix that is part of the aggregate. Because we need only one more-specific route in the BGP table in order to generate the prefix, we could have used only one **network** command. The problem with using only one **network** command is that if the network goes down, the more-specific route is withdrawn from the BGP table. If the only specific route in the BGP table is withdrawn, the aggregate is withdrawn as well. By using a **network** command for every prefix that is contained in the aggregate, the aggregate is advertised as long as one of the more-specific routes is up.

Verification

Verify that the aggregate address is in both the Router A and B BGP tables:

```
rtrA#show ip bgp
BGP table version is 18, local router ID is 172.17.1.1
Status codes: s suppressed, d damped, h history, * valid, > best, i - internal
Origin codes: i - IGP, e - EGP, ? - incomplete

   Network          Next Hop            Metric LocPrf Weight Path
*> 172.16.0.0/24    10.1.1.2                 0             0 2 i
*> 172.16.0.0/22    10.1.1.2                               0 2 i
*> 172.16.1.0/24    10.1.1.2                 0             0 2 i
*> 172.16.2.0/24    10.1.1.2                 0             0 2 i
*> 172.16.3.0/24    10.1.1.2                 0             0 2 I
rtrB#show ip bgp
BGP table version is 8, local router ID is 172.16.3.1
Status codes: s suppressed, d damped, h history, * valid, > best, i - internal
Origin codes: i - IGP, e - EGP, ? - incomplete

   Network          Next Hop            Metric LocPrf Weight Path
*> 172.16.0.0/24    0.0.0.0                  0         32768 i
*> 172.16.0.0/22    0.0.0.0                            32768 i
*> 172.16.1.0/24    0.0.0.0                  0         32768 i
*> 172.16.2.0/24    0.0.0.0                  0         32768 i
*> 172.16.3.0/24    0.0.0.0                  0         32768 i
```

Examine the specific information for the aggregate on Router A:

```
rtrA#show ip bgp 172.16.0.0 255.255.252.0
BGP routing table entry for 172.16.0.0/22, version 18
Paths: (1 available, best #1, table Default-IP-Routing-Table)
  Not advertised to any peer
  2, (aggregated by 2 172.16.3.1)
    10.1.1.2 from 10.1.1.2 (172.16.3.1)
      Origin IGP, localpref 100, valid, external, atomic-aggregate, best
```

Notice that the aggregate has the attribute **atomic-aggregate**. This indicates that the AS
information for the aggregate has been lost. This does not pose any problems in this
example, because the routes that comprise the aggregate and the aggregate itself originate
on the same router. The next example more clearly illustrates the **atomic aggregate**
attribute. Also notice that the aggregate for this example contains only the four prefixes
172.16.0.0/24 through 172.16.3.0/24. We could have used an aggregate with a shorter
mask. For example, we could use a 16-bit mask when forming the aggregate on Router B,
as shown in the following configuration. This is not recommended, though, because you are
aggregating routes that might not belong to you.

```
Router B
router bgp 2
  network 172.16.0.0 mask 255.255.255.0
  network 172.16.1.0 mask 255.255.255.0
  network 172.16.2.0 mask 255.255.255.0
  network 172.16.3.0 mask 255.255.255.0
  aggregate-address 172.16.0.0 255.255.0.0
  neighbor 10.1.1.1 remote-as 1
```

Verify that the aggregate is being advertised:

```
rtrB#show ip bgp
BGP table version is 20, local router ID is 172.17.1.1
Status codes: s suppressed, d damped, h history, * valid, > best, i - internal
Origin codes: i - IGP, e - EGP, ? - incomplete

   Network          Next Hop         Metric LocPrf Weight Path
*> 172.16.0.0/24    10.1.1.2              0          0 2 i
*> 172.16.0.0       10.1.1.2                         0 2 i
*> 172.16.1.0/24    10.1.1.2              0          0 2 i
*> 172.16.2.0/24    10.1.1.2              0          0 2 i
*> 172.16.3.0/24    10.1.1.2              0          0 2 i
```

Finally, examine the IP routing table on Router A:

```
rtrA#show ip route
Codes: C - connected, S - static, I - IGRP, R - RIP, M - mobile, B - BGP
       D - EIGRP, EX - EIGRP external, O - OSPF, IA - OSPF inter area
       N1 - OSPF NSSA external type 1, N2 - OSPF NSSA external type 2
```

(Continued)

```
        E1 - OSPF external type 1, E2 - OSPF external type 2, E - EGP
        i - IS-IS, L1 - IS-IS level-1, L2 - IS-IS level-2, * - candidate default
        U - per-user static route, o - ODR

Gateway of last resort is not set

     1.0.0.0/32 is subnetted, 1 subnets
C       1.1.1.1 is directly connected, Loopback0
     172.16.0.0/16 is variably subnetted, 5 subnets, 2 masks
B       172.16.0.0/16 [200/0] via 0.0.0.0, 00:03:01, Null0
C       172.16.0.0/24 is directly connected, Loopback1
C       172.16.1.0/24 is directly connected, Loopback2
C       172.16.2.0/24 is directly connected, Loopback3
C       172.16.3.0/24 is directly connected, Loopback4
     10.0.0.0/30 is subnetted, 1 subnets
C       10.1.1.0 is directly connected, Serial0
```

Notice that BGP automatically installs a route for the aggregate with a next hop of Null 0 into the IP routing table. Figure 1-2 illustrates the purpose of the route to Null 0.

Figure 1-2   *Route to Null 0 Is Needed to Prevent Routing Loops*

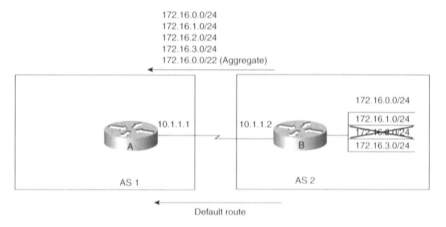

Assume that network 172.16.2.0/24 on Router B is down. Router B withdraws this route from the BGP table but still advertises the aggregate. Assume that Router B has a default route pointing to Router A and that there is no BGP route for 172.16.0.0/22 to Null 0 on Router B. When Router A receives an IP packet destined for 172.16.2.x, the packet is sent to Router B, because Router A has the aggregate 172.16.0.0/22 in its IP routing table. When Router B receives the packet, it inspects the IP routing table to determine how to route the packet. Because 172.16.2.0/24 is down, there is no route in the routing table. Router B sends the packet to the default route, which is toward Router A. When Router A receives the packet, it is sent back to B, and B sends it back to A. This process continues until the

TTL in the IP packet goes to 0. With the Null 0 route for 172.16.0.0/22 on Router B, the packet is simply dropped if network 172.16.2.0/24 is down.

Configuration Example 2: Aggregating Redistributed Routes

Instead of using the **network** command to place the more-specific routes in the BGP table, we could simply redistribute the connected routes and then aggregate them, as in Example 1. Modify the BGP configuration on Router B using redistribution instead of the **network** command. The **no auto-summary** command is needed to prevent the router from generating a classful summary of the 172.16.0.0/16 network (see Chapter 2, "Auto-Summary," for more information):

```
Router B
router bgp 2
  aggregate-address 172.16.0.0 255.255.252.0
  redistribute connected metric 20
  neighbor 10.1.1.1 remote-as 1
  no auto-summary
```

Verification

Inspect the BGP tables on Routers A and B to verify that the summary is being advertised:

```
rtrA#show ip bgp
BGP table version is 18, local router ID is 172.16.3.1
Status codes: s suppressed, d damped, h history, * valid, > best, i - internal
Origin codes: i - IGP, e - EGP, ? - incomplete

   Network          Next Hop          Metric LocPrf Weight Path
*  10.1.1.0/30      10.1.1.1             20            0 1 ?
*>                  0.0.0.0              20        32768 ?
*> 172.16.0.0/24    0.0.0.0              20        32768 ?
*> 172.16.0.0/22    0.0.0.0                      32768 i
*> 172.16.1.0/24    0.0.0.0              20        32768 ?
*> 172.16.2.0/24    0.0.0.0              20        32768 ?
*> 172.16.3.0/24    0.0.0.0              20        32768 ?
```

Configuration Example 3: Aggregating BGP Learned Routes

In Figure 1-3, Router A is learning the prefixes 172.16.0.0/24 through 172.16.3.0/24 from Router B. Because these routes are now in the BGP table on Router A, Router A can aggregate them into the 172.16.0.0/22 prefix.

Figure 1-3   *Aggregating BGP Learned Routes*

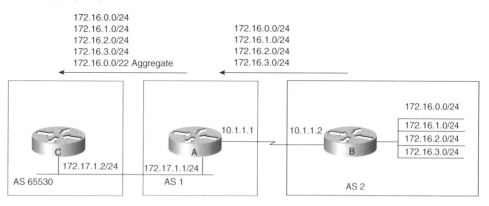

```
Router A
router bgp 1
 aggregate-address 172.16.0.0 255.255.252.0
 neighbor 10.1.1.2 remote-as 2
 neighbor 172.17.1.2 remote-as 65530
Router B
interface loopback 0
 ip address 172.16.0.1 255.255.255.0
 !
interface loopback 1
 ip address 172.16.1.1 255.255.255.0
 !
interface loopback 2
 ip address 172.16.2.1 255.255.255.0
 !
interface loopback 3
 ip address 172.16.3.1 255.255.255.0
 !
router bgp 2
network 172.16.0.0 mask 255.255.255.0
network 172.16.1.0 mask 255.255.255.0
network 172.16.2.0 mask 255.255.255.0
network 172.16.3.0 mask 255.255.255.0
 neighbor 10.1.1.1 remote-as 1
Router C
router bgp 65530
 neighbor 172.17.1.1 remote-as 1
```

Verification

The BGP tables on Routers A and C should now contain the aggregate address:

```
rtrA#show ip bgp
BGP table version is 6, local router ID is 172.17.1.1
Status codes: s suppressed, d damped, h history, * valid, > best, i - internal
Origin codes: i - IGP, e - EGP, ? - incomplete

   Network          Next Hop         Metric LocPrf Weight Path
*> 172.16.0.0/24    10.1.1.2              0             0 2 i
*> 172.16.0.0/22    0.0.0.0                           32768 i
*> 172.16.1.0/24    10.1.1.2              0             0 2 i
*> 172.16.2.0/24    10.1.1.2              0             0 2 i
*> 172.16.3.0/24    10.1.1.2              0             0 2 I
rtrC#show ip bgp
BGP table version is 32, local router ID is 172.17.1.2
Status codes: s suppressed, d damped, h history, * valid, > best, i - internal
Origin codes: i - IGP, e - EGP, ? - incomplete

   Network          Next Hop         Metric LocPrf Weight Path
*> 172.16.0.0/24    172.17.1.1                          0 1 2 i
*> 172.16.0.0/22    172.17.1.1                          0 1 i
*> 172.16.1.0/24    172.17.1.1                          0 1 2 i
*> 172.16.2.0/24    172.17.1.1                          0 1 2 i
*> 172.16.3.0/24    172.17.1.1                          0 1 2 i
```

Notice that in the BGP table on Router C, the path information for the specific routes is different from the path for the aggregate route. Router A is forming the aggregate, so it looks as though Router A "owns" this route. If you check the specific route information for the aggregate on Router C in the following output, you can see that the route carries the **atomic** attribute, signifying that there has been a loss of AS path information:

```
rtrC#show ip bgp 172.16.0.0 255.255.252.0
BGP routing table entry for 172.16.0.0/22, version 28
Paths: (1 available, best #1)
  Not advertised to any peer
  1, (aggregated by 1 172.17.1.1)
    172.17.1.1 from 172.17.1.1 (172.17.1.1)
      Origin IGP, localpref 100, valid, external, atomic-aggregate, best, ref 2
```

If you need to retain the AS path information for the aggregate, see section 1-3.

Configuration Example 4: Aggregating Using a Static Route

For the scenario in Figure 1-1, an aggregate could have been generated by creating a static route on Router B and then redistributing the static route into BGP:

```
Router B
router bgp 2
  redistribute static
  neighbor 10.1.1.1 remote-as 1
  no auto-summary
  !
ip route 172.16.0.0 255.255.252.0 Null0
```

Verification

Verify that the aggregate is being generated and advertised by checking the BGP tables on Routers A and B.

```
rtrA#show ip bgp
BGP table version is 18, local router ID is 172.17.1.1
Status codes: s suppressed, d damped, h history, * valid, > best, i - internal
Origin codes: i - IGP, e - EGP, ? - incomplete

   Network          Next Hop            Metric LocPrf Weight Path
*> 172.16.0.0/24    10.1.1.2                 0             0 2 i
*> 172.16.0.0/22    10.1.1.2                 0             0 2 ?
*> 172.16.1.0/24    10.1.1.2                 0             0 2 i
*> 172.16.2.0/24    10.1.1.2                 0             0 2 i
*> 172.16.3.0/24    10.1.1.2                 0             0 2 i
rtrB#show ip bgp
BGP table version is 6, local router ID is 172.16.3.1
Status codes: s suppressed, d damped, h history, * valid, > best, i - internal
Origin codes: i - IGP, e - EGP, ? - incomplete

   Network          Next Hop            Metric LocPrf Weight Path
*> 172.16.0.0/24    0.0.0.0                  0         32768 i
*> 172.16.0.0/22    0.0.0.0                  0         32768 ?
*> 172.16.1.0/24    0.0.0.0                  0         32768 i
*> 172.16.2.0/24    0.0.0.0                  0         32768 i
*> 172.16.3.0/24    0.0.0.0                  0         32768 i
```

Troubleshooting

Step 1 Verify that the BGP neighbors are in the Established state using the **show ip bgp neighbors** command.

If the neighbor relationship is not in the Established state, see section 8-23.

Step 2 Ensure that at least one specific route in the BGP table is contained in the range of addresses that you want to aggregate using the **show ip bgp** command.

Step 3   If at least one more-specific route is in the BGP table, go to Step 5.

Step 4   If at least one more-specific route is not in the BGP table, do the following:

— Check the syntax (address and mask) of your BGP **network** command. Go to Step 2.

— If you're redistributing routes (connected, static, or from an IGP), make sure you are using the **no auto-summary** command. Check the syntax of your redistribution command(s). Go to Step 2.

Step 5   Verify that no filters are blocking the aggregate from being advertised.

1-2: aggregate-address *address mask* as-set

Syntax Description:

- *address*—Aggregate IP address.
- *mask*—Aggregate mask.

Purpose: To create an aggregate entry in the BGP table. An aggregate is created only if a more-specific route of the aggregate exists in the BGP table. Without the **as-set** option, the AS path information for the specific routes forming the aggregate is lost. This form of the **aggregate-address** command advertises the aggregate while retaining the AS path information for the more-specific routes.

Cisco IOS Software Release: 10.0

Configuration Example: Forming an Aggregate Consisting of Prefixes from Different Autonomous Systems

In Figure 1-4, Router A is learning about networks 172.16.0.0/24 and 172.16.1.0/24 from AS 65530 and networks 172.16.2.0/24 and 172.16.3.0/24 from AS 2.

Figure 1-4   *Aggregate Consists of Routes Originated in Multiple Autonomous Systems*

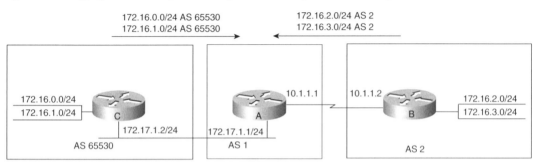

```
Router A
router bgp 1
 neighbor 10.1.1.2 remote-as 2
 neighbor 172.17.1.2 remote-as 65530
Router B
interface loopback 0
 ip address 172.16.2.1 255.255.255.0
 !
interface loopback 1
 ip address 172.16.3.1 255.255.255.0
 !
router bgp 2
network 172.16.2.0 mask 255.255.255.0
network 172.16.3.0 mask 255.255.255.0
neighbor 10.1.1.1 remote-as 1
Router C
interface loopback 0
 ip address 172.16.0.1 255.255.255.0
 !
interface loopback 1
 ip address 172.16.1.1 255.255.255.0
 !
router bgp 65530
network 172.16.0.0 mask 255.255.255.0
network 172.16.1.0 mask 255.255.255.0
neighbor 172.17.1.1 remote-as 1
 !
```

Four loopbacks have been created—two on Router B and two on Router C. A BGP router can advertise an aggregate only if at least one specific route of the aggregate is in the BGP table. The BGP **network** commands are necessary on Routers B and C in order to place more-specific routes of the aggregate into the BGP table. Before aggregating the loopback prefixes, verify that the specific routes are in the BGP tables on Routers A, B, and C:

```
rtrA#show ip bgp
BGP table version is 35, local router ID is 144.223.1.1
Status codes: s suppressed, d damped, h history, * valid, > best, i - internal
Origin codes: i - IGP, e - EGP, ? - incomplete

   Network          Next Hop          Metric LocPrf Weight Path
*> 172.16.0.0/24    172.17.1.2             0             0 65530 i
*> 172.16.1.0/24    172.17.1.2             0             0 65530 i
*> 172.16.2.0/24    10.1.1.2               0             0 2 i
*> 172.16.3.0/24    10.1.1.2               0             0 2 i
```
```
rtrB#show ip bgp
BGP table version is 13, local router ID is 172.16.3.1
Status codes: s suppressed, d damped, h history, * valid, > best, i - internal
Origin codes: i - IGP, e - EGP, ? - incomplete

   Network          Next Hop          Metric LocPrf Weight Path
*> 172.16.0.0/24    10.1.1.1                              0 1 65530 i
*> 172.16.1.0/24    10.1.1.1                              0 1 65530 i
*> 172.16.2.0/24    0.0.0.0                0         32768 i
*> 172.16.3.0/24    0.0.0.0                0         32768 I
```
```
rtrC#show ip bgp
BGP table version is 35, local router ID is 172.17.1.2
Status codes: s suppressed, d damped, h history, * valid, > best, i - internal
Origin codes: i - IGP, e - EGP, ? - incomplete

   Network          Next Hop          Metric LocPrf Weight Path
*> 172.16.0.0/24    0.0.0.0                0         32768 i
*> 172.16.1.0/24    0.0.0.0                0         32768 i
*> 172.16.2.0/24    172.17.1.1                            0 1 2 i
*> 172.16.3.0/24    172.17.1.1                            0 1 2 i
```

Now modify the BGP configuration on Router A to enable the advertisement of the aggregate:

```
Router A
router bgp 1
 aggregate-address 172.16.0.0 255.255.252.0
 neighbor 10.1.1.2 remote-as 2
 neighbor 172.17.1.2 remote-as 65530
```

The aggregate contains two routes from AS 65530 and two routes from AS 2. Router A should now be advertising the aggregate with itself as the next hop, indicating a loss of AS path information. The AS path information for the aggregate indicates that this prefix originates from AS 1. Routers B and C accept this route because their AS number does not appear in the AS_PATH attribute:

```
rtrA#show ip bgp
BGP table version is 6, local router ID is 144.223.1.1
Status codes: s suppressed, d damped, h history, * valid, > best, i - internal
Origin codes: i - IGP, e - EGP, ? - incomplete
```

(Continued)

```
   Network          Next Hop         Metric LocPrf Weight Path
*> 172.16.0.0/24    172.17.1.2          0              0 65530 i
*> 172.16.0.0/22    0.0.0.0                         32768 i
*> 172.16.1.0/24    172.17.1.2          0              0 65530 i
*> 172.16.2.0/24    10.1.1.2            0              0 2 i
*> 172.16.3.0/24    10.1.1.2            0              0 2 I

rtrA#show ip bgp 172.16.0.0 255.255.252.0
BGP routing table entry for 172.16.0.0/22, version 6
Paths: (1 available, best #1, table Default-IP-Routing-Table)
  Advertised to non peer-group peers:
  10.1.1.2 172.17.1.2
  Local, (aggregated by 1 144.223.1.1)
    0.0.0.0 from 0.0.0.0 (144.223.1.1)
      Origin IGP, localpref 100, weight 32768, valid, aggregated, local, atomic-
        aggregate, best
rtrB#show ip bgp
BGP table version is 8, local router ID is 172.16.3.1
Status codes: s suppressed, d damped, h history, * valid, > best, i - internal
Origin codes: i - IGP, e - EGP, ? - incomplete

   Network          Next Hop         Metric LocPrf Weight Path
*> 172.16.0.0/24    10.1.1.1                         0 1 65530 i
*> 172.16.0.0/22    10.1.1.1                         0 1 i
*> 172.16.1.0/24    10.1.1.1                         0 1 65530 i
*> 172.16.2.0/24    0.0.0.0             0           32768 i
*> 172.16.3.0/24    0.0.0.0             0           32768 I
rtrC#show ip bgp
BGP table version is 8, local router ID is 172.16.1.1
Status codes: s suppressed, d damped, h history, * valid, > best, i - internal
Origin codes: i - IGP, e - EGP, ? - incomplete

   Network          Next Hop         Metric LocPrf Weight Path
*> 172.16.0.0/24    0.0.0.0             0           32768 i
*> 172.16.0.0/22    172.17.1.1                        0 1 i
*> 172.16.1.0/24    0.0.0.0             0           32768 i
*> 172.16.2.0/24    172.17.1.1                        0 1 2 i
*> 172.16.3.0/24    172.17.1.1                        0 1 2 i
```

Now use the **as-set** option on Router A in order to preserve AS path information:

```
Router A
router bgp 1
aggregate-address 172.16.0.0 255.255.252.0 as-set
 neighbor 10.1.1.2 remote-as 2
 neighbor 172.17.1.2 remote-as 65530
```

Verification

Verify that the aggregate address is in the BGP table on Router A and that the AS path information has been retained:

```
rtrA#show ip bgp
BGP table version is 10, local router ID is 144.223.1.1
Status codes: s suppressed, d damped, h history, * valid, > best, i - internal
Origin codes: i - IGP, e - EGP, ? - incomplete

   Network          Next Hop         Metric LocPrf Weight Path
*> 172.16.0.0/24    172.17.1.2            0           0 65530 i
*> 172.16.0.0/22    0.0.0.0                         32768 {65530,2} i
*> 172.16.1.0/24    172.17.1.2            0           0 65530 i
*> 172.16.2.0/24    10.1.1.2             0           0 2 i
*> 172.16.3.0/24    10.1.1.2             0           0 2 i
```

The **as-set** option causes Router A to preserve the AS path information for the aggregate:

```
rtrA#show ip bgp 172.16.0.0/22
BGP routing table entry for 172.16.0.0/22, version 10
Paths: (1 available, best #1, table Default-IP-Routing-Table)
  Advertised to non peer-group peers:
  10.1.1.2 172.17.1.2
  {65530,2}, (aggregated by 1 144.223.1.1)
    0.0.0.0 from 0.0.0.0 (144.223.1.1)
      Origin IGP, localpref 100, weight 32768, valid, aggregated, local, atomic-
aggregate, best
```

Routers B and C should reject the aggregate because their AS number is now contained in the AS path attribute:

```
rtrB#show ip bgp
BGP table version is 9, local router ID is 172.16.3.1
Status codes: s suppressed, d damped, h history, * valid, > best, i - internal
Origin codes: i - IGP, e - EGP, ? - incomplete

   Network          Next Hop         Metric LocPrf Weight Path
*> 172.16.0.0/24    10.1.1.1                          0 1 65530 i
*> 172.16.1.0/24    10.1.1.1                          0 1 65530 i
*> 172.16.2.0/24    0.0.0.0              0         32768 i
*> 172.16.3.0/24    0.0.0.0              0         32768 I
rtrC#show ip bgp
BGP table version is 9, local router ID is 172.16.1.1
Status codes: s suppressed, d damped, h history, * valid, > best, i - internal
Origin codes: i - IGP, e - EGP, ? - incomplete

   Network          Next Hop         Metric LocPrf Weight Path
*> 172.16.0.0/24    0.0.0.0              0         32768 i
*> 172.16.1.0/24    0.0.0.0              0         32768 i
*> 172.16.2.0/24    172.17.1.1                        0 1 2 i
*> 172.16.3.0/24    172.17.1.1                        0 1 2 i
```

Troubleshooting

Step 1   Verify that the BGP neighbors are in the Established state using the **show ip bgp neighbors** command.

If the neighbor relationship is not in the Established state, see section 8-23.

Step 2   Ensure that at least one specific route in the BGP table is contained in the range of addresses that you want to aggregate using the **show ip bgp** command.

Step 3   If at least one more-specific route is in the BGP table, go to Step 5.

Step 4   If at least one more-specific route is not in the BGP table, do the following:

— Check the syntax (address and mask) of your BGP **network** command. Go to Step 2.

— If you're redistributing routes (connected, static, or from an IGP), make sure you are using the **no auto-summary** command. Check the syntax of your redistribution command(s). Go to Step 2.

Step 5   Verify that no filters are blocking the aggregate from being advertised.

Step 6   Verify the syntax of your route map and access list.

1-3: aggregate-address *address mask* as-set advertise-map *route-map-name*

Syntax Description:

- *address*—Aggregate IP address.

- *mask*—Aggregate mask.

- *route-map-name*—Route map used to determine the prefixes used to form the aggregate.

Purpose: To create an aggregate entry in the BGP table. An aggregate is created only if a more-specific route of the aggregate exists in the BGP table. Without the **as-set** option, the AS path information for the specific routes forming the aggregate is lost. This form of the **aggregate-address** command advertises the aggregate while retaining the AS path information for the more-specific routes. An **advertise-map** can be used to determine which AS path information is retained in the aggregate.

Cisco IOS Software Release: 10.0

Configuration Example: Forming an Aggregate Based on a Subset of Prefixes from Different Autonomous Systems

In Figure 1-5, Router A is learning about networks 172.16.0.0/24 and 172.16.1.0/24 from AS 65530 and networks 172.16.2.0/24 and 172.16.3.0./24 from AS 2. We will use the **advertise-map** option to base the aggregate on routes received from AS 65530.

Figure 1-5   *Aggregate Based on Routes from a Specific Autonomous System*

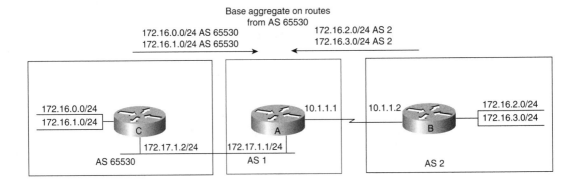

```
Router A
router bgp 1
 neighbor 10.1.1.2 remote-as 2
 neighbor 172.17.1.2 remote-as 65530
Router B
interface loopback 0
 ip address 172.16.2.1 255.255.255.0
!
interface loopback 1
 ip address 172.16.3.1 255.255.255.0
!
router bgp 2
network 172.16.2.0 mask 255.255.255.0
network 172.16.3.0 mask 255.255.255.0
neighbor 10.1.1.1 remote-as 1
Router C
interface loopback 0
 ip address 172.16.0.1 255.255.255.0
!
interface loopback 1
 ip address 172.16.1.1 255.255.255.0
!
router bgp 65530
network 172.16.0.0 mask 255.255.255.0
```

(Continued)
```
network 172.16.1.0 mask 255.255.255.0
neighbor 172.17.1.1 remote-as 1
!
```

Four loopbacks have been created—two on Router B and two on Router C. A BGP router can advertise an aggregate only if at least one specific route of the aggregate is in the BGP table. The BGP **network** commands are necessary on Routers B and C in order to place the routes into the BGP table. Before aggregating the loopback prefixes, verify that the specific routes are in the BGP table on Routers A, B, and C:

```
rtrA#show ip bgp
BGP table version is 35, local router ID is 172.17.1.1
Status codes: s suppressed, d damped, h history, * valid, > best, i - internal
Origin codes: i - IGP, e - EGP, ? - incomplete

   Network          Next Hop          Metric LocPrf Weight Path
*> 172.16.0.0/24    172.17.1.2             0            0 65530 i
*> 172.16.1.0/24    172.17.1.2             0            0 65530 i
*> 172.16.2.0/24    10.1.1.2               0            0 2 i
*> 172.16.3.0/24    10.1.1.2               0            0 2 i
rtrB#show ip bgp
BGP table version is 13, local router ID is 172.16.3.1
Status codes: s suppressed, d damped, h history, * valid, > best, i - internal
Origin codes: i - IGP, e - EGP, ? - incomplete

   Network          Next Hop          Metric LocPrf Weight Path
*> 172.16.0.0/24    10.1.1.1                       0 1 65530 i
*> 172.16.1.0/24    10.1.1.1                       0 1 65530 i
*> 172.16.2.0/24    0.0.0.0                0       32768 i
*> 172.16.3.0/24    0.0.0.0                0       32768 I
rtrC#show ip bgp
BGP table version is 35, local router ID is 172.17.1.2
Status codes: s suppressed, d damped, h history, * valid, > best, i - internal
Origin codes: i - IGP, e - EGP, ? - incomplete

   Network          Next Hop          Metric LocPrf Weight Path
*> 172.16.0.0/24    0.0.0.0                0       32768 i
*> 172.16.1.0/24    0.0.0.0                0       32768 i
*> 172.16.2.0/24    172.17.1.1                    0 1 2 i
*> 172.16.3.0/24    172.17.1.1                    0 1 2 i
```

Now modify the BGP configuration on Router A to enable the advertisement of the aggregate:

```
Router A
router bgp 1
 aggregate-address 172.16.0.0 255.255.252.0
  neighbor 10.1.1.2 remote-as 2
  neighbor 172.17.1.2 remote-as 65530
```

The aggregate contains two routes from AS 65530 and two routes from AS 2. Router A should now be advertising the aggregate with itself as the next hop, indicating a loss of AS path information. The AS path information for the aggregate indicates that this prefix originates from AS 1. Routers B and C accept this route because their AS number does not appear in the AS path attribute. Normal BGP behavior is to reject any update containing your own AS number.

```
rtrA#show ip bgp
BGP table version is 6, local router ID is 172.17.1.1
Status codes: s suppressed, d damped, h history, * valid, > best, i - internal
Origin codes: i - IGP, e - EGP, ? - incomplete

   Network          Next Hop          Metric LocPrf Weight Path
*> 172.16.0.0/24    172.17.1.2             0             0 65530 i
*> 172.16.0.0/22    0.0.0.0                          32768 i
*> 172.16.1.0/24    172.17.1.2             0             0 65530 i
*> 172.16.2.0/24    10.1.1.2               0             0 2 i
*> 172.16.3.0/24    10.1.1.2               0             0 2 I

rtrA#show ip bgp 172.16.0.0 255.255.252.0
BGP routing table entry for 172.16.0.0/22, version 6
Paths: (1 available, best #1, table Default-IP-Routing-Table)
  Advertised to non peer-group peers:
  10.1.1.2 172.17.1.2
  Local, (aggregated by 1 172.17.1.1)
    0.0.0.0 from 0.0.0.0 (172.17.1.1)
      Origin IGP, localpref 100, weight 32768, valid, aggregated, local, atomic-
      aggregate, best
rtrB#show ip bgp
BGP table version is 8, local router ID is 172.16.3.1
Status codes: s suppressed, d damped, h history, * valid, > best, i - internal
Origin codes: i - IGP, e - EGP, ? - incomplete

   Network          Next Hop          Metric LocPrf Weight Path
*> 172.16.0.0/24    10.1.1.1                            0 1 65530 i
*> 172.16.0.0/22    10.1.1.1                            0 1 i
*> 172.16.1.0/24    10.1.1.1                            0 1 65530 i
*> 172.16.2.0/24    0.0.0.0                0         32768 i
*> 172.16.3.0/24    0.0.0.0                0         32768 I
rtrC#show ip bgp
BGP table version is 8, local router ID is 172.16.1.1
Status codes: s suppressed, d damped, h history, * valid, > best, i - internal
Origin codes: i - IGP, e - EGP, ? - incomplete

   Network          Next Hop          Metric LocPrf Weight Path
*> 172.16.0.0/24    0.0.0.0                0         32768 i
*> 172.16.0.0/22    172.17.1.1                          0 1 i
*> 172.16.1.0/24    0.0.0.0                0         32768 i
*> 172.16.2.0/24    172.17.1.1                          0 1 2 i
*> 172.16.3.0/24    172.17.1.1                          0 1 2 i
```

Now use the **as-set** option on Router A in order to preserve AS path information.

```
Router A
router bgp 1
aggregate-address 172.16.0.0 255.255.252.0 as-set
 neighbor 10.1.1.2 remote-as 2
 neighbor 172.17.1.2 remote-as 65530
```

Verify that the AS path information has been preserved for the aggregate address on Router A:

```
rtrA#show ip bgp
BGP table version is 10, local router ID is 172.17.1.1
Status codes: s suppressed, d damped, h history, * valid, > best, i - internal
Origin codes: i - IGP, e - EGP, ? - incomplete

   Network          Next Hop            Metric LocPrf Weight Path
*> 172.16.0.0/24    172.17.1.2               0          0 65530 i
*> 172.16.0.0/22    0.0.0.0                         32768 {65530,2} i
*> 172.16.1.0/24    172.17.1.2               0          0 65530 i
*> 172.16.2.0/24    10.1.1.2                 0          0 2 i
*> 172.16.3.0/24    10.1.1.2                 0          0 2 i
```

The **as-set** option causes Router A to preserve the AS path information for the aggregate:

```
rtrA#show ip bgp 172.16.0.0/22
BGP routing table entry for 172.16.0.0/22, version 10
Paths: (1 available, best #1, table Default-IP-Routing-Table)
  Advertised to non peer-group peers:
  10.1.1.2 172.17.1.2
  {65530,2}, (aggregated by 1 172.17.1.1)
    0.0.0.0 from 0.0.0.0 (172.17.1.1)
      Origin IGP, localpref 100, weight 32768, valid, aggregated, local, atomic-
aggregate, best
```

Routers B and C should reject the aggregate, because their AS number is now contained in the AS path attribute:

```
rtrB#show ip bgp
BGP table version is 9, local router ID is 172.16.3.1
Status codes: s suppressed, d damped, h history, * valid, > best, i - internal
Origin codes: i - IGP, e - EGP, ? - incomplete

   Network          Next Hop            Metric LocPrf Weight Path
*> 172.16.0.0/24    10.1.1.1                            0 1 65530 i
*> 172.16.1.0/24    10.1.1.1                            0 1 65530 i
*> 172.16.2.0/24    0.0.0.0                  0      32768 i
*> 172.16.3.0/24    0.0.0.0                  0      32768 I
```

continues

(Continued)

```
rtrC#show ip bgp
BGP table version is 9, local router ID is 172.16.1.1
Status codes: s suppressed, d damped, h history, * valid, > best, i - internal
Origin codes: i - IGP, e - EGP, ? - incomplete

   Network          Next Hop         Metric LocPrf Weight Path
*> 172.16.0.0/24    0.0.0.0               0         32768 i
*> 172.16.1.0/24    0.0.0.0               0         32768 i
*> 172.16.2.0/24    172.17.1.1                       0 1 2 i
*> 172.16.3.0/24    172.17.1.1                       0 1 2 i
```

Assume that you want to advertise the aggregate to AS 2 but not to AS 65530. You can accomplish this by retaining AS 65530 in the AS path information for the aggregate while suppressing AS 2. The **advertise-map** option is used to achieve this behavior. Modify the BGP configuration on Router A so that the aggregate contains only AS path 65530:

```
Router A
router bgp 1
 aggregate-address 172.16.0.0 255.255.252.0 as-set advertise-map select-as
 neighbor 10.1.1.2 remote-as 2
 neighbor 172.17.1.2 remote-as 65530
 !
access-list 1 permit 172.16.0.0 0.0.0.255
access-list 1 permit 172.16.1.0 0.0.0.255
route-map select-as permit 10
 match as-path 1
```

The **route map select-as** permits only those routes that originated from AS 65530 to be used in forming the aggregate. Therefore, the aggregate AS path information contains only AS number 65530. We could use an IP as-path access filter to accomplish the same result:

```
router bgp 1
 aggregate-address 172.16.0.0 255.255.252.0 as-set advertise-map select-as
 neighbor 10.1.1.2 remote-as 2
 neighbor 172.17.1.2 remote-as 65530
 !
ip as-path access-list 1 permit ^65530$
 !
route-map select-as permit 10
 match as-path 1
```

Verification

Verify that the AS path information for the aggregate contains only AS path 65530:

```
rtrA#show ip bgp
BGP table version is 6, local router ID is 172.17.1.1
Status codes: s suppressed, d damped, h history, * valid, > best, i - internal
Origin codes: i - IGP, e - EGP, ? - incomplete
```

(Continued)

```
   Network          Next Hop          Metric LocPrf Weight Path
*> 172.16.0.0/24    172.17.1.2             0             0 65530 i
*> 172.16.0.0/22    0.0.0.0                          32768 65530 i
*> 172.16.1.0/24    172.17.1.2             0             0 65530 i
*> 172.16.2.0/24    10.1.1.2               0             0 2 i
*> 172.16.3.0/24    10.1.1.2               0             0 2 I

rtrA#show ip bgp 172.16.0.0/22
BGP routing table entry for 172.16.0.0/22, version 5
Paths: (1 available, best #1, table Default-IP-Routing-Table)
  Advertised to non peer-group peers:
  10.1.1.2 172.17.1.2
  65530, (aggregated by 1 172.17.1.1)
    0.0.0.0 from 0.0.0.0 (172.17.1.1)
      Origin IGP, localpref 100, weight 32768, valid, aggregated, local, atomic-
aggregate, best
```

Also verify that the aggregate is being accepted by Router B and rejected by Router C:

```
rtrB#show ip bgp
BGP table version is 34, local router ID is 172.16.3.1
Status codes: s suppressed, d damped, h history, * valid, > best, i - internal
Origin codes: i - IGP, e - EGP, ? - incomplete

   Network          Next Hop          Metric LocPrf Weight Path
*> 172.16.0.0/24    10.1.1.1                             0 1 65530 i
*> 172.16.0.0/22    10.1.1.1                             0 1 65530 i
*> 172.16.1.0/24    10.1.1.1                             0 1 65530 i
*> 172.16.2.0/24    0.0.0.0                0         32768 i
*> 172.16.3.0/24    0.0.0.0                0         32768 I
rtrC#show ip bgp
BGP table version is 25, local router ID is 172.16.1.1
Status codes: s suppressed, d damped, h history, * valid, > best, i - internal
Origin codes: i - IGP, e - EGP, ? - incomplete

   Network          Next Hop          Metric LocPrf Weight Path
*> 172.16.0.0/24    0.0.0.0                0         32768 i
*> 172.16.1.0/24    0.0.0.0                0         32768 i
*> 172.16.2.0/24    172.17.1.1                           0 1 2 i
*> 172.16.3.0/24    172.17.1.1                           0 1 2 i
```

Troubleshooting

Step 1   Verify that the BGP neighbors are in the Established state using the **show ip bgp neighbors** command.

If the neighbor relationship is not in the Established state, see section 8-23.

Step 2   Ensure that at least one specific route in the BGP table is contained in the range of addresses that you want to aggregate using the **show ip bgp** command.

Step 3   If at least one more-specific route is in the BGP table, go to Step 5.

Step 4   If there is not at least one more-specific route in the BGP table, do the following:

— Check the syntax (address and mask) of your BGP **network** command. Go to Step 2.

— If you're redistributing routes (connected, static, or from an IGP), make sure you are using the **no auto-summary** command. Check the syntax of your redistribution command(s). Go to Step 2.

Step 5   Verify that no filters are blocking the aggregate from being advertised.

Step 6   Verify the syntax of your route map and access list or AS path list.

1-4: aggregate-address *address mask* attribute-map *route-map-name*

1-5: aggregate-address *address mask* route-map *route-map-name*

Syntax Description:

- *address*—Aggregate IP address.
- *mask*—Aggregate mask.
- *route-map-name*—Route map used to modify the aggregate's attributes.

Purpose: To create an aggregate entry in the BGP table. An aggregate is created only if a more-specific route of the aggregate exists in the BGP table. This form of the **aggregate-address** command can be used to modify the aggregate's BGP attributes. The form of the command using the keyword **route-map** is equivalent to using the keyword **attribute-map**.

Cisco IOS Software Release: 10.0

Configuration Example: Modifying the Aggregate's Attributes

Figure 1-6 shows Router A learning two routes from Router B and two routes from Router C. Router B aggregates these four routes and modifies the aggregate's metric.

Figure 1-6   *An Attribute Map Is Used to Modify the Attributes of an Aggregate Route*

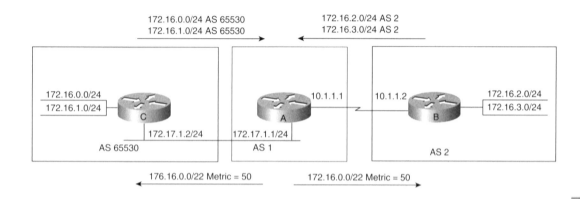

```
Router A
router bgp 1
 neighbor 10.1.1.2 remote-as 2
 neighbor 172.17.1.2 remote-as 65530
```
```
Router B
interface loopback 0
 ip address 172.16.2.1 255.255.255.0
!
interface loopback 1
 ip address 172.16.3.1 255.255.255.0
!
router bgp 2
network 172.16.2.0 mask 255.255.255.0
network 172.16.3.0 mask 255.255.255.0
neighbor 10.1.1.1 remote-as 1
```
```
Router C
interface loopback 0
 ip address 172.16.0.1 255.255.255.0
!
interface loopback 1
 ip address 172.16.1.1 255.255.255.0
!
router bgp 65530
network 172.16.0.0 mask 255.255.255.0
network 172.16.1.0 mask 255.255.255.0
neighbor 172.17.1.1 remote-as 1
!
```

Four loopbacks have been created—two on Router B and two on Router C. A BGP router can advertise an aggregate only if at least one specific route of the aggregate is in the BGP table. The BGP **network** commands are necessary on Routers B and C in order to place the routes into the BGP table. Before aggregating the loopback prefixes, you need to verify that the specific routes are in the BGP table on Routers A, B, and C:

```
rtrA#show ip bgp
BGP table version is 35, local router ID is 144.223.1.1
Status codes: s suppressed, d damped, h history, * valid, > best, i - internal
Origin codes: i - IGP, e - EGP, ? - incomplete

   Network          Next Hop           Metric LocPrf Weight Path
*> 172.16.0.0/24    172.17.1.2              0             0 65530 i
*> 172.16.1.0/24    172.17.1.2              0             0 65530 i
*> 172.16.2.0/24    10.1.1.2                0             0 2 i
*> 172.16.3.0/24    10.1.1.2                0             0 2 i
rtrB#show ip bgp
BGP table version is 13, local router ID is 172.16.3.1
Status codes: s suppressed, d damped, h history, * valid, > best, i - internal
Origin codes: i - IGP, e - EGP, ? - incomplete

   Network          Next Hop           Metric LocPrf Weight Path
*> 172.16.0.0/24    10.1.1.1                              0 1 65530 i
*> 172.16.1.0/24    10.1.1.1                              0 1 65530 i
*> 172.16.2.0/24    0.0.0.0                 0         32768 i
*> 172.16.3.0/24    0.0.0.0                 0         32768 I
rtrC#show ip bgp
BGP table version is 35, local router ID is 172.17.1.2
Status codes: s suppressed, d damped, h history, * valid, > best, i - internal
Origin codes: i - IGP, e - EGP, ? - incomplete

   Network          Next Hop           Metric LocPrf Weight Path
*> 172.16.0.0/24    0.0.0.0                 0         32768 i
*> 172.16.1.0/24    0.0.0.0                 0         32768 i
*> 172.16.2.0/24    172.17.1.1                            0 1 2 i
*> 172.16.3.0/24    172.17.1.1                            0 1 2 i
```

Now modify the BGP configuration on Router A to enable the advertisement of the aggregate and to verify that the aggregate is being advertised to Routers B and C:

```
Router A
router bgp 1
 aggregate-address 172.16.0.0 255.255.252.0
 neighbor 10.1.1.2 remote-as 2
 neighbor 172.17.1.2 remote-as 65530
```

Verify that the aggregate is being advertised:

```
rtrA#show ip bgp
BGP table version is 6, local router ID is 144.223.1.1
Status codes: s suppressed, d damped, h history, * valid, > best, i - internal
Origin codes: i - IGP, e - EGP, ? - incomplete
```

(Continued)

```
   Network          Next Hop           Metric LocPrf Weight Path
*> 172.16.0.0/24    172.17.1.2              0             0 65530 i
*> 172.16.0.0/22    0.0.0.0                           32768 i
*> 172.16.1.0/24    172.17.1.2              0             0 65530 i
*> 172.16.2.0/24    10.1.1.2                0             0 2 i
*> 172.16.3.0/24    10.1.1.2        0       0       2     I
rtrB#show ip bgp
BGP table version is 8, local router ID is 172.16.3.1
Status codes: s suppressed, d damped, h history, * valid, > best, i - internal
Origin codes: i - IGP, e - EGP, ? - incomplete

   Network          Next Hop           Metric LocPrf Weight Path
*> 172.16.0.0/24    10.1.1.1                          0 1 65530 i
*> 172.16.0.0/22    10.1.1.1                          0 1 i
*> 172.16.1.0/24    10.1.1.1                          0 1 65530 i
*> 172.16.2.0/24    0.0.0.0                 0       32768 i
*> 172.16.3.0/24    0.0.0.0                 0       32768 I
rtrC#show ip bgp
BGP table version is 8, local router ID is 172.16.1.1
Status codes: s suppressed, d damped, h history, * valid, > best, i - internal
Origin codes: i - IGP, e - EGP, ? - incomplete

   Network          Next Hop           Metric LocPrf Weight Path
*> 172.16.0.0/24    0.0.0.0                 0       32768 i
*> 172.16.0.0/22    172.17.1.1                        0 1 i
*> 172.16.1.0/24    0.0.0.0                 0       32768 i
*> 172.16.2.0/24    172.17.1.1                        0 1 2 i
*> 172.16.3.0/24    172.17.1.1                        0 1 2 i
```

Now use an **attribute-map** on Router A to modify the attribute's MED or metric:

```
Router A
router bgp 1
 aggregate-address 172.16.0.0 255.255.252.0 attribute-map attrib
 neighbor 10.1.1.2 remote-as 2
 neighbor 172.17.1.2 remote-as 65530
 !
route-map attrib permit 10
 set metric 50
```

Verification

Verify that the metric for the attribute has been modified:

```
rtrA#show ip bgp
BGP table version is 6, local router ID is 172.17.1.1
Status codes: s suppressed, d damped, h history, * valid, > best, i - internal
Origin codes: i - IGP, e - EGP, ? - incomplete
```

continues

(Continued)

```
     Network          Next Hop          Metric LocPrf Weight Path
 *> 172.16.0.0/24     172.17.1.2             0             0 65530 i
 *> 172.16.0.0/22     0.0.0.0               50         32768 i
 *> 172.16.1.0/24     172.17.1.2             0             0 65530 i
 *> 172.16.2.0/24     10.1.1.2               0             0 2 i
 *> 172.16.3.0/24     10.1.1.2               0             0 2 I
rtrB#show ip bgp
BGP table version is 60, local router ID is 172.16.3.1
Status codes: s suppressed, d damped, h history, * valid, > best, i - internal
Origin codes: i - IGP, e - EGP, ? - incomplete

     Network          Next Hop          Metric LocPrf Weight Path
 *> 172.16.0.0/24     10.1.1.1                             0 1 65530 i
 *> 172.16.0.0/22     10.1.1.1              50             0 1 i
 *> 172.16.1.0/24     10.1.1.1                             0 1 65530 i
 *> 172.16.2.0/24     0.0.0.0                0         32768 i
 *> 172.16.3.0/24     0.0.0.0                0         32768 I
rtrC#show ip bgp
BGP table version is 48, local router ID is 172.16.1.1
Status codes: s suppressed, d damped, h history, * valid, > best, i - internal
Origin codes: i - IGP, e - EGP, ? - incomplete

     Network          Next Hop          Metric LocPrf Weight Path
 *> 172.16.0.0/24     0.0.0.0                0         32768 i
 *> 172.16.0.0/22     172.17.1.1            50             0 1 i
 *> 172.16.1.0/24     0.0.0.0                0         32768 i
 *> 172.16.2.0/24     172.17.1.1                           0 1 2 i
 *> 172.16.3.0/24     172.17.1.1                           0 1 2 i
```

Troubleshooting

Step 1   Verify that the BGP neighbors are in the Established state using the **show ip bgp neighbors** command.

   If the neighbor relationship is not in the Established state, see section 8-23.

Step 2   Ensure that at least one specific route in the BGP table is contained in the range of addresses that you want to aggregate using the **show ip bgp** command.

Step 3   If at least one more-specific route is in the BGP table, go to Step 5.

Step 4   If there is not at least one more-specific route in the BGP table, do the following:

   — Check the syntax (address and mask) of your BGP **network** command. Go to Step 2.

— If you're redistributing routes (connected, static, or from an IGP), make sure you are using the **no auto-summary** command. Check the syntax of your redistribution command(s). Go to Step 2.

Step 5   Verify that no filters are blocking the aggregate from being advertised.

Step 6   Verify the syntax of your route map.

1-6: aggregate-address *address mask* summary-only

Syntax Description:

- *address*—Aggregate IP address.

- *mask*—Aggregate mask.

Purpose: To create an aggregate entry in the BGP table. An aggregate is created only if a more-specific route of the aggregate exists in the BGP table. This form of the **aggregate-address** command advertises the aggregate while suppressing all the more-specific routes.

Cisco IOS Software Release: 10.0

Configuration Example: Advertise an Aggregate While Suppressing the More-Specific Routes

In Figure 1-7, Router B is generating an aggregate for 172.16.0.0/22 while suppressing the specific routes that comprise the aggregate.

Figure 1-7   *Suppressing the Specific Routes of the Aggregate*

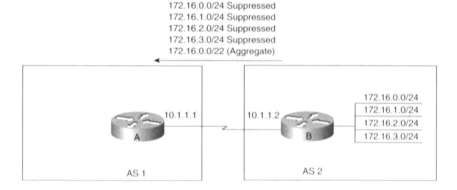

```
Router A
router bgp 1
neighbor 10.1.1.2 remote-as 2
```

```
Router B
interface loopback 0
 ip address 172.16.0.1 255.255.255.0
!
interface loopback 1
 ip address 172.16.1.1 255.255.255.0
!
interface loopback 2
 ip address 172.16.2.1 255.255.255.0
!
interface loopback 3
 ip address 172.16.3.1 255.255.255.0
!
router bgp 2
network 172.16.0.0 mask 255.255.255.0
network 172.16.1.0 mask 255.255.255.0
network 172.16.2.0 mask 255.255.255.0
network 172.16.3.0 mask 255.255.255.0
neighbor 10.1.1.1 remote-as 1
!
```

Four loopbacks have been created on Router B to simulate the locally sourced routes that
will be aggregated. A BGP router can advertise an aggregate only if at least one specific
route of the aggregate is in the BGP table. The BGP **network** commands are necessary on
Router B in order to place more-specific routes of the aggregate into the BGP table. Before
aggregating the loopback prefixes, you need to verify that the specific routes are in the BGP
tables on Routers A and B:

```
rtrA#show ip bgp
BGP table version is 16, local router ID is 172.17.1.1
Status codes: s suppressed, d damped, h history, * valid, > best, i - internal
Origin codes: i - IGP, e - EGP, ? - incomplete

   Network          Next Hop          Metric LocPrf Weight Path
*> 172.16.0.0/24    10.1.1.2               0             0 2 i
*> 172.16.1.0/24    10.1.1.2               0             0 2 i
*> 172.16.2.0/24    10.1.1.2               0             0 2 i
*> 172.16.3.0/24    10.1.1.2               0             0 2 i
```
```
rtrB#show ip bgp
BGP table version is 6, local router ID is 172.16.3.1
Status codes: s suppressed, d damped, h history, * valid, > best, i - internal
Origin codes: i - IGP, e - EGP, ? - incomplete

   Network          Next Hop          Metric LocPrf Weight Path
*> 172.16.0.0/24    0.0.0.0                0         32768 i
*> 172.16.1.0/24    0.0.0.0                0         32768 i
*> 172.16.2.0/24    0.0.0.0                0         32768 i
*> 172.16.3.0/24    0.0.0.0                0         32768 i
```

Now modify the BGP configuration on Router B to enable the advertisement of the aggregate while suppressing the more-specific routes:

```
Router B
router bgp 2
 network 172.16.0.0 mask 255.255.255.0
 network 172.16.1.0 mask 255.255.255.0
 network 172.16.2.0 mask 255.255.255.0
 network 172.16.3.0 mask 255.255.255.0
 aggregate-address 172.16.0.0 255.255.252.0 summary-only
 neighbor 10.1.1.1 remote-as 1
```

The configuration for Router B contains a **network** command for every prefix that is part of the aggregate. Because you need only one more-specific route in the BGP table in order to generate the prefix, you could use only one **network** command. The problem with using only one **network** command is that if the network goes down, the more-specific route is withdrawn from the BGP table. If the only specific route in the BGP table is withdrawn, the aggregate is withdrawn as well. If you use a **network** command for every prefix that is contained in the aggregate, the aggregate is advertised as long as one of the more-specific routes is up.

Verification

Verify that the aggregate address is in both the Router A and B BGP tables and that the more-specific routes have been suppressed:

```
rtrA#show ip bgp
BGP table version is 13, local router ID is 172.17.1.1
Status codes: s suppressed, d damped, h history, * valid, > best, i - internal
Origin codes: i - IGP, e - EGP, ? - incomplete

   Network          Next Hop  Metric  LocPrf  Weight  Path
*> 172.16.0.0/22    10.1.1.2  0                 2      I
rtrB#show ip bgp
BGP table version is 11, local router ID is 172.16.3.1
Status codes: s suppressed, d damped, h history, * valid, > best, i - internal
Origin codes: i - IGP, e - EGP, ? - incomplete

   Network            Next Hop         Metric LocPrf Weight Path
s> 172.16.0.0/24      0.0.0.0          0             32768 i
*> 172.16.0.0/22      0.0.0.0                        32768 i
s> 172.16.1.0/24      0.0.0.0          0             32768 i
s> 172.16.2.0/24      0.0.0.0          0             32768 i
s> 172.16.3.0/24      0.0.0.0          0             32768 i
```

Examine the specific information for one of the specific routes on Router B:

```
rtrB#show ip bgp 172.16.2.0
BGP routing table entry for 172.16.2.0/24, version 9
Paths: (1 available, best #1)
```

continues

Section 1-6

(Continued)

```
Advertisements of this net are suppressed by an aggregate.
  Not advertised to any peer
  Local
    0.0.0.0 from 0.0.0.0 (172.16.3.1)
      Origin IGP, metric 0, localpref 100, weight 32768, valid, sourced, local,
best, ref 2
```

Troubleshooting

Step 1   Verify that the BGP neighbors are in the Established state using the **show ip bgp neighbors** command.

> If the neighbor relationship is not in the Established state, see section 8-23.

Step 2   Ensure that at least one specific route in the BGP table is contained in the range of addresses that you want to aggregate using the **show ip bgp** command.

Step 3   If at least one more-specific route is in the BGP table, go to Step 5.

Step 4   If there is not at least one more-specific route in the BGP table, do the following:

> — Check the syntax (address and mask) of your BGP **network** command. Go to Step 2.

> — If you're redistributing routes (connected, static, or from an IGP), make sure you are using the **no auto-summary** command. Check the syntax of your redistribution command(s). Go to Step 2.

Step 5   Verify that no filters are blocking the aggregate from being advertised.

Step 6   Verify that the specific routes of the aggregate are being suppressed using the **show ip bgp** command.

1-7: aggregate-address *address mask* suppress-map *route-map-name*

Syntax Description:

- *address*—Aggregate IP address.
- *mask*—Aggregate mask.
- *route-map-name*—Name of the route map that is used to determine which specific prefixes will be suppressed.

Purpose: To create an aggregate entry in the BGP table. An aggregate is created only if a more-specific route of the aggregate exists in the BGP table. This form of the **aggregate-address** command advertises the aggregate while suppressing the more-specific routes indicated by the route map.

Cisco IOS Software Release: 10.0

Configuration Example: Suppressing a Subset of the More-Specific Routes Used to Form the Aggregate

In Figure 1-8, Router B is generating an aggregate for 172.16.0.0/22 while suppressing one of the more-specific prefixes.

Figure 1-8 *Suppressing Specific Prefixes*

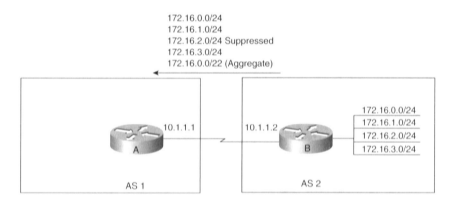

172.16.0.0/24
172.16.1.0/24
172.16.2.0/24 Suppressed
172.16.3.0/24
172.16.0.0/22 (Aggregate)

10.1.1.1   10.1.1.2

A   B

AS 1   AS 2

172.16.0.0/24
172.16.1.0/24
172.16.2.0/24
172.16.3.0/24

```
Router A
router bgp 1
neighbor 10.1.1.2 remote-as 2
Router B
interface loopback 0
 ip address 172.16.0.1 255.255.255.0
!
interface loopback 1
 ip address 172.16.1.1 255.255.255.0
!
interface loopback 2
 ip address 172.16.2.1 255.255.255.0
!
interface loopback 3
 ip address 172.16.3.1 255.255.255.0
!
router bgp 2
network 172.16.0.0 mask 255.255.255.0
network 172.16.1.0 mask 255.255.255.0
```

Section 1-7

continues

(Continued)

```
network 172.16.2.0 mask 255.255.255.0
network 172.16.3.0 mask 255.255.255.0
neighbor 10.1.1.1 remote-as 1
!
```

Four loopbacks have been created on Router B to simulate the locally sourced routes that will be aggregated. A BGP router can advertise an aggregate only if at least one specific route of the aggregate is in the BGP table. The BGP **network** commands are necessary on Router B in order to place more-specific routes of the aggregate into the BGP table. Before aggregating the loopback prefixes, you need to verify that the specific routes are in the BGP tables on Routers A and B:

```
rtrA#show ip bgp
BGP table version is 16, local router ID is 172.17.1.1
Status codes: s suppressed, d damped, h history, * valid, > best, i - internal
Origin codes: i - IGP, e - EGP, ? - incomplete

   Network          Next Hop          Metric LocPrf Weight Path
*> 172.16.0.0/24    10.1.1.2               0             0 2 i
*> 172.16.1.0/24    10.1.1.2               0             0 2 i
*> 172.16.2.0/24    10.1.1.2               0             0 2 i
*> 172.16.3.0/24    10.1.1.2               0             0 2 i
rtrB#show ip bgp
BGP table version is 6, local router ID is 172.16.3.1
Status codes: s suppressed, d damped, h history, * valid, > best, i - internal
Origin codes: i - IGP, e - EGP, ? - incomplete

   Network          Next Hop          Metric LocPrf Weight Path
*> 172.16.0.0/24    0.0.0.0                0          32768 i
*> 172.16.1.0/24    0.0.0.0                0          32768 i
*> 172.16.2.0/24    0.0.0.0                0          32768 i
*> 172.16.3.0/24    0.0.0.0                0          32768 i
```

Now modify the BGP configuration on Router B to enable the advertisement of the aggregate while suppressing the more-specific route 172.16.2.0/24:

```
Router B
router bgp 2
 network 172.16.0.0 mask 255.255.255.0
 network 172.16.1.0 mask 255.255.255.0
 network 172.16.2.0 mask 255.255.255.0
 network 172.16.3.0 mask 255.255.255.0
 aggregate-address 172.16.0.0 255.255.252.0 suppress-map suppress
 neighbor 10.1.1.1 remote-as 1
!
access-list 1 permit 172.16.2.0 0.0.0.255
route-map suppress permit 10
 match ip address 1
```

The form of the route map used permits routes to be suppressed. This example permits prefix 172.16.2.0/24 to be suppressed. The prefixes that are contained in the aggregate that are not specifically matched by the route map will not be suppressed.

Verification

Verify that the aggregate address is in both the Router A and B BGP tables and that the more-specific route 172.16.2.0/24 has been suppressed:

```
rtrA#show ip bgp
BGP table version is 29, local router ID is 172.17.1.1
Status codes: s suppressed, d damped, h history, * valid, > best, i - internal
Origin codes: i - IGP, e - EGP, ? - incomplete

   Network          Next Hop         Metric LocPrf Weight Path
*> 172.16.0.0/24    10.1.1.2              0             0 2 i
*> 172.16.0.0/22    10.1.1.2                            0 2 i
*> 172.16.1.0/24    10.1.1.2              0             0 2 i
*> 172.16.3.0/24    10.1.1.2              0             0 2 i
rtrB#show ip bgp
BGP table version is 7, local router ID is 172.16.3.1
Status codes: s suppressed, d damped, h history, * valid, > best, i - internal
Origin codes: i - IGP, e - EGP, ? - incomplete

   Network          Next Hop         Metric LocPrf Weight Path
*> 172.16.0.0/24    0.0.0.0              0          32768 i
*> 172.16.0.0/22    0.0.0.0                         32768 i
*> 172.16.1.0/24    0.0.0.0              0          32768 i
s> 172.16.2.0/24    0.0.0.0              0          32768 i
*> 172.16.3.0/24    0.0.0.0              0          32768 i
```

Examine the specific information for prefix 172.16.2.0/24 on Router B:

```
rtrB#show ip bgp 172.16.2.0
BGP routing table entry for 172.16.2.0/24, version 7
Paths: (1 available, best #1)
Advertisements of this net are suppressed by an aggregate.
  Not advertised to any peer
  Local
    0.0.0.0 from 0.0.0.0 (172.16.3.1)
      Origin IGP, metric 0, localpref 100, weight 32768, valid, sourced, local,
best, ref 2
```

Troubleshooting

Step 1 Verify that the BGP neighbors are in the Established state using the **show ip bgp neighbors** command.

If the neighbor relationship is not in the Established state, see section 8-23.

Step 2 Ensure that at least one specific route in the BGP table is contained in the range of addresses that you want to aggregate using the **show ip bgp** command.

Step 3 If at least one more-specific route is in the BGP table, go to Step 5.

Step 4 If there is not at least one more-specific route in the BGP table, do the following:

— Check the syntax (address and mask) of your BGP **network** command. Go to Step 2.

— If you're redistributing routes (connected, static, or from an IGP), make sure you are using the **no auto-summary** command. Check the syntax of your redistribution command(s). Go to Step 2.

Step 5 Verify that no filters are blocking the aggregate from being advertised.

Step 6 Verify the syntax of your route map and access list.

CHAPTER 2

Auto-Summary

2-1: auto-summary

Syntax Description:

This command has no arguments. **auto-summary** is enabled by default.

Purpose: When **auto-summary** is enabled, routes injected into BGP via redistribution are summarized on a classful boundary. A 32-bit IP address consists of a network address and a host address. The subnet mask determines the number of bits used for the network address and the number of bits used for the host address. The IP address classes have a natural or standard subnet mask, as shown in Table 2-1.

Table 2-1   *IP Address Classes*

Class	Address Range	Natural Mask
A	1.0.0.0 to 126.0.0.0	255.0.0.0 or /8
B	128.1.0.0 to 191.254.0.0	255.255.0.0 or /16
C	192.0.1.0 to 223.255.254.0	255.255.255.0 or /24

Reserved addresses include 128.0.0.0, 191.255.0.0, 192.0.0.0, and 223.255.255.0

When using the standard subnet mask, Class A addresses have one octet for the network, Class B addresses have two octets for the network, and Class C addresses have three octets for the network. As an example, consider the Class B address 156.26.32.1 with a 24-bit subnet mask. The 24-bit subnet mask selects three octets, 156.26.32, for the network. The last octet is the host address. If the network 156.26.32.1/24 is learned via an IGP and is then redistributed into BGP, the network is automatically summarized to the natural mask for a Class B network. The network that BGP advertises is 156.26.0.0/16. BGP is advertising that it can reach the entire Class B address space from 156.26.0.0 to 156.26.255.255. If the only network that can be reached via the BGP router is 156.26.32.0/24, BGP is advertising 254 networks that cannot be reached via this router.

auto-summary does not apply to routes injected into BGP via the **network** command or through IBGP or EBGP.

Cisco IOS Software Release: 10.0

Configuration Example: Automatic Route Summarization

This example demonstrates the effect of automatic route summarization. In Figure 2-1, static routes, connected routes, and routes learned via OSPF are being redistributed into BGP as shown in the following configurations. The redistributed routes are summarized to a classful boundary by BGP because **auto-summary** is enabled by default.

Figure 2-1   *Automatic BGP Route Summarization Applies Only to Redistributed Routes*

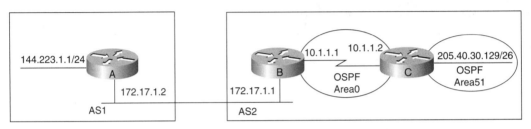

```
Router A
interface loopback 0
 ip address 144.223.1.1 255.255.255.0
 !
router bgp 1
 network 144.223.1.0 mask 255.255.255.0
 neighbor 172.17.1.1 remote-as 2
```
```
Router B
router ospf 1
 network 10.0.0.0 0.255.255.255 area 0
 !
router bgp 2
 redistribute ospf 1
 redistribute static
 redistribute connected
 neighbor 172.17.1.2 remote-as 1
 !
ip route 198.8.4.128 255.255.255.128 Ethernet 0
```
```
Router C
interface loopback 0
 ip address 205.40.30.129 255.255.255.192
 !
router ospf 1
 network 10.0.0.0 0.255.255.255 area 0
 network 205.0.0.0 0.255.255.255 area 51
```

On Router A, prefix 144.223.1.0/24 is being injected into BGP via the **network** command. If this prefix were automatically summarized to a classful boundary, the prefix in the BGP table would be 144.223.0.0/16. Because the **network** command was used to inject this route into BGP, summarization should not have occurred.

```
rtrA#show ip bgp
BGP table version is 14, local router ID is 144.223.1.1
Status codes: s suppressed, d damped, h history, * valid, > best, i - internal
Origin codes: i - IGP, e - EGP, ? - incomplete

   Network          Next Hop          Metric LocPrf Weight Path
*> 10.0.0.0         172.17.1.1             0             0 2 ?
*> 144.223.1.0/24   0.0.0.0                0         32768 i
*> 172.16.0.0       172.17.1.1             0             0 2 ?
*> 198.8.4.0        172.17.1.1             0             0 2 ?
*> 205.40.30.0      172.17.1.1             0             0 2 ?
```

Router B is learning about network 205.40.30.128 from router C via OSPF. Router B also has a route to network 198.8.4.128 via a static route, as shown in the IP routing table.

```
rtrB#show ip route
Codes: C - connected, S - static, I - IGRP, R - RIP, M - mobile, B - BGP
       D - EIGRP, EX - EIGRP external, O - OSPF, IA - OSPF inter area
       N1 - OSPF NSSA external type 1, N2 - OSPF NSSA external type 2
       E1 - OSPF external type 1, E2 - OSPF external type 2, E - EGP
       i - IS-IS, L1 - IS-IS level-1, L2 - IS-IS level-2, ia - IS-IS inter area
       * - candidate default, U - per-user static route, o - ODR
       P - periodic downloaded static route

Gateway of last resort is not set

     172.17.0.0/24 is subnetted, 1 subnets
C       172.17.1.0 is directly connected, Ethernet0/0
     172.16.0.0/24 is subnetted, 1 subnets
C       172.16.2.0 is directly connected, Loopback0
     144.223.0.0/24 is subnetted, 1 subnets
B       144.223.1.0 [20/0] via 172.17.1.2, 00:27:30
     10.0.0.0/30 is subnetted, 1 subnets
C       10.1.1.0 is directly connected, Serial2/0
     205.40.30.0/25 is subnetted, 1 subnets
O IA    205.40.30.128 [110/49] via 10.1.1.2, 00:00:12, Serial2/0
     198.8.4.0/25 is subnetted, 1 subnets
S       198.8.4.128 is directly connected, Ethernet0/0
```

The OSPF and static routes on Router B are being redistributed into BGP. **auto-summary** will summarize these prefixes to a classful boundary:

```
rtrB#show ip bgp
BGP table version is 12, local router ID is 172.16.2.1
Status codes: s suppressed, d damped, h history, * valid, > best, i - internal
Origin codes: i - IGP, e - EGP, ? - incomplete

   Network          Next Hop          Metric LocPrf Weight Path
*> 10.0.0.0         0.0.0.0                0         32768 ?
*> 144.223.1.0/24   172.17.1.2             0             0 1 i
*> 172.16.0.0       0.0.0.0                0         32768 ?
*> 198.8.4.0        0.0.0.0                0         32768 ?
*> 205.40.30.0      0.0.0.0                0         32768 ?
```

Router B advertises the 198.8.4.0 and 205.40.30.0 prefixes to Router A via BGP:

```
rtrA#show ip bgp
BGP table version is 14, local router ID is 144.223.1.1
Status codes: s suppressed, d damped, h history, * valid, > best, i - internal
Origin codes: i - IGP, e - EGP, ? - incomplete

   Network          Next Hop         Metric LocPrf Weight Path
*> 10.0.0.0         172.17.1.1            0             0 2 ?
*> 144.223.1.0/24   0.0.0.0              0         32768 i
*> 172.16.0.0       172.17.1.1            0             0 2 ?
*> 198.8.4.0        172.17.1.1            0             0 2 ?
*> 205.40.30.0      172.17.1.1            0             0 2 ?
```

auto-summary can cause routing problems if the advertising router does not own the entire summarized prefix. For example, if you redistribute only one subnet of a Class B address into BGP, BGP advertises the entire Class B address space if **auto-summary** is enabled. Typically, you want to disable **auto-summary** on your BGP routers. Modify the configuration on Router B so that **auto-summary** is disabled.

```
Router B
router bgp 2
 redistribute ospf 1
 redistribute static
 redistribute connected
 neighbor 172.17.1.2 remote-as 1
 no auto-summary
```

Verification

Verify that Router B is no longer creating summaries for the redistributed routes.

```
router B#show ip bgp
BGP table version is 20, local router ID is 172.16.2.1
Status codes: s suppressed, d damped, h history, * valid, > best, i - internal
Origin codes: i - IGP, e - EGP, ? - incomplete

   Network          Next Hop         Metric LocPrf Weight Path
*> 10.1.1.0/30      0.0.0.0              0         32768 ?
*> 144.223.1.0/24   172.17.1.2           0             0 1 i
*> 172.16.2.0/24    0.0.0.0              0         32768 ?
*> 198.8.4.128/25   0.0.0.0              0         32768 ?
*> 205.40.30.128/25 10.1.1.2            49         32768 ?
```

Troubleshooting

Step 1 Verify that the BGP neighbors are in the Established state using the **show ip bgp neighbors** command.

If the neighbor relationship is not in the Established state, see section 8-23.

Step 2 If routes are being redistributed into BGP, use the **no auto-summary** command. Verify that redistributed routes are not summarized to a classful boundary using the **show ip bgp** command.

CHAPTER 3

BGP-Specific Commands

3-1: bgp always-compare-med

Syntax Description:

This command has no arguments.

Purpose: If multiple BGP routes to the same destination exist, BGP selects the best path based on the route attributes in the following order:

1 Ignore a route if the next hop is not known.

2 Ignore IBGP routes that are not synchronized.

3 Prefer the route with the largest weight.

4 Prefer the route with the largest local preference.

5 Prefer the route that was locally originated.

6 Prefer the route with the shortest AS path.

If you're using **bgp bestpath as-path ignore**, skip this step. When you use the **as-set** option for aggregated routes, **as_set** counts as 1 regardless of the number of AS entries in the set. Confederation sub-AS numbers are not used to determine the AS-path length.

7 Prefer the route with the lowest origin (IGP < EGP < Incomplete).

8 Prefer the route with the lowest MED.

This comparison is only between routes advertised by the same external AS.

NOTE   If you're using **bgp always-compare-med**, compare MEDs for all paths. If used, this command needs to be configured on every BGP router in the AS.

If you're using **bgp bestpath med-confed**, the MEDs are compared only for routes that have an AS confederation sequence in their AS-PATH attribute.

If a prefix is received with no MED value, the prefix is assigned a MED value of 0. If you're using **bgp bestpath med missing-as-worst**, a prefix with a missing MED value is assigned a MED value of 4,294,967,294.

9 Prefer EBGP routes to IBGP routes.

10 Prefer the route with the nearest IGP neighbor.

11 Prefer the oldest route.

12 Prefer the path received from the router with the lowest router ID.

BGP normally does not compare MED values for routes from different autonomous systems. This command allows for the comparison of MED values for routes from different autonomous systems.

Cisco IOS Software Release: 11.0

Configuration Example: Comparing MED Values from Different Autonomous Systems

In Figure 3-1, Router B is learning about network 193.16.1.0/24 from Routers A and C. AS 4 is being simulated using loopbacks, a static route, and route maps.

Figure 3-1 *MEDs From Different Autonomous Systems Are Normally Not Compared*

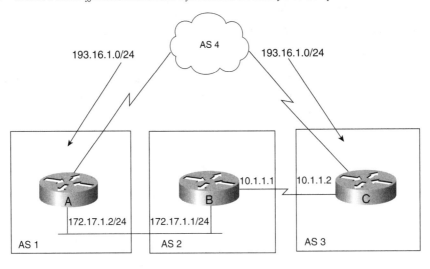

```
Router A
interface Loopback0
 ip address 5.5.5.5 255.255.255.255
 !
interface FastEthernet0
 ip address 172.17.1.2 255.255.255.0
 !
router bgp 1
 redistribute static route-map setmed
 neighbor 172.17.1.1 remote-as 2
 neighbor 172.17.1.1 route-map setas out
 no auto-summary
 !
ip route 193.16.1.0 255.255.255.0 Loopback0
route-map setmed permit 10
 set metric 200
route-map setmas permit 10
 set as-path prepend 4
```

```
Router B
interface Ethernet0/0
 ip address 172.17.1.1 255.255.255.0
 !
interface Serial2/0
 ip address 10.1.1.1 255.255.255.252
 clockrate 64000
 !
router bgp 2
 neighbor 10.1.1.2 remote-as 3
 neighbor 172.17.1.2 remote-as 1
```

```
Router C
interface Loopback1
 ip address 6.6.6.6 255.255.255.255
 !
interface Serial0
 ip address 10.1.1.2 255.255.255.252
 !
router bgp 3
 redistribute static route-map setmed
neighbor 10.1.1.1 remote-as 2
neighbor 10.1.1.1 route-map setas
no auto-summary
 !
route-map setmed permit 10
 set metric 100
route-map setas permit 10
 set as-path prepend 4
ip route 193.16.1.0 255.255.255.0 Loopback1
```

Router A is advertising network 193.16.1.0/24 with a metric or MED of 200, and Router C is advertising network 193.16.1.0/24 with a metric or MED of 100. Because Routers A and C are in different autonomous systems, Router B does not use the MED value to determine the best path. From the best path selection criteria, we can see that Router B uses the router

ID to determine the best path to 193.16.1.0/24. The BGP ID of a neighbor BGP router can be found by using the **show ip bgp neighbors** command. A router's own BGP ID can be found using the **show ip bgp summary** or **show ip bgp** commands.

```
rtrA#show ip bgp summary
BGP router identifier 5.5.5.5, local AS number 1
BGP table version is 3, main routing table version 3
1 network entries and 1 paths using 133 bytes of memory
1 BGP path attribute entries using 52 bytes of memory
0 BGP route-map cache entries using 0 bytes of memory
0 BGP filter-list cache entries using 0 bytes of memory
BGP activity 2/3 prefixes, 5/4 paths

Neighbor        V    AS MsgRcvd MsgSent   TblVer  InQ OutQ Up/Down  State/PfxRcd

172.17.1.1      4     2   122     123        3     0    0 01:45:46           0
rtrB#show ip bgp neighbors
BGP neighbor is 10.1.1.2,  remote AS 3, external link
  BGP version 4, remote router ID 6.6.6.6
  BGP state = Established, up for 01:49:19

BGP neighbor is 172.17.1.2,  remote AS 1, external link
  BGP version 4, remote router ID 5.5.5.5
  BGP state = Established, up for 01:46:44
rtrC#show ip bgp summary
BGP router identifier 6.6.6.6, local AS number 3
BGP table version is 3, main routing table version 3
1 network entries and 2 paths using 153 bytes of memory
2 BGP path attribute entries using 192 bytes of memory
BGP activity 1/0 prefixes, 3/1 paths

Neighbor        V    AS MsgRcvd MsgSent   TblVer  InQ OutQ Up/Down  State/PfxRcd

10.1.1.1        4     2   139     141        3     0    0 01:52:18           1
```

Router A has a lower router ID than Router C. If all other path selection criteria are equal, the route learned from Router A is used. Inspect the BGP table on Router B to ensure that 193.16.1.0/24 is being learned from both Routers A and C.

```
rtrB#show ip bgp
BGP table version is 3, local router ID is 172.17.1.1
Status codes: s suppressed, d damped, h history, * valid, > best, i - internal
Origin codes: i - IGP, e - EGP, ? - incomplete

   Network          Next Hop          Metric LocPrf Weight Path
*  193.16.1.0       10.1.1.2             100            0 3 4 ?
*>      172.17.1.2                       200            0 1 4 ?
```

The route learned from Router A should be installed in the IP routing table even though this route has a higher MED than the route learned from Router C.

```
rtrB#show ip route
Codes: C - connected, S - static, I - IGRP, R - RIP, M - mobile, B - BGP
       D - EIGRP, EX - EIGRP external, O - OSPF, IA - OSPF inter area
       N1 - OSPF NSSA external type 1, N2 - OSPF NSSA external type 2
       E1 - OSPF external type 1, E2 - OSPF external type 2, E - EGP
       i - IS-IS, L1 - IS-IS level-1, L2 - IS-IS level-2, ia - IS-IS inter area
       * - candidate default, U - per-user static route, o - ODR
       P - periodic downloaded static route

Gateway of last resort not set

     172.17.0.0/24 is subnetted, 1 subnets
C       172.17.1.0 is directly connected, Ethernet0/0
     172.16.0.0/24 is subnetted, 1 subnets
10.0.0.0/30 is subnetted, 1 subnets
C       10.1.1.0 is directly connected, Serial2/0
B    193.16.1.0/24 [20/200] via 172.17.1.2, 00:10:36
```

Modify the BGP configuration on Router B to allow the comparison of MED values from different autonomous systems.

```
Router B
router bgp 2
bgp always-compare-med
 neighbor 10.1.1.2 remote-as 3
 neighbor 172.17.1.2 remote-as 1
```

Verification

Verify that the best path to 193.16.1.0/24 has changed to the route with the lowest MED.

```
rtrB#show ip bgp
BGP table version is 4, local router ID is 172.17.1.1
Status codes: s suppressed, d damped, h history, * valid, > best, i - internal
Origin codes: i - IGP, e - EGP, ? - incomplete

   Network          Next Hop          Metric LocPrf Weight Path
*> 193.16.1.0       10.1.1.2             100            0 3 4 ?
*                   172.17.1.2           200            0 1 4 ?

rtrB#show ip route
Codes: C - connected, S - static, I - IGRP, R - RIP, M - mobile, B - BGP
       D - EIGRP, EX - EIGRP external, O - OSPF, IA - OSPF inter area
       N1 - OSPF NSSA external type 1, N2 - OSPF NSSA external type 2
       E1 - OSPF external type 1, E2 - OSPF external type 2, E - EGP
       i - IS-IS, L1 - IS-IS level-1, L2 - IS-IS level-2, ia - IS-IS inter area
       * - candidate default, U - per-user static route, o - ODR
       P - periodic downloaded static route

Gateway of last resort is not set

     172.17.0.0/24 is subnetted, 1 subnets
C       172.17.1.0 is directly connected, Ethernet0/0
```

continues

(Continued)

```
     172.16.0.0/24 is subnetted, 1 subnets
S       172.16.4.0 is directly connected, Serial2/0
     10.0.0.0/30 is subnetted, 1 subnets
C       10.1.1.0 is directly connected, Serial2/0
B    193.16.1.0/24 [20/100] via 10.1.1.2, 00:02:08
```

Troubleshooting

Step 1   Verify that the BGP neighbors are in the Established state using the **show ip bgp neighbors** command.

If the neighbor relationship is not in the Established state, see section 8-23.

Step 2   Make sure you understand the algorithm for route selection listed at the beginning of this section. A route with a lower MED might not be selected if other attributes with a higher precedence are used to select the best route.

3-2: bgp bestpath as-path ignore

Syntax Description:

This command has no arguments.

Purpose: If multiple BGP routes to the same destination exist, BGP selects the best path based on the route attributes in the following order:

1   Ignore a route if the next hop is not known.

2   Ignore IBGP routes that are not synchronized.

3   Prefer the route with the largest weight.

4   Prefer the route with the largest local preference.

5   Prefer the route that was locally originated.

6   Prefer the route with the shortest AS path.

If you're using **bgp bestpath as-path ignore**, skip this step. When you use the **as-set** option for aggregated routes, **as_set** counts as 1 regardless of the number of AS entries in the set. Confederation sub-AS numbers are not used to determine the AS-path length.

7   Prefer the route with the lowest origin (IGP < EGP < Incomplete).

8   Prefer the route with the lowest MED. This comparison is only between routes advertised by the same external AS.

If you're using **bgp always-compare-med**, compare MEDs for all paths. If used, this command needs to be configured on every BGP router in the AS.

If you're using **bgp bestpath med-confed**, the MEDs are compared only for routes that have an AS confederation sequence in their AS-path attribute.

If a prefix is received with no MED value, the prefix is assigned a MED value of 0. If you're using **bgp bestpath med missing-as-worst**, a prefix with a missing MED value is assigned a MED value of 4,294,967,294.

9 Prefer EBGP routes to IBGP routes.

10 Prefer the route with the nearest IGP neighbor.

11 Prefer the oldest route.

12 Prefer the path received from the router with the lowest router ID.

The shortest AS-path normally is used to select the best path if there are multiple routes to the same destination. This command allows the router to ignore AS-path information when making a best path determination.

Cisco IOS Software Release: 12.0

Configuration Example: Ignoring the AS-Path Attribute When Making a Best Path Selection

In Figure 3-2, Router B is learning about network 193.16.1.0/24 from Routers A and C. ASs 4 and 5 are simulated using loopbacks, a static route, and a route map. The simulated autonomous systems are used to create a longer AS-path attribute for the route being advertised by Router A.

Figure 3-2   *The AS-Path Attribute Is Normally Used to Make a Best Path Determination*

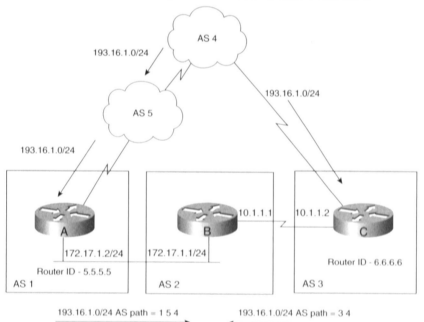

```
Router A
interface Loopback0
 ip address 5.5.5.5 255.255.255.255
 !
interface FastEthernet0
 ip address 172.17.1.2 255.255.255.0
 !
router bgp 1
 redistribute static
 neighbor 172.17.1.1 remote-as 2
 neighbor 172.17.1.1 route-map setas out
 no auto-summary
 !
ip route 193.16.1.0 255.255.255.0 Loopback0
route-map setas permit 10
 set as-path prepend 5 4
```
```
Router B
interface Ethernet0/0
 ip address 172.17.1.1 255.255.255.0
 !
interface Serial2/0
 ip address 10.1.1.1 255.255.255.252
 clockrate 64000
 !
router bgp 2
 neighbor 10.1.1.2 remote-as 3
 neighbor 172.17.1.2 remote-as 1
```
```
Router C
interface Loopback1
 ip address 6.6.6.6 255.255.255.255
 !
interface Serial0
 ip address 10.1.1.2 255.255.255.252
 !
router bgp 3
 redistribute static
 neighbor 10.1.1.1 remote-as 2
 neighbor 10.1.1.1 route-map setas out
 no auto-summary
 !
route-map setas permit 10
 set as-path prepend 4
ip route 193.16.1.0 255.255.255.0 Loopback1
```

Router A is advertising network 193.16.1.0/24 with an AS-path of 1 5 4, and Router C is advertising network 193.16.1.0/24 with an AS-path of 3 4. Router B selects the path for 193.16.1.0/24 from Router C as the best path because the AS-path is shorter than the AS-path from Router A.

```
rtrB#show ip bgp
BGP table version is 2, local router ID is 172.17.1.1
Status codes: s suppressed, d damped, h history, * valid, > best, i - internal
Origin codes: i - IGP, e - EGP, ? - incomplete

   Network          Next Hop          Metric LocPrf Weight Path
*  193.16.1.0       172.17.1.2             0               0 1 5 4 ?
*>                  10.1.1.2               0               0 3 4 ?

rtrB#show ip route
Codes: C - connected, S - static, I - IGRP, R - RIP, M - mobile, B - BGP
       D - EIGRP, EX - EIGRP external, O - OSPF, IA - OSPF inter area
       N1 - OSPF NSSA external type 1, N2 - OSPF NSSA external type 2
       E1 - OSPF external type 1, E2 - OSPF external type 2, E - EGP
       i - IS-IS, L1 - IS-IS level-1, L2 - IS-IS level-2, ia - IS-IS inter area
       * - candidate default, U - per-user static route, o - ODR
       P - periodic downloaded static route

Gateway of last resort is not set

     172.17.0.0/24 is subnetted, 1 subnets
C        172.17.1.0 is directly connected, Ethernet0/0
     172.16.0.0/24 is subnetted, 1 subnets
10.0.0.0/30 is subnetted, 1 subnets
C        10.1.1.0 is directly connected, Serial2/0
B    193.16.1.0/24 [20/0] via 10.1.1.2, 00:19:15
```

Modify the BGP configuration on Router B so that the AS-path is not used to make the best path selection.

```
Router B
router bgp 2
 bgp bestpath as-path ignore
 neighbor 10.1.1.2 remote-as 3
 neighbor 172.17.1.2 remote-as 1
```

Verification

Router A has a lower router ID than Router C. If all other path selection criteria are equal, the route learned from Router A is used. Because the AS-path attribute is being ignored, the best path should be toward Router A due to its lower router ID value. The router ID values can be found using the **show ip bgp** command on Routers A and C:

```
rtrA#show ip bgp
BGP table version is 5, local router ID is 5.5.5.5
Status codes: s suppressed, d damped, h history, * valid, > best, i - internal
Origin codes: i - IGP, e - EGP, ? - incomplete

   Network          Next Hop          Metric LocPrf Weight Path
*  193.16.1.0       172.17.1.1                         0 2 3 4 ?
*>                  0.0.0.0                0         32768 ?
```

continues

(Continued)

```
rtrC#show ip bgp
BGP table version is 3, local router ID is 6.6.6.6
Status codes: s suppressed, d damped, h history, * valid, > best, i - internal
Origin codes: i - IGP, e - EGP, ? - incomplete

   Network          Next Hop          Metric LocPrf Weight Path
*> 193.16.1.0       0.0.0.0                0          32768 ?
```

Verify that the best path to 193.16.1.0/24 has changed to the route advertised by Router A:

```
rtrB#show ip bgp
BGP table version is 2, local router ID is 172.17.1.1
Status codes: s suppressed, d damped, h history, * valid, > best, i - internal
Origin codes: i - IGP, e - EGP, ? - incomplete

   Network          Next Hop          Metric LocPrf Weight Path
* >193.16.1.0       172.17.1.2             0              0 1 5 4 ?
*                   10.1.1.2               0              0 3 4 ?

rtrB#show ip route
Codes: C - connected, S - static, I - IGRP, R - RIP, M - mobile, B - BGP
       D - EIGRP, EX - EIGRP external, O - OSPF, IA - OSPF inter area
       N1 - OSPF NSSA external type 1, N2 - OSPF NSSA external type 2
       E1 - OSPF external type 1, E2 - OSPF external type 2, E - EGP
       i - IS-IS, L1 - IS-IS level-1, L2 - IS-IS level-2, ia - IS-IS inter area
       * - candidate default, U - per-user static route, o - ODR
       P - periodic downloaded static route

Gateway of last resort is not set

     172.17.0.0/24 is subnetted, 1 subnets
C       172.17.1.0 is directly connected, Ethernet0/0
     172.16.0.0/24 is subnetted, 1 subnets
10.0.0.0/30 is subnetted, 1 subnets
C       10.1.1.0 is directly connected, Serial2/0
B    193.16.1.0/24 [20/0] via 172.17.1.2, 00:08:48
```

Troubleshooting

Step 1 Verify that the BGP neighbors are in the Established state using the **show ip bgp neighbors** command.

If the neighbor relationship is not in the Established state, see section 8-23.

Step 2 The BGP decision algorithm might determine the best path based on parameters that have a higher priority than AS-path (weight, local preference, and locally originated). Make sure you understand the BGP decision process.

3-3: bgp bestpath med confed

Syntax Description:

This command has no arguments.

Purpose: If multiple BGP routes to the same destination exist, BGP selects the best path based on the route attributes in the following order:

1 Ignore a route if the next hop is not known.

2 Ignore IBGP routes that are not synchronized.

3 Prefer the route with the largest weight.

4 Prefer the route with the largest local preference.

5 Prefer the route that was locally originated.

6 Prefer the route with the shortest AS path.

   If you're using **bgp bestpath as-path ignore**, skip this step. When you use the **as-set** option for aggregated routes, **as_set** counts as 1 regardless of the number of AS entries in the set. Confederation sub-AS numbers are not used to determine the AS-path length.

7 Prefer the route with the lowest origin (IGP < EGP < Incomplete).

8 Prefer the route with the lowest MED. This comparison is only between routes advertised by the same external AS.

   If you're using **bgp always-compare-med**, compare MEDs for all paths. If used, this command needs to be configured on every BGP router in the AS.

NOTE   If you're using **bgp bestpath med-confed**, the MEDs are compared only for routes that have an AS confederation sequence in their AS-path attribute.

   If a prefix is received with no MED value, the prefix is assigned a MED value of 0. If you're using **bgp bestpath med missing-as-worst**, a prefix with a missing MED value is assigned a MED value of 4,294,967,294.

9 Prefer EBGP routes to IBGP routes.

10 Prefer the route with the nearest IGP neighbor.

11 Prefer the oldest route.

12 Prefer the path received from the router with the lowest router ID.

This command allows the comparison of MEDs from BGP routers in a confederation.

Cisco IOS Software Release: 12.0

Configuration Example: BGP MED Comparison in a Confederation

In Figure 3-3, Router B is learning about network 150.150.150.0/24 from Routers A and D.

Figure 3-3 *Using MEDs with a BGP Confederation*

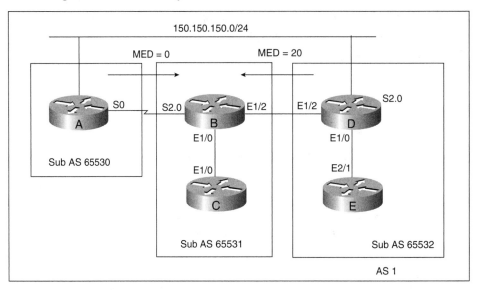

```
Router A
interface ethernet0
 ip address 150.150.150.1 255.255.255.0
!
interface Serial0
 ip address 193.16.0.2 255.255.255.252
!
router bgp 65530
 bgp confederation identifier 1
 bgp confederation peers 65531
 network 150.150.150.0 mask 255.255.255.0
 neighbor 193.16.0.1 remote-as 65531
!
Router B
interface Ethernet1/0
 ip address 172.16.0.1 255.255.255.252
!
interface Ethernet1/2
 ip address 172.16.0.17 255.255.255.252
!
interface Serial2/0
 ip address 193.16.0.1 255.255.255.252
 clockrate 64000
!
```

(Continued)

```
router bgp 65531
 bgp confederation identifier 1
 bgp confederation peers 65530 65532
 neighbor 172.16.0.2 remote-as 65531
 neighbor 172.16.0.18 remote-as 65532
 neighbor 193.16.0.2 remote-as 65530
```
```
Router D
interface Ethernet1/0
 ip address 172.16.0.14 255.255.255.252
!
interface Ethernet1/2
 ip address 172.16.0.18 255.255.255.252
!
interface Ethernet1/3
 ip address 150.150.150.2 255.255.255.0
!
interface Serial2/0
 ip address 193.16.0.9 255.255.255.252
 clockrate 64000
!
router bgp 65532
 bgp confederation identifier 1
 bgp confederation peers 65531
 network 150.150.150.0 mask 255.255.255.0
 neighbor 172.16.0.13 remote-as 65532
 neighbor 172.16.0.17 remote-as 65531
```

Router B is receiving an advertisement for network 150.150.150.0/24 from Routers A and D:

```
rtrB#show ip bgp
BGP table version is 6, local router ID is 172.16.88.4
Status codes: s suppressed, d damped, h history, * valid, > best, i - internal
Origin codes: i - IGP, e - EGP, ? - incomplete

   Network          Next Hop          Metric LocPrf Weight Path
*> 150.150.150.0/24 172.16.0.18            0    100      0 (65532) i
*                   193.16.0.2             0    100      0 (65530) i
```

The best-path algorithm has selected the route from Router D as the best. In order to demonstrate the comparison of MED values in a confederation, set the MED for routes from Router D to 20:

```
Router D
router bgp 65532
 neighbor 172.16.0.17 route-map setmed out
!
route-map setmed permit 10
 set metric 20
```

At this point, the MED values are not used in the best-path determination. Verify that the new MED value has been configured.

```
rtrB#show ip bgp
BGP table version is 6, local router ID is 172.16.88.4
Status codes: s suppressed, d damped, h history, * valid, > best, i - internal
Origin codes: i - IGP, e - EGP, ? - incomplete

   Network          Next Hop         Metric LocPrf Weight Path
*> 150.150.150.0/24 172.16.0.18          20    100      0 (65532) i
*                   193.16.0.2            0    100      0 (65530) i
```

Now modify the BGP configuration on Router B so that the MEDs from the confederation will be compared when determining the best path:

```
Router B
router bgp 2
 bgp bestpath med confed
```

Verification

Verify that the best-path algorithm has selected the route from Router A as the best due to a lower MED value:

```
rtrB#show ip bgp
BGP table version is 6, local router ID is 172.16.88.4
Status codes: s suppressed, d damped, h history, * valid, > best, i - internal
Origin codes: i - IGP, e - EGP, ? - incomplete

   Network          Next Hop         Metric LocPrf Weight Path
*  150.150.150.0/24 172.16.0.18          20    100      0 (65532) i
*>                  193.16.0.2            0    100      0 (65530) i
```

Troubleshooting

Step 1   Verify that the BGP neighbors are in the Established state using the **show ip bgp neighbors** command.

If the neighbor relationship is not in the Established state, see section 8-23.

Step 2   If the command **bgp bestpath med confed** does not produce the desired result, check the other path attributes, such as weight and local preference. The other attributes might be selecting the best path before MED values are compared.

3-4: bgp bestpath med missing-as-worst

Syntax Description:

This command has no arguments.

Purpose: If multiple BGP routes to the same destination exist, BGP selects the best path based on the route attributes in the following order:

1 Ignore a route if the next hop is not known.

2 Ignore IBGP routes that are not synchronized.

3 Prefer the route with the largest weight.

4 Prefer the route with the largest local preference.

5 Prefer the route that was locally originated.

6 Prefer the route with the shortest AS path.

   If using **bgp bestpath as-path ignore**, skip this step. When using the **as-set** option for aggregated routes, **as_set** counts as 1 regardless of the number of AS entries in the set. Confederation sub-AS numbers are not used to determine the AS-path length.

7 Prefer the route with the lowest origin (IGP < EGP < Incomplete).

8 Prefer the route with the lowest MED. This comparison is only between routes advertised by the same external AS.

   If you're using **bgp always-compare-med**, compare MEDs for all paths. If used, this command needs to be configured on every BGP router in the AS.

   If you're using **bgp bestpath med-confed**, the MEDs are compared only for routes that have an AS confederation sequence in their AS-path attribute.

   If a prefix is received with no MED value, the prefix is assigned a MED value of 0. If you're using **bgp bestpath med missing-as-worst**, a prefix with a missing MED value is assigned a MED value of 4,294,967,294.

9 Prefer EBGP routes to IBGP routes.

10 Prefer the route with the nearest IGP neighbor.

11 Prefer the oldest route.

12 Prefer the path received from the router with the lowest router ID.

By default, Cisco IOS Software sets the MED value to 0 for a prefix that does not have the MED value set. If all other attributes are equal, the route with a MED of 0 is considered the best. Using this command causes the router to consider prefixes with a missing MED to have a MED of infinity.

Cisco IOS Software Release: 12.0

Configuration Example: Comparing MEDs from Different Autonomous Systems

In Figure 3-4, Router B is learning about network 150.150.150.0/24 from Routers A and C. Router C is using a MED of 20, and Router A is not setting the MED value. By default, BGP sets the missing MED value to 0. Because Routers A and C are in different autonomous systems, the MED values for 150.150.150.0/24 are not compared. For this example, we will force Router B to compare the MED values using the command **bgp always-compare-med**.

Figure 3-4 *By Default, BGP Sets a Missing MED Value to 0*

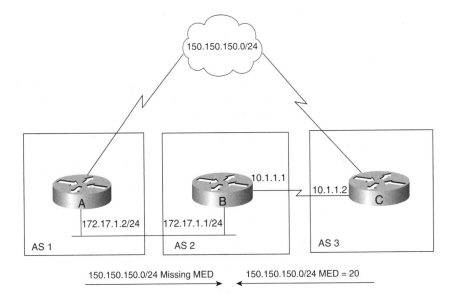

```
Router A
router bgp 1
 network 150.150.150.0 mask 255.255.255.0
 neighbor 172.17.1.1 remote-as 2
!
ip route 150.150.150.0 255.255.255.0 serial0
Router B
router bgp 2
 bgp always-compare-med
 neighbor 172.17.1.2 remote-as 1
 neighbor 10.1.1.2 remote-as 3
```

(Continued)

```
Router C
router bgp 3
 neighbor 10.1.1.1 route-map setmed out
 network 150.150.150.0 mask 255.255.255.0
 neighbor 10.1.1.1 remote-as 2
 neighbor 10.1.1.1 route-map setmed out
 !
ip route 150.150.150.0 255.255.255.0 serial1
 !
route-map setmed permit 10
 set metric 20
```

Router B is receiving an advertisement for network 150.150.150.0/24 from Routers A and C:

```
rtrB#show ip bgp
BGP table version is 3, local router ID is 172.16.2.1
Status codes: s suppressed, d damped, h history, * valid, > best, i - internal
Origin codes: i - IGP, e - EGP, ? - incomplete

   Network          Next Hop          Metric LocPrf Weight Path
*> 150.150.150.0/24 172.17.1.2            0               0 1 i
*                   10.1.1.2            20               0 3 I
```

The best-path algorithm has selected the route from Router A as the best because we are comparing MEDs. Router A does not send a MED value for network 150.150.150.0/24. By default, BGP sets the MED value for prefixes from Router A to 0.

Now modify the BGP configuration on Router B so that the missing MEDs are treated as infinity:

```
Router B
router bgp 2
 bgp bestpath med missing-as-worst
```

Verification

Verify that the best-path algorithm has selected the route from Router C as the best due to a lower MED value:

```
rtrB#show ip bgp
BGP table version is 3, local router ID is 172.16.2.1
Status codes: s suppressed, d damped, h history, * valid, > best, i - internal
Origin codes: i - IGP, e - EGP, ? - incomplete

   Network          Next Hop          Metric LocPrf Weight Path
*  150.150.150.0/24 172.17.1.2            0               0 1 i
*>                  10.1.1.2            20               0 3 i
```

Troubleshooting

Step 1   Verify that the BGP neighbors are in the Established state using the **show ip bgp neighbors** command.

If the neighbor relationship is not in the Established state, see section 8-23.

Step 2   If the command **bgp bestpath missing-as-worst** does not produce the desired result, check the other path attributes, such as weight and local preference. The other attributes might be selecting the best path before MED values are compared.

3-5: bgp client-to-client reflection

Syntax Description:

This command has no arguments.

Purpose: When a router is configured as a route reflector, client-to-client reflection is enabled by default. If the route reflector's clients are fully meshed, client-to-client reflection can be disabled on the route reflector using the **no** form of the command.

Cisco IOS Software Release: 11.1

Configuration Example: Route Reflectors and Peer Groups

An obvious question is why use a route reflector if the clients have a full IBGP mesh? If client-to-client reflection is enabled, the clients cannot be part of a peer group. Figure 3-5 demonstrates a situation in which we want to scale the IBGP connections using route reflectors, but we also want Routers A, B, and C to be part of the same peer group. Therefore, client-to-client reflection needs to be disabled on Router B. The total number of IBGP connections is still reduced, even though the clients are fully meshed. Routers B and D need to be configured as route reflectors. If B and D were not route reflectors, a full mesh would be required between all five routers. A route reflector is set up by configuring Routers A and C as route reflector clients on Router B. But because the clients are fully meshed, route reflection can be disabled on Router B.

Figure 3-5   *Route Reflectors and Peer Groups*

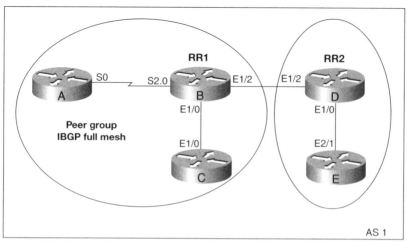

```
Router A
interface Serial0
 ip address 193.16.0.2 255.255.255.252†
 !
router eigrp 1
 network 193.16.0.0
 no auto-summary
 !
router bgp 1
 neighbor 193.16.0.1 remote-as 1
```
```
Router B
interface Ethernet1/0
 ip address 172.16.0.1 255.255.255.252
 !
interface Ethernet1/2
 ip address 172.16.0.17 255.255.255.252
 !
interface Serial2/0
 ip address 193.16.0.1 255.255.255.252
 clockrate 64000
 !
router eigrp 1
 network 172.16.0.0
 network 193.16.0.0
 no auto-summary
 !
```

continues

(Continued)

```
router bgp 1
 neighbor 172.16.0.18 remote-as 1
 no bgp client-to-client reflection
 neighbor group1 peer-group
 neighbor group1 remote-as 1
 neighbor group1 route-reflector-client
 neighbor 172.16.0.2 peer-group group1
 neighbor 193.16.0.2 peer-group group1
```

```
Router C
interface Ethernet1/0
 ip address 172.16.0.2 255.255.255.252
!
router eigrp 1
 network 172.16.0.0
 no auto-summary
!
router bgp 1
 neighbor 172.16.0.1 remote-as 1
 neighbor 193.16.0.2 remote-as 1
```

```
Router D
interface Ethernet1/0
 ip address 172.16.0.14 255.255.255.252
!
interface Ethernet1/2
 ip address 172.16.0.18 255.255.255.252
!
router eigrp 1
 network 172.16.0.0
 network 193.16.0.0
 no auto-summary
!
router bgp 1
 neighbor 172.16.0.13 remote-as 1
 neighbor 172.16.0.13 route-reflector-client
 neighbor 172.16.0.17 remote-as 1
```

```
Router E
interface Ethernet2/1
 ip address 172.16.0.13 255.255.255.252
!
router eigrp 1
 network 172.16.0.0
 no auto-summary
!
router bgp 1
 neighbor 172.16.0.14 remote-as 1
```

Verification

Verify that the neighbors have been configured in the proper peer group and that the route reflector is enabled:

```
rtrB#show ip bgp n
BGP neighbor is 172.16.0.2,  remote AS 1, internal link
 Member of peer-group group1 for session parameters
  BGP version 4, remote router ID 172.16.88.3
  BGP state = Established, up for 00:11:33
  Last read 00:00:34, hold time is 180, keepalive interval is 60 seconds
  Neighbor capabilities:
    Route refresh: advertised and received
    Address family IPv4 Unicast: advertised and received
  Received 115 messages, 0 notifications, 0 in queue
  Sent 110 messages, 0 notifications, 0 in queue
  Route refresh request: received 0, sent 0
  Minimum time between advertisement runs is 5 seconds

 For address family: IPv4 Unicast
  BGP table version 4, neighbor version 4
  Index 1, Offset 0, Mask 0x2
  Route-Reflector Client
  group1 peer-group member

BGP neighbor is 193.16.0.2,  remote AS 1, internal link
 Member of peer-group group1 for session parameters
  BGP version 4, remote router ID 193.16.0.2
  BGP state = Established, up for 00:12:07
  Last read 00:00:08, hold time is 180, keepalive interval is 60 seconds
  Neighbor capabilities:
    Route refresh: advertised
    Address family IPv4 Unicast: advertised and received
  Received 108 messages, 0 notifications, 0 in queue
  Sent 108 messages, 0 notifications, 0 in queue
  Route refresh request: received 0, sent 0
  Minimum time between advertisement runs is 5 seconds

 For address family: IPv4 Unicast
  BGP table version 4, neighbor version 4
  Index 1, Offset 0, Mask 0x2
  Route-Reflector Client
  group1 peer-group member
  0 accepted prefixes consume 0 bytes
  Prefix advertised 0, suppressed 0, withdrawn 0
```

Troubleshooting

Step 1   Verify that the BGP neighbors are in the Established state using the **show ip bgp neighbors** command.

If the neighbor relationship is not in the Established state, see section 8-23. For IBGP and loopbacks, see section 8-33.

Section 3-5

Step 2 Verify that the IBGP neighbors have been configured as route reflector clients and that they are in the proper peer group using the **show ip bgp neighbors** command.

Step 3 Verify that BGP client-to-client reflection has been disabled.

3-6: bgp cluster-id *32-bit_id*

Syntax Description:

32-bit_id—Route reflector cluster ID entered as either a 32-bit number or an IP address.

Purpose: EBGP loop detection is based on the AS-path attribute. If a BGP router receives an update from an EBGP peer containing the local AS number, the update is ignored. The AS-path method of loop detection does not work when you're using route reflectors, because the reflector and the clients are in the same AS. A route reflector generates an originator ID assigned from the router ID. When you're using multiple route reflectors, the route reflectors in the same cluster must be configured with the same ID, called the cluster ID. A cluster consists of the router reflectors and their clients. The cluster IDs contained in the cluster list are used for loop detection within the local AS when route reflectors are being used.

Cisco IOS Software Release: 11.0

Configuration Example: Redundant Route Reflectors

Figure 3-6 shows a cluster consisting of two clients and two route reflectors. Two route reflectors are configured for redundancy and therefore must have the same cluster ID.

Figure 3-6 *Redundant Route Reflectors*

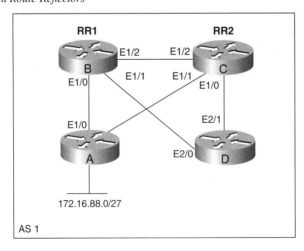

```
Router A
interface Loopback0
 ip address 172.16.88.3 255.255.255.224
 !
interface Ethernet1/0
 ip address 172.16.0.2 255.255.255.252
 !
interface Ethernet1/1
 ip address 172.16.0.9 255.255.255.252
 !
router eigrp 1
 network 172.16.0.0
 no auto-summary
 !
router bgp 1
 network 172.16.88.0 mask 255.255.255.224
 neighbor 172.16.0.1 remote-as 1
 neighbor 172.16.0.10 remote-as 1
```

```
Router B
interface Ethernet1/0
 ip address 172.16.0.1 255.255.255.252
 !
interface Ethernet1/1
 ip address 172.16.0.5 255.255.255.252
 !
interface Ethernet1/2
 ip address 172.16.0.17 255.255.255.252
 !
router eigrp 1
 network 172.16.0.0
 network 193.16.0.0
 no auto-summary
 !
router bgp 1
 bgp cluster-id 1
 neighbor 172.16.0.2 remote-as 1
 neighbor 172.16.0.2 route-reflector-client
 neighbor 172.16.0.6 remote-as 1
 neighbor 172.16.0.6 route-reflector-client
 neighbor 172.16.0.18 remote-as 1
```

```
Router C
interface Ethernet1/0
 ip address 172.16.0.14 255.255.255.252
 !
interface Ethernet1/1
 ip address 172.16.0.10 255.255.255.252
 !
interface Ethernet1/2
 ip address 172.16.0.18 255.255.255.252
 !
```

continues

Section 3-6

(Continued)

```
router eigrp 1
 network 10.0.0.0
 network 172.16.0.0
 network 193.16.0.0
 no auto-summary
!
router bgp 1
 bgp cluster-id 1
 neighbor 172.16.0.9 remote-as 1
 neighbor 172.16.0.9 route-reflector-client
 neighbor 172.16.0.13 remote-as 1
 neighbor 172.16.0.13 route-reflector-client
 neighbor 172.16.0.17 remote-as 1
```

```
Router D
interface Ethernet2/0
 ip address 172.16.0.6 255.255.255.252
!
interface Ethernet2/1
 ip address 172.16.0.13 255.255.255.252
!
router eigrp 1
 network 172.16.0.0
 no auto-summary
!
router bgp 1
 neighbor 172.16.0.5 remote-as 1
 neighbor 172.16.0.14 remote-as 1
```

Verification

Verify that Routers A and D are clients of Routers B and C:

```
rtrB#show ip bgp neighbor 172.16.0.2
BGP neighbor is 172.16.0.2,  remote AS 1, internal link
  BGP version 4, remote router ID 172.16.88.3
  BGP state = Established, up for 00:28:35
  Last read 00:00:36, hold time is 180, keepalive interval is 60 seconds
  Neighbor capabilities:
    Route refresh: advertised and received
    Address family IPv4 Unicast: advertised and received
  Received 32 messages, 0 notifications, 0 in queue
  Sent 31 messages, 0 notifications, 0 in queue
  Route refresh request: received 0, sent 0
  Minimum time between advertisement runs is 5 seconds

  For address family: IPv4 Unicast
  BGP table version 2, neighbor version 2
  Index 3, Offset 0, Mask 0x8
  Route-Reflector Client
  1 accepted prefixes consume 36 bytes
  Prefix advertised 0, suppressed 0, withdrawn 0
```

(Continued)

```
rtrB#show ip bgp neighbor 172.16.0.6
BGP neighbor is 172.16.0.6,  remote AS 1, internal link
  BGP version 4, remote router ID 172.16.2.1
  BGP state = Established, up for 00:32:22
  Last read 00:00:23, hold time is 180, keepalive interval is 60 seconds
  Neighbor capabilities:
    Route refresh: advertised and received
    Address family IPv4 Unicast: advertised and received
  Received 35 messages, 0 notifications, 0 in queue
  Sent 36 messages, 0 notifications, 0 in queue
  Route refresh request: received 0, sent 0
  Minimum time between advertisement runs is 5 seconds

 For address family: IPv4 Unicast
  BGP table version 2, neighbor version 2
  Index 1, Offset 0, Mask 0x2
  Route-Reflector Client
  0 accepted prefixes consume 0 bytes
  Prefix advertised 1, suppressed 0, withdrawn 0
```

Verify that the cluster ID has been configured:

```
rtrD#show ip bgp 172.16.88.0
BGP routing table entry for 172.16.88.0/27, version 3
Paths: (2 available, best #1, table Default-IP-Routing-Table)
  Not advertised to any peer
  Local
    172.16.0.2 (metric 307200) from 172.16.0.5 (172.16.88.3)
      Origin IGP, metric 0, localpref 100, valid, internal, synchronized, best
      Originator: 172.16.88.3, Cluster list: 0.0.0.1
  Local
    172.16.0.9 (metric 307200) from 172.16.0.14 (172.16.88.3)
      Origin IGP, metric 0, localpref 100, valid, internal, synchronized
      Originator: 172.16.88.3, Cluster list: 0.0.0.1
```

Troubleshooting

Step 1   Verify that the BGP neighbors are in the Established state using the **show ip bgp neighbors** command.

If the neighbor relationship is not in the Established state, see section 8-23. For IBGP and loopbacks, see section 8-33.

Step 2   Verify that the route reflector clients have been configured using the **show ip bgp neighbors** command.

Step 3   Verify that the same cluster ID has been configured on each route reflector in the cluster.

Section 3-6

3-7: bgp confederation identifier *AS-number*

3-8: bgp confederation peers *1_or_more_AS-numbers*

Syntax Description:

- *AS-number*—AS number used with EBGP neighbors.

- *1_or_more_AS-numbers*—AS number(s) of directly connected peers that are in a different sub-AS.

Purpose: IBGP neighbors do not propagate routing information learned from one IBGP neighbor to another IBGP neighbor. If you are running IBGP, every IBGP speaker must have a connection to every other IBGP speaker in the AS. This becomes a scaling problem as the number of IBGP speakers increases. The number of IBGP connections for n speakers is $[n(n-1)]/2$. Table 3-1 lists the number of connections needed for two to ten IBGP speakers.

Table 3-1   *IBGP Connections Needed for a Full Mesh*

Number of IBGP Speakers	Number of Connections
2	1
3	3
4	6
5	10
6	15
7	21
8	28
9	36
10	45

A confederation is one technique used to overcome the scaling issue with IBGP. The AS is divided into multiple subautonomous systems. Within a confederation sub-AS, a full IBGP mesh is required. BGP connections between confederations behave like EBGP peers, but they exchange routing information as if they were using IBGP. This means that the BGP attributes next hop, metric, and local preference are preserved. To an EBGP neighbor, the confederation appears as a single AS.

Cisco IOS Software Release: 10.3

Configuration Example: BGP Confederation

Autonomous system 1 in Figure 3-7 contains five BGP routers. For an IBGP full mesh, we would need ten IBGP connections. In order to reduce the number of BGP connections within the AS, a BGP confederation is used. AS 1 is divided into three subautonomous systems using AS numbers from the private AS range 64512 to 65535.

Figure 3-7   *BGP Confederation*

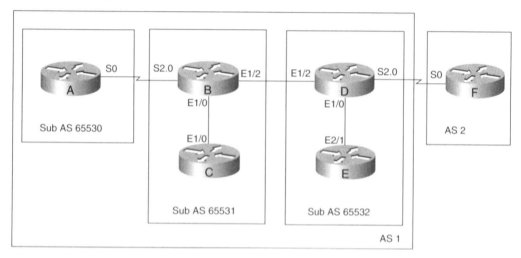

```
Router A
interface Serial0
 ip address 193.16.0.2 255.255.255.252
 !
router bgp 65530
 bgp confederation identifier 1
 bgp confederation peers 65531
 neighbor 193.16.0.1 remote-as 65531
Router B
interface Ethernet1/0
 ip address 172.16.0.1 255.255.255.252
 !
interface Ethernet1/2
 ip address 172.16.0.17 255.255.255.252
 !
interface Serial2/0
 ip address 193.16.0.1 255.255.255.252
 clockrate 64000
 !
```

Sections 3-7 – 3-8

continues

(Continued)

```
router bgp 65531
 bgp confederation identifier 1
 bgp confederation peers 65530 65532
 neighbor 172.16.0.2 remote-as 65531
 neighbor 172.16.0.18 remote-as 65532
 neighbor 193.16.0.2 remote-as 65530
Router C
interface Ethernet1/0
 ip address 172.16.0.2 255.255.255.252
!
router bgp 65531
 bgp confederation identifier 1
 neighbor 172.16.0.1 remote-as 65531
Router D
interface Ethernet1/0
 ip address 172.16.0.14 255.255.255.252
!
interface Ethernet1/2
 ip address 172.16.0.18 255.255.255.252
!
interface Serial2/0
 ip address 193.16.0.9 255.255.255.252
 clockrate 64000
!
router bgp 65532
 bgp confederation identifier 1
 bgp confederation peers 65531
 neighbor 172.16.0.13 remote-as 65532
 neighbor 172.16.0.17 remote-as 65531
 neighbor 193.16.0.10 remote-as 2
Router E
interface Ethernet2/1
 ip address 172.16.0.13 255.255.255.252
!
router bgp 65532
 bgp confederation identifier 1
 neighbor 172.16.0.14 remote-as 65532
Router F
interface Serial0
 ip address 193.16.0.10 255.255.255.252
!
router bgp 2
 neighbor 193.16.0.9 remote-as 1
```

The configuration of a BGP confederation is relatively straightforward. The BGP process number used for each router in the confederation is the AS number used to identify the sub-AS:

```
router bgp 65530, 65531, or 65532
```

Every router in the confederation is configured with the AS number that you want to use with EBGP peers   in this case, AS 1:

```
bgp confederation identifier 1
```

Finally, if a router has BGP connections to routers in a different sub-AS, you must use the **bgp confederation peers** command:

```
Router A
router bgp 65530
 bgp confederation peers 65531
```
```
Router B
router bgp 65531
 bgp confederation peers 65530 65532
```
```
Router D
router bgp 65532
 bgp confederation peers 65531
```

Routes advertised by BGP within the confederation carry the AS number of each sub-AS that the route advertisement has passed through. For example, create a loopback interface on Router A, and advertise this prefix in BGP:

```
Router A
interface loopback 0
 ip address 150.150.150.1 255.255.255.0
 !
router bgp 65530
 network 150.150.150.0 mask 255.255.255.0
```

Now trace the route through the confederation to Router F:

```
rtrA#show ip bgp
BGP table version is 33, local router ID is 193.16.0.2
Status codes: s suppressed, d damped, h history, * valid, > best, i - internal
Origin codes: i - IGP, e - EGP, ? - incomplete

   Network          Next Hop          Metric LocPrf Weight Path
*> 150.150.150.0/24 0.0.0.0               0         32768 I
```
```
rtrB#show ip bgp
BGP table version is 6, local router ID is 172.16.88.4
Status codes: s suppressed, d damped, h history, * valid, > best, i - internal
Origin codes: i - IGP, e - EGP, ? - incomplete

   Network          Next Hop          Metric LocPrf Weight Path
*> 150.150.150.0/24 193.16.0.2           20    100      0 (65530) I
```
```
rtrD#show ip bgp
BGP table version is 10, local router ID is 172.16.88.1
Status codes: s suppressed, d damped, h history, * valid, > best, i - internal
Origin codes: i - IGP, e - EGP, ? - incomplete

   Network          Next Hop          Metric LocPrf Weight Path
*> 150.150.150.0/24 193.16.0.2           20    100      0 (65531 65530) I
```

continues

Sections 3-7 – 3-8

(Continued)

```
rtrF#show ip bgp
BGP table version is 23, local router ID is 193.16.0.10
Status codes: s suppressed, d damped, h history, * valid, > best, i - internal
Origin codes: i - IGP, e - EGP, ? - incomplete

  Network          Next Hop          Metric LocPrf Weight Path
*> 150.150.150.0/24 193.16.0.9                          0 1 i
```

Within the confederation, each sub-AS that the route has traversed is contained in the AS-path attribute. Outside the confederation, the AS-path attribute contains only the AS number of the confederation identifier.

Verification

Examine the neighbor relationship between BGP routers in a different sub-AS. For this case, we will examine the relationship between Routers A and B:

```
rtrA#show ip bgp neighbors
BGP neighbor is 193.16.0.1,  remote AS 65531, external link
  Index 1, Offset 0, Mask 0x2
  BGP version 4, remote router ID 172.16.88.4
  Neighbor under common administration
  BGP state = Established, table version = 30, up for 00:58:23
  Last read 00:00:24, hold time is 180, keepalive interval is 60 seconds
rtrB#show ip bgp neighbors 193.16.0.2
BGP neighbor is 193.16.0.2,  remote AS 65530, external link
  BGP version 4, remote router ID 193.16.0.2
  Neighbor under common administration
  BGP state = Established, up for 01:05:34
  Last read 00:00:34, hold time is 180, keepalive interval is 60 seconds
```

The BGP neighbor relationship between Routers A and B is external because they are in a different sub-AS. The neighbors are under a common administration because they are confederation peers. The BGP relationship between neighbors in the same sub-AS is a normal IBGP relationship, as shown by the output for Routers B and C:

```
rtrB#show ip bgp neighbors 172.16.0.2
BGP neighbor is 172.16.0.2,  remote AS 65531, internal link
  BGP version 4, remote router ID 172.16.88.3
  BGP state = Established, up for 01:09:25
  Last read 00:00:25, hold time is 180, keepalive interval is 60 seconds
rtrC#show ip bgp neighbors
BGP neighbor is 172.16.0.1,  remote AS 65531, internal link
  BGP version 4, remote router ID 172.16.88.4
  BGP state = Established, up for 01:10:50
  Last read 00:00:50, hold time is 180, keepalive interval is 60 seconds
```

Finally, examine the relationship between Routers D and F:

```
rtrD#show ip bgp neighbors 193.16.0.10
BGP neighbor is 193.16.0.10,  remote AS 2, external link
  BGP version 4, remote router ID 193.16.0.10
  BGP state = Established, up for 1d02h
  Last read 00:00:15, hold time is 180, keepalive interval is 60 seconds
rtrF#show ip bgp neighbors
BGP neighbor is 193.16.0.9,  remote AS 1, external link
  Index 1, Offset 0, Mask 0x2
  BGP version 4, remote router ID 172.16.88.1
  BGP state = Established, table version = 21, up for 1d02h
  Last read 00:00:09, hold time is 180, keepalive interval is 60 seconds
```

Router F sees router D as belonging to AS 1, the confederation identifier. The sub-AS numbers are hidden from true external peers.

Troubleshooting

Step 1   Verify that the BGP neighbors are in the Established state using the **show ip bgp neighbors** command.

If the neighbor relationship is not in the Established state, see section 8-23. For IBGP and loopbacks, see section 8-33.

Step 2   Verify the syntax of the confederation commands. Each router in the confederation should use the command **bgp confederation identifier** *as-number*. BGP connections between subautonomous systems should use the command **bgp confederation peers** *1_or_more_AS-numbers*.

3-9: bgp dampening

3-10: bgp dampening *half-life*

3-11: bgp dampening *half-life reuse suppress max-suppress-time*

3-12: bgp dampening route-map *route-map-name*

Syntax Description:

- *half-life*—Time for the penalty to decrease to one-half of its current value. The range of values is 1 to 45 minutes. The default is 15 minutes.

- *reuse*—When the penalty for a suppressed route decays below the *reuse* value, the route becomes unsuppressed. The range of values is 1 to 20,000. The default value is 750.

- *suppress*—When the penalty for a route exceeds the *suppress* value, the route is suppressed. The range of values is 1 to 20,000. The default value is 2000.

- *max-suppress-time*—Maximum time that a dampened route is suppressed. The range of values is 1 to 255 minutes. The default value is four times the *half-life* value.

- *route-map-name*—Name of the route map used to select prefixes and dampening parameters.

Purpose: A route flap occurs when a prefix transitions from the up to the down state. When the prefix goes from up to down, BGP must send a WITHDRAWN message. When the prefix goes from down to up, BGP sends an UPDATE message. If the prefix is constantly flapping, this can cause high CPU utilization while the BGP routes are converging. Additionally, if you are redistributing BGP into your IGP, the flapping route can cause instability in the IGP. Dampening is a method to control the effect of a flapping route. The mechanics of route dampening are illustrated in Figure 3-8.

Figure 3-8   *BGP Dampening Parameters and Operation*

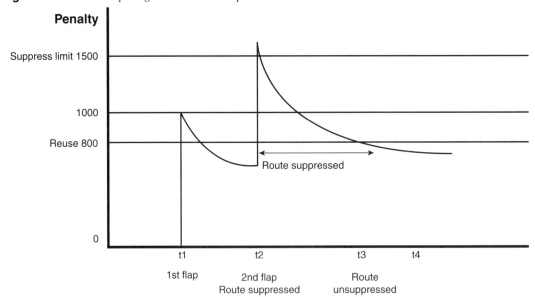

Assume that BGP route dampening has been applied to a particular route. At time t1 in Figure 3-8, a route flap occurs. Remember that a route flap is when a prefix goes from the up to the down state. When a route flaps, a penalty of 1000 is applied to the route. This is a fixed parameter that cannot be changed. At time t1, the flapping route incurs a penalty of 1000. Because the penalty is less than the suppress limit, which has been configured to be 1500, the flapping route is not dampened. Because the route has not been dampened, BGP sends a WITHDRAWN message when the route goes from up to down and then an UPDATE message when the route goes from down to up. When route dampening is enabled, BGP must maintain a history of flapping routes. The penalty associated with the route decreases over time. The rate of decrease in the penalty is a function of the half-life. The half-life is the amount of time for the penalty to decrease to half of its current value. If the half-life is 15 minutes, the penalty decreases to 500 in 7.5 minutes. At time t2, the penalty decreases to 600, and another route flap occurs. The route is again penalized, with an additional value of 1000 added to the current value of the penalty. The total penalty associated with the route is now 1600. When the total penalty of a route becomes greater than the suppress limit, the route is dampened. A dampened route means that BGP no longer sends UPDATE messages when the prefix goes from the down to the up state. The flapping prefix remains in the WITHDRAWN state. The route remains in the WITHDRAWN state until its penalty decreases below the reuse limit. When the penalty decreases below the reuse limit, BGP sends an UPDATE message for the route. Routes learned via IBGP are not dampened.

Cisco IOS Software Release: 11.0

Configuration Example 1: Default Dampening

Figure 3-9 shows the configuration and monitoring of route dampening. Routers A and B are configured as EBGP neighbors. Router A is advertising network 172.16.2.0/24 to Router B via EBGP. This prefix is a loopback interface that we will cause to flap by administratively shutting down and reenabling the interface.

Figure 3-9   *BGP Dampening Parameters and Operation*

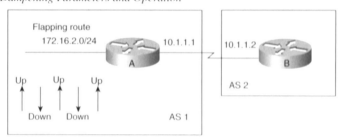

```
Router A
interface loopback 0
 ip address 172.16.2.1 255.255.255.0
 !
router bgp 1
 neighbor 10.1.1.2 remote-as 2
 network 172.16.2.0 mask 255.255.255.0
Router B
router bgp 2
 bgp dampening
 neighbor 10.1.1.1 remote-as 1
```

BGP dampening has been configured using the general form of the **bgp dampening** command. This applies route dampening to every BGP route with the following defaults:

- *half-life*—15 minutes
- *reuse*—750
- *suppress-limit*—2000
- *half-life*—15 minutes
- *max-suppress-time*—4 * *half-life* = 60 minutes

Router B should have an entry for prefix 172.16.2.0/24 in its BGP table:

```
Router B#show ip bgp
BGP table version is 2, local router ID is 5.5.5.5
Status codes: s suppressed, d damped, h history, * valid, > best, i - internal
Origin codes: i - IGP, e - EGP, ? - incomplete

   Network          Next Hop          Metric LocPrf Weight Path
*> 172.16.2.0/24    10.1.1.1               0             0 1 i
```

Shut down network 172.16.2.0 on Router A by shutting down the loopback 0 interface. Examine the BGP table on Router B:

```
2511#show ip bgp
BGP table version is 3, local router ID is 5.5.5.5
Status codes: s suppressed, d damped, h history, * valid, > best, i - internal
Origin codes: i - IGP, e - EGP, ? - incomplete

   Network          Next Hop          Metric LocPrf Weight Path
 h 172.16.2.0/24    10.1.1.1               0             0 1 i
```

The prefix 172.16.2.0/24 is still in the BGP table, but it is an invalid route. Because dampening is enabled on Router B, Router B must maintain a history for every route that has flapped. View the dampening parameters for prefix 172.16.2.0/24:

```
rtrB#show ip bgp 172.16.2.0/24
BGP routing table entry for 172.16.2.0/24, version 3
Paths: (1 available, no best path)
  Not advertised to any peer
  1 (history entry)
    10.1.1.1 from 10.1.1.1 (172.16.88.2)
      Origin IGP, metric 0, localpref 100, external, ref 2
      Dampinfo: penalty 996, flapped 1 times in 00:00:08
```

Reenable the loopback interface on Router A, and then reinspect the parameters for prefix 172.16.2.0/24 on Router B:

```
rtrB#show ip bgp
BGP table version is 4, local router ID is 10.1.1.2
Status codes: s suppressed, d damped, h history, * valid, > best, i - internal
Origin codes: i - IGP, e - EGP, ? - incomplete

   Network          Next Hop          Metric LocPrf Weight Path
*> 172.16.2.0/24    10.1.1.1               0             0 1 I

rtrB#show ip bgp 172.16.2.0/24
BGP routing table entry for 172.16.2.0/24, version 4
Paths: (1 available, best #1)
  Not advertised to any peer
  1
    10.1.1.1 from 10.1.1.1 (172.16.88.2)
      Origin IGP, metric 0, localpref 100, valid, external, best, ref 2
      Dampinfo: penalty 871, flapped 1 times in 00:03:06
```

The route is now being advertised, and BGP is maintaining a history of the route. Notice that the penalty has decreased to 871. Now shut down the loopback interface on Router A and check the route's parameters on Router B:

```
rtrB#show ip bgp
BGP table version is 5, local router ID is 10.1.1.2
Status codes: s suppressed, d damped, h history, * valid, > best, i - internal
Origin codes: i - IGP, e - EGP, ? - incomplete

   Network          Next Hop          Metric LocPrf Weight Path
h 172.16.2.0/24     10.1.1.1               0             0 1 i

rtrB#show ip bgp 172.16.2.0/24
BGP routing table entry for 172.16.2.0/24, version 5
Paths: (1 available, no best path)
  Not advertised to any peer
  1 (history entry)
    10.1.1.1 from 10.1.1.1 (172.16.88.2)
      Origin IGP, metric 0, localpref 100, external, ref 2
      Dampinfo: penalty 1760, flapped 2 times in 00:05:52
```

The route is down, and BGP is maintaining a history of the flapping route. Because the total penalty is below the default suppress limit of 2000, when the route comes up, it is advertised. Reenable the loopback interface on Router A:

```
rtrB#show ip bgp
BGP table version is 6, local router ID is 10.1.1.2
Status codes: s suppressed, d damped, h history, * valid, > best, i - internal
Origin codes: i - IGP, e - EGP, ? - incomplete

   Network          Next Hop           Metric LocPrf Weight Path
*> 172.16.2.0/24    10.1.1.1                0               0 1 I

rtrB#show ip bgp 172.16.2.0/24
BGP routing table entry for 172.16.2.0/24, version 6
Paths: (1 available, best #1)
  Not advertised to any peer
  1
    10.1.1.1 from 10.1.1.1 (172.16.88.2)
      Origin IGP, metric 0, localpref 100, valid, external, best, ref 2
      Dampinfo: penalty 1553, flapped 2 times in 00:08:39
```

Shut down and then reenable the loopback on Router A. This puts the penalty above the suppress limit of 2000, and the route will be suppressed even though it is up:

```
rtrB#show ip bgp
BGP table version is 7, local router ID is 10.1.1.2
Status codes: s suppressed, d damped, h history, * valid, > best, i - internal
Origin codes: i - IGP, e - EGP, ? - incomplete

   Network          Next Hop           Metric LocPrf Weight Path
*d 172.16.2.0/24    10.1.1.1                0               0 1 I

rtrB#show ip bgp 172.16.2.0/24
BGP routing table entry for 172.16.2.0/24, version 7
Paths: (1 available, no best path)
  Not advertised to any peer
  1, (suppressed due to dampening)
    10.1.1.1 from 10.1.1.1 (172.16.88.2)
      Origin IGP, metric 0, localpref 100, valid, external, ref 2
      Dampinfo: penalty 2275, flapped 3 times in 00:12:12, reuse in 00:24:00
```

Even though the route is now up, it will not be advertised or injected into the IP routing table. The penalty for this prefix has exceeded the suppress limit, and we can see from the BGP table on Router B that the route is dampened. The specific BGP information for the dampened route shows that the route will be reused in 24 minutes, assuming that it does not flap again. Because the route is now dampened, WITHDRAWN and UPDATE messages will not be sent if the route flaps. If we are patient and wait 24 minutes, we will see BGP restore the route, and it will be installed in the IP routing table. Dampened paths can be viewed using the **show ip bgp dampened-paths** command:

```
rtrB#show ip bgp dampened-paths
BGP table version is 7, local router ID is 10.1.1.2
Status codes: s suppressed, d damped, h history, * valid, > best, i - internal
Origin codes: i - IGP, e - EGP, ? - incomplete

   Network          From           Reuse     Path
*d 172.16.2.0/24    10.1.1.1       00:19:30 1 i
```

Now wait 19 minutes and 30 seconds. BGP will reuse the route as long as the route does not flap while we are waiting. We can verify that the route is being reused by examining the BGP and IP routing tables:

```
rtrB#show ip bgp
BGP table version is 8, local router ID is 10.1.1.2
Status codes: s suppressed, d damped, h history, * valid, > best, i - internal
Origin codes: i - IGP, e - EGP, ? - incomplete

   Network          Next Hop           Metric LocPrf Weight Path
*> 172.16.2.0/24    10.1.1.1                0             0 1 i

rtrB#show ip route
Codes: C - connected, S - static, I - IGRP, R - RIP, M - mobile, B - BGP
       D - EIGRP, EX - EIGRP external, O - OSPF, IA - OSPF inter area
       N1 - OSPF NSSA external type 1, N2 - OSPF NSSA external type 2
       E1 - OSPF external type 1, E2 - OSPF external type 2, E - EGP
       i - IS-IS, L1 - IS-IS level-1, L2 - IS-IS level-2, * - candidate default
       U - per-user static route, o - ODR

Gateway of last resort is not set

     172.16.0.0/24 is subnetted, 1 subnets
B       172.16.2.0 [20/0] via 10.1.1.1, 00:00:12
     10.0.0.0/30 is subnetted, 1 subnets
C       10.1.1.0 is directly connected, Serial0
```

Configuration Example 2: Configuring Dampening Parameters

The first example used the BGP dampening defaults. Two forms of the **dampening** command are available to customize the dampening parameters. The first form allows you to configure the half-life while using the defaults for suppress limit, reuse, and maximum suppress time:

```
bgp dampening 30
```

The preceding command sets the half-life to 30 minutes and uses the defaults for suppress limit (2000), reuse (750), and maximum suppress time (4 times the half-life). The second form allows you to customize all the dampening parameters except the penalty. The penalty has a fixed value of 1000:

```
bgp dampening half-life reuse suppress max-suppress-time
```

When you use the preceding form of this command, the maximum suppress time cannot be less than the half-life.

Configuration Example 3: Configuring Dampening Parameters Using a Route Map

The previous forms of the **dampening** command apply to every EBGP learned route. A route map allows you to apply different dampening parameters to different prefixes based on IP address or AS-path information. In the first example, we will apply dampening to prefixes 172.16.2.0/24 and 192.16.4.0/24 based on the IP address of the route using IP access lists:

```
router bgp 2
 bgp dampening route-map dampen
 neighbor 10.1.1.1 remote-as 1
!
access-list 1 permit 172.16.2.0 0.0.0.255
access-list 2 permit 192.16.4.0 0.0.0.255
!
route-map dampen permit 10
 match ip address 1
 set dampening 15 750 2000 60
route-map dampen permit 20
 match ip address 2
 set dampening 20 800 2200 80
```

In the second example, we will apply different parameters to routes originating from AS 1 and AS 3:

```
router bgp 2
 bgp dampening route-map dampen
 neighbor 10.1.1.1 remote-as 1
!
ip as-path access-list 1 permit ip as-path access-list 1 permit ^1$
ip as-path access-list 2 permit ip as-path access-list 1 permit ^3$
!
route-map dampen permit 10
 match as-path 1
 set dampening 15 750 2000 60
route-map dampen permit 20
 match as-path 2
 set dampening 20 800 2200 80
```

Verification

When using BGP dampening, you can tell if dampening is working only if a prefix is flapping. If route flaps are occurring, dampening can be verified using the commands described in the following examples.

Use the **show ip bgp** command to verify that BGP is maintaining a history of flapping routes:

```
rtrB#show ip bgp
BGP table version is 5, local router ID is 10.1.1.2
Status codes: s suppressed, d damped, h history, * valid, > best, i - internal
Origin codes: i - IGP, e - EGP, ? - incomplete

   Network          Next Hop           Metric LocPrf Weight Path
 h 172.16.2.0/24    10.1.1.1                0             0 1 i
```

Use the **show ip bgp** *prefix* command to view the dampening parameters for a flapping route:

```
rtrB#show ip bgp 172.16.2.0/24
BGP routing table entry for 172.16.2.0/24, version 5
Paths: (1 available, no best path)
  Not advertised to any peer
  1 (history entry)
    10.1.1.1 from 10.1.1.1 (172.16.88.2)
      Origin IGP, metric 0, localpref 100, external, ref 2
      Dampinfo: penalty 1760, flapped 2 times in 00:05:52
```

Use the **show ip bgp dampened-paths** command to view which prefixes are dampened:

```
rtrB#show ip bgp dampened-paths
BGP table version is 7, local router ID is 10.1.1.2
Status codes: s suppressed, d damped, h history, * valid, > best, i - internal
Origin codes: i - IGP, e - EGP, ? - incomplete

   Network          From              Reuse      Path
*d 172.16.2.0/24    10.1.1.1          00:19:30 1 i
```

Use the **show ip bgp flap-statistics** command to view statistics for flapping prefixes:

```
rtrB#show ip bgp flap-statistics
BGP table version is 9, local router ID is 10.1.1.2
Status codes: s suppressed, d damped, h history, * valid, > best, i - internal
Origin codes: i - IGP, e - EGP, ? - incomplete

   Network          From              Flaps Duration Reuse      Path
*d 172.16.2.0/24    10.1.1.1          3     00:02:55 00:28:10 1
```

Troubleshooting

Step 1   Verify that the BGP neighbors are in the Established state using the **show ip bgp neighbors** command.

If the neighbor relationship is not in the Established state, see section 8-23.

Step 2   If you're using either **bgp dampening**, **bgp dampening** *half-life,* or **bgp dampening** *half-life reuse suppress max-suppress-time,* dampening is applied to flapping routes.

Step 3   If you're using **bgp dampening route-map** *route-map-name,* verify the syntax of your route map, access list, prefix list, or AS path list.

3-13: bgp default local-preference *local-preference*

Syntax Description:

- *local-preference*—Value to use as the default local preference. The range of values is 0 to 4294967295.

Purpose: Routes originating on a BGP router that are advertised within the local AS have a default local preference of 100. This command allows you to set the local preference of locally advertised routes to a value other than the default value of 100. The new value for the local preference is applicable only within the local autonomous system.

Cisco IOS Software Release: 10.0

Configuration Example: Default Local Preference

Router B in Figure 3-10 is modifying the default local preference. The value of the local preference on Router B affects only routes advertised to Router C, because Routers B and C are in the same autonomous system.

Figure 3-10   *Modifying Local Preference for Locally Advertised Routes*

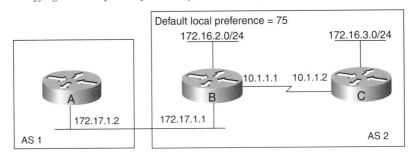

```
Router A
interface FastEthernet0
 ip address 172.17.1.2 255.255.255.0
 !
router bgp 1
 neighbor 172.17.1.1 remote-as 2
```
```
Router B
interface Loopback0
 ip address 172.16.2.1 255.255.255.0
 !
interface Ethernet0/0
 ip address 172.17.1.1 255.255.255.0
 !
interface Serial2/0
 ip address 10.1.1.1 255.255.255.252
 clockrate 64000
 !
router bgp 2
 bgp default local-preference 75
 network 172.16.2.0 mask 255.255.255.0
 neighbor 10.1.1.2 remote-as 2
 neighbor 172.17.1.2 remote-as 1
```
```
Router C
interface Loopback0
 ip address 172.16.3.1 255.255.255.0
 !
interface Serial0
 ip address 10.1.1.2 255.255.255.252
 !
router bgp 2
 network 172.16.3.0 mask 255.255.255.0
 neighbor 10.1.1.1 remote-as 2
```

Verification

Routes advertised by Router B to Router C should have a local preference value of 75:

```
rtrC#show ip bgp 172.16.2.0
BGP routing table entry for 172.16.2.0/24, version 0
Paths: (1 available, no best path)
  Not advertised to any peer
  Local
    10.1.1.1 from 10.1.1.1 (172.16.2.1)
      Origin IGP, metric 0, localpref 75, valid, internal, not synchronized, ref 2
```

Routes advertised by Router B to Router A should have a local preference value of 100, the default value:

```
rtrA#show ip bgp 172.16.2.0
BGP routing table entry for 172.16.2.0/24, version 6
continued
Paths: (1 available, best #1)
  Not advertised to any peer
172.17.1.1 from 172.17.1.1 (172.16.2.1)
      Origin IGP, metric 0, localpref 100, valid, external, best, ref 2
```

Routes learned by Router B from Router C should also have a local preference of 100:

```
rtrB#show ip bgp 172.16.3.0
BGP routing table entry for 172.16.3.0/24, version 0
Paths: (1 available, no best path)
  Not advertised to any peer
  Local
    10.1.1.2 from 10.1.1.2 (10.1.1.2)
      Origin IGP, metric 0, localpref 100, valid, internal
```

Troubleshooting

Step 1 Verify that the BGP neighbors are in the Established state using the **show ip bgp neighbors** command.

If the neighbor relationship is not in the Established state, see section 8-23.

Step 2 Verify the new local preference settings by checking the routes advertised to IBGP peers using the **show ip bgp** and **show ip bgp** *prefix* commands.

3-14: bgp deterministic-med

Syntax Description:

This command has no arguments.

Purpose: If **bgp always-compare-med** is enabled, the metric or MED is compared to every path regardless of the neighbor AS. Without **bgp deterministic-med** or **bgp always-compare-med**, the order of the paths can make a difference when selecting the best path. When you're using **bgp deterministic-med**, the router sorts the paths based on neighbor AS and MED so that the paths are sorted the same way every time. This produces a deterministic best-path selection.

Cisco IOS Software Release: 12.0

3-15: bgp fast-external-fallover

Syntax Description:

This command has no arguments.

Purpose: Fast external fallover is enabled by default. When an interface that is used for a BGP connection goes down, the BGP session is immediately terminated. If the interface is flapping, instability can be caused, because the neighbors will constantly be transitioning between the idle and established states. There will also be a flood of BGP UPDATE and WITHDRAWN messages. If you have a flapping interface, use the **no** form of this command.

Cisco IOS Software Release: 11.0

Configuration Example: Demonstration of Fast External Fallover

This configuration example demonstrates using the **bgp fast-external-fallover** command. In Figure 3-11, the Ethernet interface on Router B is flapping. We will investigate the result of using both **fast-external-fallover** and **no fast-external-fallover**.

Figure 3-11 *A Flapping Interface Can Cause Instability*

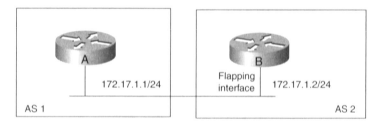

```
Router A
router bgp 1
 neighbor 172.17.1.2 remote-as 2
```
```
Router B
router bgp 2
 fast-external-fallover
 neighbor 172.17.1.1 remote-as 1
```

Verify that Routers A and B have formed a BGP connection:

```
rtrB#show ip bgp neighbors
BGP neighbor is 172.17.1.1,  remote AS 1, external link
  Index 1, Offset 0, Mask 0x2
    BGP version 4, remote router ID 172.17.1.1
    BGP state = Established, table version = 58, up for 00:14:02
```

Enable event debugging on Router B using the command **debug ip bgp events**. In configuration mode on Router B, shut down the Ethernet interface and observe the debug output:

```
1d17h: BGP: 172.17.1.1 reset requested
1d17h: BGP: 172.17.1.1 reset due to Interface flap
1d17h: BGP: 172.17.1.1 went from Established to Idle
```

Using the default **bgp fast-external-fallover**, you can see that when the interface goes down, the BGP session is immediately reset. Enable the Ethernet interface on Router B, and configure the **no** form of this command on Router B:

```
Router B
router bgp 2
 no bgp fast-external-fallover
 neighbor 172.17.1.1 remote-as 1
```

Verification

After Routers A and B have established a BGP connection, shut down the Ethernet interface on Router B, and observe the debug output:

```
1d17h: %LINK-5-CHANGED: Interface Ethernet0, changed state to administratively down
1d17h: %LINEPROTO-5-UPDOWN: Line protocol on Interface Ethernet0, changed state to
down
```

The BGP session did not drop, and the BGP neighbor relationship remained in the established state. Of course, if the interface remains down longer than the configured BGP hold time, the connection is dropped:

```
1d17h: BGP: 172.17.1.1 reset due to Peer timeout
1d17h: BGP: 172.17.1.1 went from Established to Idle
```

But if the interface goes up before the hold time expires, the session is not terminated.

Troubleshooting

Step 1   Verify that the BGP neighbors are in the Established state using the **show ip bgp neighbors** command.

   If the neighbor relationship is not in the Established state, see section 8-23. For IBGP and loopbacks, see section 8-33.

Step 2   Verify that the desired form of the **bgp fast-external-fallover** command has been configured. By default, **bgp fast-external-fallover** is enabled.

3-16: bgp log-neighbor-changes

Syntax Description:

This command has no arguments.

Purpose: To enable the logging of changes in a BGP neighbor's status. If the UNIX syslog facility is enabled, messages can be sent to a UNIX host running the syslog daemon. If you are not using the UNIX syslog facility, the status change messages are stored in the router's internal buffer. Events that are logged include the following:

- BGP protocol initialization
- No memory for path entry
- No memory for attribute entry
- No memory for prefix entry
- No memory for aggregate entry
- No memory for dampening info
- No memory for BGP updates
- BGP notification received
- Erroneous BGP update received
- User reset request
- Peer time-out
- Password change
- Error during connection collision
- Peer closing down the session
- Peer exceeding maximum prefix limit
- Interface flap
- Router ID changed
- Neighbor deleted
- Member added to peer group
- Administrative shutdown
- Remote AS changed
- RR client configuration modification
- Soft reconfiguration modification

Cisco IOS Software Release: 11.1 CC and 12.0

Section 3-16

Configuration Example 1: Enabling BGP Neighbor Status Change Logging to the Console

To enable the display of BGP neighbor status change events on the console, use the following configuration:

```
router bgp 1
bgp log-neighbor-changes
 neighbor 172.17.1.1 remote-as 2
```

Verification

When the state of a BGP neighbor changes, the event should be displayed on the console. For example, if you execute the command **clear ip bgp *** on a BGP neighbor, the following output should be displayed:

```
rtr#
01:10:52: %BGP-5-ADJCHANGE: neighbor 172.17.1.2 Down - Peer closed the session
01:11:22: %BGP-5-ADJCHANGE: neighbor 172.17.1.2 Up
```

Configuration Example 2: Enabling BGP Neighbor Status Change Logging to Memory

To enable the logging of BGP neighbor status change events to memory, use the following configuration:

```
logging buffered 4096 debugging
!
router bgp 1
bgp log-neighbor-changes
 neighbor 172.17.1.1 remote-as 2
```

The parameters **4096** and **debugging** are default values and are supplied by the router when you use the command **logging buffered**. The default values vary by platform.

Verification

The **show logging** command displays the status of buffered logging. If logging is enabled, the contents of the buffer are displayed:

```
rtr#show logging
Syslog logging: enabled (0 messages dropped, 0 flushes, 0 overruns)
    Console logging: level debugging, 48 messages logged
    Monitor logging: level debugging, 0 messages logged
    Buffer logging: level debugging, 3 messages logged
    Trap logging: level informational, 51 message lines logged
```

(Continued)

```
Log Buffer (4096 bytes):

01:18:16: %SYS-5-CONFIG_I: Configured from console by console
01:18:31: %BGP-5-ADJCHANGE: neighbor 172.17.1.2 Down - Peer closed the session
01:19:00: %BGP-5-ADJCHANGE: neighbor 172.17.1.2 Up
```

Troubleshooting

Step 1   Verify that the BGP neighbors are in the Established state using the **show ip bgp neighbors** command.

If the neighbor relationship is not in the Established state, see section 8-23.

Step 2   Verify that buffered logging is enabled using the **show logging** command.

3-17: bgp router-id *ip-address*

Syntax Description:

- *ip-address*—IP address to use for the BGP router ID.

Purpose: To explicitly set the BGP router ID. BGP normally uses the highest IP address assigned to an interface as the router ID. If loopback interfaces are used, the BGP router ID is the highest address assigned to a loopback interface, regardless of the IP addresses assigned to any physical interface.

Cisco IOS Software Release: 10.0

Configuration Example: BGP Router IDs

The scenario in Figure 3-12 is used to demonstrate the three possibilities for determining a BGP router ID. Initially, configure Router B without using loopback interfaces.

Figure 3-12 *Scenario Used to Demonstrate BGP Router IDs*

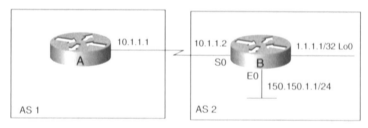

```
Router A
router bgp 1
 neighbor 10.1.1.2 remote-as 2
```
```
Router B
interface ethernet 0
 ip address 150.150.1.1 255.255.255.0
!
interface serial 0
 ip address 10.1.1.2
!
router bgp 2
neighbor 10.1.1.1 remote-as 1
```

There are two physical interfaces on Router B— Ethernet 0 and Serial 0. The BGP router ID is the highest assigned IP address, 150.150.1.1:

```
rtrB#show ip bgp summuary
BGP router identifier 150.150.1.1, local AS number 2
BGP table version is 1, main routing table version 1

Neighbor      V    AS MsgRcvd MsgSent   TblVer  InQ OutQ Up/Down  State/PfxRcd

10.1.1.1      4    2      0       0        0    0    0  never     Idle
```

Now add a loopback interface on Router B:

```
Router B
interface loopback 0
 ip add 1.1.1.1 255.255.255.255
```

The BGP router ID should now be 1.1.1.1 even though this is not the highest IP address assigned to Router B. The loopback address takes precedence over physical addresses when it comes to assigning the router ID:

```
rtrB#show ip bgp summary
BGP router identifier 1.1.1.1, local AS number 2
BGP table version is 1, main routing table version 1

Neighbor      V    AS MsgRcvd MsgSent   TblVer  InQ OutQ Up/Down  State/PfxRcd

10.1.1.1      4    2      1       2        0    0    0  never     OpenConfirm
```

Now override the BGP route ID using the command **bgp router-id** *ip-address*:

```
Router B
router bgp 2
 bgp router-id 5.5.5.5
 neighbor 10.1.1.1 remote-as 1
```

Verification

Verify that the BGP router ID has been changed to 5.5.5.5:

```
rtrB#show ip bgp summuary
BGP router identifier 5.5.5.5, local AS number 2
BGP table version is 1, main routing table version 1

Neighbor        V     AS MsgRcvd MsgSent    TblVer   InQ OutQ Up/Down  State/PfxRcd

10.1.1.1        4     2      7       6         0    0     0 00:00:18 Active
```

Troubleshooting

Step 1 Verify that the BGP neighbors are in the Established state using the **show ip bgp neighbors** command.

If the neighbor relationship is not in the Established state, see section 8-23.

Step 2 The BGP router ID should be changed if you are using the **bgp router-id** *ip-address* command. Verify using the **show ip bgp summary** command.

4

Default Information

4-1: default-information originate

Syntax Description:

This command has no arguments.

Purpose: To allow BGP to advertise the default route 0.0.0.0. A default route can also be advertised on a per-neighbor basis. See sections 8-3 and 8-4.

Cisco IOS Software Release: 10.0

Configuration Example: BGP Default Route Advertisement

Router B in Figure 4-1 needs to be configured to advertise a default route to Router A via BGP. The configuration requires a combination of commands that we will step through to illustrate the process.

Figure 4-1 *Using BGP to Advertise a Default Route*

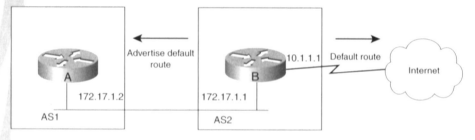

```
Router A
router bgp 1
 neighbor 172.17.1.1 remote-as 2


Router B

router bgp 2
 default-information originate
 neighbor 172.17.1.2 remote-as 1
```

Check the BGP tables on Routers A and B to determine if the default route is being advertised:

```
rtrA#show ip bgp
There are no routes in the BGP routing table.
rtrB#show ip bgp
There are no routes in the BGP routing table.
```

A default route is not being advertised by Router B. Let's try modifying the configuration on Router B so that a static default route points to the serial interface:

```
Router B
router bgp 2
 default-information originate
 neighbor 172.17.1.2 remote-as 1
 !
ip route 0.0.0.0 0.0.0.0 serial 2/0
```

Verify the static route on Router B, and then check to see if this route is being propagated by BGP:

```
rtrB#show ip route static
S*   0.0.0.0/0 is directly connected, Serial2/0

rtrA#show ip bgp

rtrB#show ip bgp
```

We still do not have the default route being propagated via BGP. We need to redistribute the static route into BGP on Router B. Before redistributing the route into BGP, remove the **default-information originate** command from the BGP configuration on Router B:

```
Router B
router bgp 2
 redistribute static
 neighbor 172.17.1.2 remote-as 1
 !
ip route 0.0.0.0 0.0.0.0 serial2/0
```

Is the default route being advertised? Check the BGP tables on Routers A and B:

```
rtrA#show ip bgp
There are no routes in the BGP routing table.
rtrB#show ip bgp
There are no routes in the BGP routing table.
```

Finally, add all the commands we have used so far to the BGP configuration on Router B:

```
Router B
router bgp 2
 redistribute static
 neighbor 172.17.1.2 remote-as 1
 default-information originate
 !
ip route 0.0.0.0 0.0.0.0 serial2/0
```

Verification

Examine the BGP tables on Routers A and B to see if we were able to advertise the default route:

```
rtrA#show ip bgp
BGP table version is 5, local router ID is 144.223.1.1
Status codes: s suppressed, d damped, h history, * valid, > best, i - internal
Origin codes: i - IGP, e - EGP, ? - incomplete

   Network          Next Hop          Metric LocPrf Weight Path
*> 0.0.0.0          172.17.1.1             0            0 2 ?
```
```
rtrB#show ip bgp
BGP table version is 3, local router ID is 172.16.2.1
Status codes: s suppressed, d damped, h history, * valid, > best, i - internal
Origin codes: i - IGP, e - EGP, ? - incomplete

   Network          Next Hop          Metric LocPrf Weight Path
*> 0.0.0.0          0.0.0.0                0        32768 ?
```

We have demonstrated that advertising a default route via BGP requires three steps:

Step 1 Create a static default route.

Step 2 Redistribute static into BGP.

Step 3 Use the BGP command **default-information originate**.

Troubleshooting

Step 1 Verify that the BGP neighbors are in the Established state using the **show ip bgp neighbors** command.

   If the neighbor relationship is not in the Established state, see section 8-23. For IBGP and loopbacks, see section 8-33.

Step 2 Verify that a static default route has been configured.

Step 3 Verify that static routes are being redistributed into BGP.

Step 4 Verify that **default-information originate** has been configured on the advertising BGP router.

4-2: default-metric *metric*

Syntax Description:

- *metric*—A metric or MED to assign to redistributed routes. The value range is 1 to 4,294,967,295.

Purpose: To assign a metric or MED to routes that are redistributed into BGP. There are three methods for assigning the metric or MED for redistributed routes. The first is to not assign a metric when redistributing routes into BGP. If a metric value is not assigned, the value 0 is applied to the metric for redistributed routes. This occurs when you use the **redistribute** command with no metric assignment (see section 10-1). The second method is to assign a metric or MED value when redistributing a protocol into BGP (see section 10-2). The third method uses the **default-metric** command to assign a metric or MED to redistributed routes that have not had their metric value assigned by the **redistribute** command:

- **redistribute ospf 1**—Assigns a metric of 0 to OSPF routes.

- **redistribute ospf 1 metric 5**—Assigns a metric of 5 to OSPF routes.

- **redistribute ospf 1 metric 5**

  redistribute static

  default-metric 10—Assigns a metric of 5 to OSPF routes and a metric of 10 to static routes.

Cisco IOS Software Release: 10.0

Configuration Example: Assigning Metrics to Redistributed Routes

In Figure 4-2, Router B is redistributing OSPF and static routes into BGP. The OSPF routes are assigned a metric of 5 using the **redistribute ospf 1 metric 5** command. The static routes are assigned a metric of 0 because we are not using the **default-metric** command or assigning a metric with the **redistribute** command.

Figure 4-2 *Assigning Metrics to Redistributed Routes*

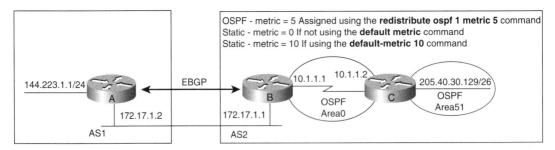

```
Router A
router bgp 1
 neighbor 172.17.1.1 remote-as 2
Router B
router ospf 1
 network 10.0.0.0 0.255.255.255 area 0
 !
router bgp 2
 redistribute ospf 1 metric 5
 redistribute static
 neighbor 172.17.1.2 remote-as 1
 no auto-summary
 !
ip route 198.8.4.128 255.255.255.128 Ethernet 0
Router C
interface loopback 0
 ip address 205.40.30.129 255.255.255.192
 !
router ospf 1
 network 10.0.0.0 0.255.255.255 area 0
 network 205.0.0.0 0.255.255.255 area 51
```

Without the **default-metric** command on Router B, the static routes are assigned a metric of 0:

```
rtrB#show ip bgp
BGP table version is 5, local router ID is 172.16.2.1
Status codes: s suppressed, d damped, h history, * valid, > best, i - internal
Origin codes: i - IGP, e - EGP, ? - incomplete

   Network          Next Hop          Metric LocPrf Weight Path
*> 10.1.1.0/30      0.0.0.0                0          32768 ?
*> 172.16.2.0/24    0.0.0.0                0          32768 ?
*> 198.8.4.128/25   0.0.0.0                0          32768 ?
*> 205.40.30.128/25 10.1.1.2               5          32768 ?
```

Now modify the BGP configuration on Router B and assign a default metric of 10:

```
Router B
router bgp 2
 redistribute static
 redistribute ospf 1 metric 5
 neighbor 172.17.1.2 remote-as 1
 default-metric 10
 no auto-summary
```

Verification

Verify that the default metric has been applied only to the static route and not to the OSPF routes:

```
rtrB#show ip bgp
BGP table version is 5, local router ID is 172.16.2.1
Status codes: s suppressed, d damped, h history, * valid, > best, i - internal
Origin codes: i - IGP, e - EGP, ? - incomplete

   Network          Next Hop          Metric LocPrf Weight Path
*> 10.1.1.0/30      0.0.0.0                0         32768 ?
*> 172.16.2.0/24    0.0.0.0                0         32768 ?
*> 198.8.4.128/25   0.0.0.0               10         32768 ?
*> 205.40.30.128/25 10.1.1.2              5          32768 ?
```

Troubleshooting

Step 1   Verify that the BGP neighbors are in the Established state using the **show ip bgp neighbors** command.

   If the neighbor relationship is not in the Established state, see section 8-23.

Step 2   The default metric will only be applied to redistributed routes that are not assigned a metric using the **redistribute** command.

Step 3   When redistributing routes, use the **no auto-summary** command (see section 2-1).

CHAPTER **5**

BGP Administrative Distance

5-1: distance *admin-distance ip-source-address ip-address-mask*

5-2: distance *admin-distance ip-source-address ip-address-mask ip-access-list-number*

Syntax Description:

- *admin-distance*—Administrative distance assigned to learned routes. The value range is 1 to 255.
- *ip-source-address*—IP address of the source of the routing update.
- *ip-address-maskl*—Address mask for the source of the routing update.
- *ip-access-list-number*—Optional standard IP access list used to apply the administrative distance to selected routes.

Purpose: To modify the administrative distance of BGP routes. When a particular route is learned via multiple routing protocols, the administrative distance is used to select the best route. The lower administrative distance is preferred. The administrative distances used for the IP routing protocols are as follows:

- Connected—0
- Static—1
- EBGP—20
- EIGRP—90
- IGRP—100
- OSPF—110
- IS-IS—115
- RIP—120
- IBGP—200

Cisco IOS Software Release: 10.0

Configuration Example 1: Modifying the Distance of All Routes Received from a Particular Neighbor

In Figure 5-1, Router A is advertising 144.223.1.0/24 and 144.223.2.0/24 via EBGP, and Router C is advertising 205.40.30.0/24 via IBGP.

Figure 5-1   *Default Administrative Distance for EBGP and IBGP*

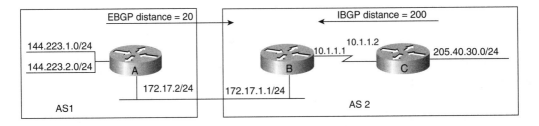

```
Router A
interface loopback 0
 ip address 144.223.1.1 255.255.255.0
 !
interface loopback 1
 ip address 144.223.2.1 255.255.255.0
 !
router bgp 1
network 144.223.1.0 mask 255.255.255.0
network 144.223.2.0 mask 255.255.255.0
 neighbor 172.17.1.1 remote-as 2
```
```
Router B
router bgp 2
 no synchronization
 neighbor 172.17.1.2 remote-as 1
 neighbor 10.1.1.2 remote-as 2
```
```
Router C
interface loopback 0
 ip address 205.40.30.1 255.255.255.0
 !
router bgp 2
 network 205.40.30.0
 neighbor 10.1.1.1 remote-as 2
```

The default administrative distance is 20 for EBGP and 200 for IBGP. This can be verified by inspecting the IP routing table on Router B:

```
rtrB#show ip route bgp
144.223.0.0/24 is subnetted, 2 subnets
B        144.223.2.0 [20/0] via 172.17.1.2, 00:00:51
B        144.223.1.0 [20/0] via 172.17.1.2, 01:13:14
B     205.40.30.0/24 [200/0] via 10.1.1.2, 01:13:14
```

For this example, we will set the administrative distance to 50 for all routes received by Router B from Router C. Using the first form of the command, all we need to do is use the IP address of Router C. Modify the BGP configuration on Router B as shown:

```
Router B
router bgp 2
 no synchronization
 neighbor 172.17.1.2 remote-as 1
 neighbor 10.1.1.2 remote-as 2
 distance 50 10.1.1.2 0.0.0.0
```

Using a mask of 0.0.0.0 matches all 32 bits of the IP address. Multiple addresses can be matched using a different mask. For example, using 10.1.1.0 0.0.0.255 matches all neighbors on subnet 10.1.1.0/24. To match all neighbors, use the address/mask pair 0.0.0.0 255.255.255.255.

Verification

Verify that the administrative distance of the route learned from Router C has been set to 50:

```
rtrB#show ip route bgp
144.223.0.0/24 is subnetted, 2 subnets
B        144.223.2.0 [20/0] via 172.17.1.2, 00:00:51
B        144.223.1.0 [20/0] via 172.17.1.2, 01:13:14
B     205.40.30.0/24 [50/0] via 10.1.1.2, 01:13:14
```

Configuration Example 2: Modifying the Distance of a Specific Route Received from a Particular Neighbor

For the configuration in Figure 5-1, we will set the administrative distance to 80 for the 144.223.1.0/24 route being advertised by Router A. Modify the BGP configuration on Router B as shown:

```
router bgp 2
 no synchronization
 neighbor 172.17.1.1 remote-as 1
 neighbor 10.1.1.2 remote-as 2
 distance 50 10.1.1.2 0.0.0.0
 distance 80 172.17.1.0 0.0.0.255 1
 !
access-list 1 permit 144.223.1.0 0.0.0.255
```

Verification

Verify that the 144.223.1.0 route now has an administrative distance of 80 and that the administrative distance for the 144.223.2.0 route is unchanged:

```
rtrB#show ip route bgp
144.223.0.0/24 is subnetted, 2 subnets
B       144.223.2.0 [20/0] via 172.17.1.2, 00:02:22
B       144.223.1.0 [80/0] via 172.17.1.2, 00:02:22
B    205.40.30.0/24 [50/0] via 10.1.1.2, 00:02:22
```

Troubleshooting

Step 1   Verify that the BGP neighbors are in the Established state using the **show ip bgp neighbors** command.

   If the neighbor relationship is not in the Established state, see section 8-23.

Step 2   Verify that the address/mask pair matches the proper neighbor

Step 3   If using an access list, verify the syntax of the list and that you are referencing the proper list.

5-3: distance bgp *external internal local*

Syntax Description:

- *external*—Routes learned via EBGP.
- *internal*—Routes learned via IBGP
- *local*—Routes entered into the BGP table via the aggregate-address command.

Defaults: external 20, internal 200, local 200

Purpose: To modify the administrative distance of BGP routes. When a particular route is learned via multiple routing protocols, the administrative distance is used to select the best route. The lower administrative distance is preferred. The administrative distances used for the IP routing protocols are:

- Connected—0
- Static—1
- EBGP—20
- EIGRP—90
- IGRP—100
- OSPF—110
- IS-IS—115
- RIP—120
- IBGP—200

Cisco IOS Software Release: 10.0

Configuration Example: Modifying the Distance for External, Internal, and Local BGP Routes

In Figure 5-2, Router A is advertising 144.223.1.0/24 via EBGP and Router C is advertising 205.40.30.0/24 via IBGP. From the perspective of Router B the EBGP route is external and the IBGP route is local. If we create an aggregate on Router B then a route to Null0 for the aggregate will be installed in the IP routing table. The Null0 route is considered a BGP local route.

Figure 5-2   *External, Internal, and Local BGP Routes*

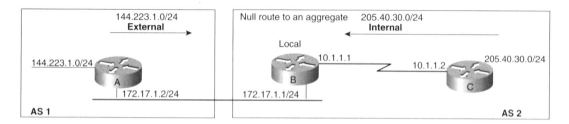

```
Router A
interface loopback 0
 ip address 144.223.1.1 255.255.255.0
 !
router bgp 1
network 144.223.1.0 mask 255.255.255.0
neighbor 172.17.1.1 remote-as 2
```
```
Router B
router bgp 2
 no synchronization
 aggregate-address 144.223.0.0 255.255.252.0 summary-only
 neighbor 172.17.1.2 remote-as 1
 neighbor 10.1.1.2 remote-as 2
```
```
Router C
interface loopback 0
 ip address 205.40.30.1 255.255.255.0
 !
router bgp 2
 network 205.40.30.0
 neighbor 10.1.1.1 remote-as 2
```

The BGP table on Router B should contain 3 routes. The route from Router A is external, the route from Router C is internal and the route to Null0 for 144.223.0.0 is local.

```
rtrB#show ip bgp
BGP table version is 5, local router ID is 172.16.2.1
Status codes: s suppressed, d damped, h history, * valid, > best, i - internal
Origin codes: i - IGP, e - EGP, ? - incomplete

   Network          Next Hop          Metric LocPrf Weight Path
*> 144.223.0.0/22   0.0.0.0                          32768 i
s> 144.223.1.0/24   172.17.1.2             0             0 1 i
*>i205.40.30.0      10.1.1.2               0    100       0 I
```

```
rtrB#show ip bgp 144.223.1.0
BGP routing table entry for 144.223.1.0/24, version 5
Paths: (1 available, best #1, table Default-IP-Routing-Table, Advertisements sup
pressed by an aggregate.)
  Not advertised to any peer
  1
    172.17.1.2 from 172.17.1.2 (144.223.1.1)
      Origin IGP, metric 0, localpref 100, valid, external, best
```

```
rtrB#show ip bgp 205.40.30.0
BGP routing table entry for 205.40.30.0/24, version 2
Paths: (1 available, best #1, table Default-IP-Routing-Table)
  Advertised to non peer-group peers:
  172.17.1.2
  Local
    10.1.1.2 from 10.1.1.2 (205.40.30.1)
      Origin IGP, metric 0, localpref 100, valid, internal, best
```

```
p2#show ip bgp 144.223.0.0
BGP routing table entry for 144.223.0.0/22, version 4
Paths: (1 available, best #1, table Default-IP-Routing-Table)
  Advertised to non peer-group peers:
  10.1.1.2 172.17.1.2
  Local, (aggregated by 2 172.16.2.1)
    0.0.0.0 from 0.0.0.0 (172.16.2.1)
      Origin IGP, localpref 100, weight 32768, valid, aggregated, local, atomic-
aggregate, best
```

The administrative distance for these routes can be seen in the IP routing table entries for Router B:

```
rtrB#show ip route bgp
     144.223.0.0/16 is variably subnetted, 2 subnets, 2 masks
B       144.223.1.0/24 [20/0] via 172.17.1.2, 00:05:58
B       144.223.0.0/22 [200/0] via 0.0.0.0, 00:05:58, Null0
B    205.40.30.0/24 [200/0] via 10.1.1.2, 00:06:07
```

Modify the BGP configuration on Router B to set the administrative distance of external routes to 15, internal routes to 25, and local routes to 35:

```
router bgp 2
 no synchronization
 aggregate-address 144.223.0.0 255.255.252.0 summary-only
 neighbor 172.17.1.2 remote-as 1
 neighbor 10.1.1.2 remote-as 2
 distance bgp 15 25 35
```

Verification

Verify that the administrative distance for the external, internal, and local BGP routes has been modified:

```
rtrB#show ip route bgp
B       144.223.1.0/24 [15/0] via 172.17.1.2, 00:03:30
B       144.223.0.0/22 [35/0] via 0.0.0.0, 00:03:30, Null0
B     205.40.30.0/24 [25/0] via 10.1.1.2, 00:03:30
```

Troubleshooting

Step 1 Verify that the BGP neighbors are in the Established state using the **show ip bgp neighbors** command.

If the neighbor relationship is not in the Established state then see section 8-23.

Step 2 If the neighbors are established then this command should work. Understand the difference between external, internal, and local BGP routes.

CHAPTER 6

BGP Route Filtering

6-1: distribute-list

Purpose: This form of the **distribute-list** command works only with Interior Gateway Protocols. Even though this command appears as a BGP router configuration option, do not use this command when configuring BGP. Use the **neighbor** {*ip-address* | *peer-group*} **distribute-list** {**in** | **out**} command described in sections 8-6 and 8-7.

CHAPTER 7

BGP Maximum Paths

7-1: maximum-paths *number-of-paths*

Syntax Description:

- *number-of-paths*—Number of BGP learned paths to the same destination that will be installed in the IP routing table. The value can be 1 to 6.

Purpose: By default, BGP installs only the best path to a destination in the IP routing table. The **maximum-paths** command allows up to six paths to the same destination to be installed in the IP routing table.

IOS Release: 11.2

Configuration Example

In Figure 7-1, Router A is learning two paths to network 172.17.1.x via EBGP. By default, BGP will install only one of these paths in the IP routing table. If all the attributes of the paths are equal, such as MED, Local Preference, and Weight, the route that will be installed is the one learned from the router with the lowest router ID. Initially, the routers will be configured without using the **maximum-paths** command, as shown in the following listing. This is done to demonstrate that only one route to 172.17.1.0 will be installed.

Figure 7-1 *Configuration Used to Demonstrate the* **maximum-paths** *Command*

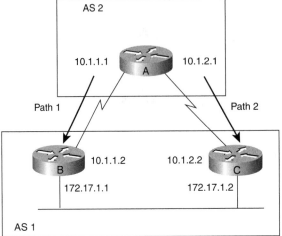

```
Router A
ip subnet-zero
!
interface Serial0
 ip address 10.1.1.1 255.255.255.252
!
interface Serial1
 ip address 10.1.2.1 255.255.255.252
!
router bgp 2
 neighbor 10.1.1.2 remote-as 1
 neighbor 10.1.2.2 remote-as 1
```
```
Router B
ip subnet-zero
!
interface Ethernet0
 ip address 172.17.1.1 255.255.255.0
!
interface Serial0
 ip address 10.1.1.2 255.255.255.252
 clockrate 64000
!
router bgp 1
 network 172.17.1.0 mask 255.255.255.0
 network 10.1.1.0 mask 255.255.255.252
 neighbor 10.1.1.1 remote-as 2
 neighbor 172.17.1.2 remote-as 1
 no synchronization
```
```
Router C
ip subnet-zero
 !
```

(Continued)

```
interface Ethernet0
 ip address 172.17.1.2 255.255.255.0
!
interface Serial0
 ip address 10.1.2.2 255.255.255.252
 clockrate 64000
!
router bgp 1
 network 172.17.1.0 mask 255.255.255.0
 network 10.1.2.0 mask 255.255.255.252
 neighbor 10.1.2.1 remote-as 2
 neighbor 172.17.1.1 remote-as 1
 no synchronization
```

The BGP table on Router A should contain two paths to network 172.17.1.0:

```
rtrA#show ip bgp
BGP table version is 4, local router ID is 10.1.1.1
Status codes: s suppressed, d damped, h history, * valid, > best, i - internal
Origin codes: i - IGP, e - EGP, ? - incomplete

   Network          Next Hop         Metric LocPrf Weight Path
*  172.17.1.0/24    10.1.2.2              0           0 1 i
*>                  10.1.1.2              0           0 1 I
```

Notice that the path to 172.17.1.0/24 learned from 10.1.1.2 is considered the best path, as denoted by the > symbol. This is the best path because the BGP neighbor advertising this path has a lower router ID than the neighbor advertising the other path, as seen in the **show ip bgp neighbors** command on Router A:

```
rtrA#show ip bgp neighbors
BGP neighbor is 10.1.1.2,  remote AS 1, external link
  Index 1, Offset 0, Mask 0x2
  BGP version 4, remote router ID 172.17.1.1
  BGP state = Established, table version = 6, up for 00:01:38
  Last read 00:00:37, hold time is 180, keepalive interval is 60 seconds
  Minimum time between advertisement runs is 30 seconds
  Received 24 messages, 0 notifications, 0 in queue
  Sent 20 messages, 0 notifications, 0 in queue
  Prefix advertised 0, suppressed 0, withdrawn 0
  Connections established 3; dropped 2
  Last reset 00:02:00, due to Peer closed the session
  1 accepted prefixes consume 32 bytes
  0 history paths consume 0 bytes
Connection state is ESTAB, I/O status: 1, unread input bytes: 0
Local host: 10.1.1.1, Local port: 179
Foreign host: 10.1.1.2, Foreign port: 11006

BGP neighbor is 10.1.2.2,  remote AS 1, external link
```

continues

(Continued)

```
 Index 2, Offset 0, Mask 0x4
 BGP version 4, remote router ID 172.17.1.2
 BGP state = Established, table version = 6, up for 00:02:54
 Last read 00:00:55, hold time is 180, keepalive interval is 60 seconds
 Minimum time between advertisement runs is 30 seconds
 Received 23 messages, 0 notifications, 0 in queue
 Sent 20 messages, 0 notifications, 0 in queue
 Prefix advertised 0, suppressed 0, withdrawn 0
 Connections established 3; dropped 2
 Last reset 00:03:19, due to Peer closed the session
 1 accepted prefixes consume 32 bytes
 0 history paths consume 0 bytes
```

Only one of the paths to 172.17.1.0/24 will be installed in the IP routing table on Router A:

```
rtrA#show ip route
Codes: C - connected, S - static, I - IGRP, R - RIP, M - mobile, B - BGP
       D - EIGRP, EX - EIGRP external, O - OSPF, IA - OSPF inter area
       N1 - OSPF NSSA external type 1, N2 - OSPF NSSA external type 2
       E1 - OSPF external type 1, E2 - OSPF external type 2, E - EGP
       i - IS-IS, L1 - IS-IS level-1, L2 - IS-IS level-2, * - candidate default
       U - per-user static route, o - ODR, P - periodic downloaded static route
       T - traffic engineered route

Gateway of last resort is not set

     172.17.0.0/24 is subnetted, 1 subnets
B       172.17.1.0 [20/0] via 10.1.1.2
     10.0.0.0/30 is subnetted, 2 subnets
C       10.1.2.0 is directly connected, Serial1
C       10.1.1.0 is directly connected, Serial0
```

Now add the **maximum-paths 2** command to the configuration on Router A:

```
Router A
router bgp 2
 neighbor 10.1.1.2 remote-as 1
 neighbor 10.1.2.2 remote-as 1
 maximim-paths 2
```

Verification

Verify that both routes to 172.17.1.0/24 learned via EBGP are being installed in the IP routing table on Router A:

```
rtrA#show ip route
Codes: C - connected, S - static, I - IGRP, R - RIP, M - mobile, B - BGP
       D - EIGRP, EX - EIGRP external, O - OSPF, IA - OSPF inter area
       N1 - OSPF NSSA external type 1, N2 - OSPF NSSA external type 2
```

(Continued)
```
        E1 - OSPF external type 1, E2 - OSPF external type 2, E - EGP
        i - IS-IS, L1 - IS-IS level-1, L2 - IS-IS level-2, * - candidate default
        U - per-user static route, o - ODR, P - periodic downloaded static route
        T - traffic engineered route

Gateway of last resort is not set

        172.17.0.0/24 is subnetted, 1 subnets
B          172.17.1.0 [20/0] via 10.1.1.2
                       [20/0] via 10.1.2.2
        10.0.0.0/30 is subnetted, 2 subnets
C          10.1.2.0 is directly connected, Serial1
C          10.1.1.0 is directly connected, Serial0
```

Troubleshooting

Step 1 Verify that the BGP neighbors are in the Established state using the **show ip bgp neighbors** command.

If the neighbor relationship is not in the Established state, see section 8-23.

Step 2 Verify that the router is learning multiple paths to the same destination using the **show ip bgp** command.

Step 3 If multiple paths are not being learned via BGP, check your BGP neighbor configuration, especially the syntax for the network and/or redistribution commands. Also check for any filters that might be blocking the desired routes.

Step 4 Verify that multiple routes to the same destination have been installed in the IP routing table using the **show ip route** command.

CHAPTER **8**

Neighbor Configuration

8-1: neighbor {*ip-address* | *peer-group-name*} **advertise-map** *route-map-name1* **non-exist-map** *route-map-name2*

Syntax Description:

- *ip-address*—Neighbor's IP address.

- *peer-group-name*—Name of the peer group. See section 8-19.

- *route-map-name1*—Route map that identifies the secondary prefix to advertise only if the primary prefix referenced by *route-map-name2* disappears.

- *route-map-name2*—Route map that identifies the primary prefix to advertise. If this route disappears, the secondary prefix referenced by *route-map-name1* is advertised.

Purpose: The primary prefix referenced by *route-map-name2* is advertised to BGP peers if the prefix is in the BGP table. If the network is directly connected, the **network** or **redistribute connected** command can be used to place the primary network in the BGP table. If the primary prefix is learned via an IGP, the **redistribute** *IGP* command installs the prefix in the BGP table. The prefix may be learned from a BGP peer and is automatically placed in the BGP table. The primary prefix is advertised until it disappears from the BGP table. This can happen if the network goes down or if the advertisement for this network is no longer being received. When the route disappears, the prefix referenced by *route-map-name1* is advertised. If the primary network reappears in the BGP table, it is again advertised, and the secondary prefix is suppressed.

Cisco IOS Software Release: 12.0

Configuration Example: Advertise the Primary Route While Suppressing the Secondary Route

The goal of this example is to illustrate the mechanics of the neighbor **advertise-map** command. In Figure 8-1, Router A advertises network 156.26.32.0/24 if the route is up. If network 156.26.32.0/24 goes down, network 144.223.8.0/24 is advertised.

Figure 8-1 *Illustration of the* **neighbor advertise-map** *Command*

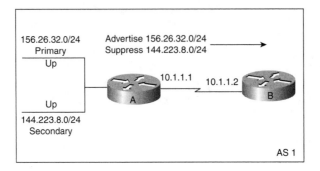

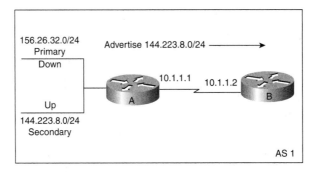

```
Router A
interface loopback 0
 description primary prefix
 ip address 156.26.32.1 255.255.255.0
!
interface loopback 1
 description secondary prefix
 ip address 144.223.8.1 255.255.255.0
!
router bgp 1
 network 156.26.32.0 mask 255.255.255.0
 network 144.223.8.0 mask 255.255.255.0
 neighbor 10.1.1.2 remote-as 1
 neighbor 10.1.1.2 advertise-map secondary non-exist-map primary
!
access-list 1 permit 156.26.1.0 0.0.0.255
access-list 2 permit 144.223.8.0 0.0.0.255
!
route-map primary permit 10
 match ip address 1
!
```

(Continued)
```
route-map secondary permit 10
  match ip address 2
```
```
Router B
router bgp 1
  neighbor 10.1.1.1 remote-as 1
!
```

Two loopbacks have been created on Router A to simulate the primary and secondary prefixes. Both prefixes must be in the BGP table. The two **network** commands on Router A install the prefixes in the BGP table. If both of the loopback interfaces are up, the primary and secondary prefixes are in the BGP table on Router A. The **advertise-map** command prevents the secondary prefix from being advertised to BGP peers as long as the primary prefix is in the BGP table. If the primary prefix disappears from the BGP table, the secondary prefix is advertised.

Verification

Verify that the primary and secondary prefixes are in the BGP table on Router A:

```
rtrA#show ip bgp
BGP table version is 15, local router ID is 156.26.32.1
Status codes: s suppressed, d damped, h history, * valid, > best, i - internal
Origin codes: i - IGP, e - EGP, ? - incomplete

   Network          Next Hop            Metric LocPrf Weight Path
*> 144.223.8.0/24   0.0.0.0                  0          32768 i
*> 156.26.32.0/24   0.0.0.0                  0          32768 i
```

Verify that only the primary prefix is being advertised to Router B:

```
rtrB#show ip bgp
BGP table version is 23, local router ID is 10.1.1.2
Status codes: s suppressed, d damped, h history, * valid, > best, i - internal
Origin codes: i - IGP, e - EGP, ? - incomplete

   Network          Next Hop            Metric LocPrf Weight Path
*  i156.26.32.0/24  10.1.1.1               0    100     0 i
```

You can also view the effect of **advertise-map** by examining specific entries in the BGP table.

```
rtrA#show ip bgp 144.223.8.0
BGP routing table entry for 144.223.8.0/24, version 29
Paths: (1 available, best #1)
  Not advertised to any peer
  Local
    0.0.0.0 from 0.0.0.0 (156.26.32.1)
      Origin IGP, metric 0, localpref 100, weight 32768, valid, sourced, local,2
```

continues

(Continued)

```
rtrA#show ip bgp 156.26.32.0
BGP routing table entry for 156.26.32.0/24, version 28
Paths: (1 available, best #1)
  Advertised to non peer-group peers:
    10.1.1.2
  Local
    0.0.0.0 from 0.0.0.0 (156.26.32.1)
      Origin IGP, metric 0, localpref 100, weight 32768, valid, sourced, local,2
```

To demonstrate the operation of the **advertise-map** command, we need to make the primary prefix disappear from the BGP table on Router A by shutting down loopback interface 0 on Router A:

```
int loopback 0
 ip address 156.26.32.1 255.255.255.0
 shutdown
```

The primary route should disappear from the BGP table on Router A:

```
rtrA#show ip bgp
BGP table version is 16, local router ID is 156.26.32.1
Status codes: s suppressed, d damped, h history, * valid, > best, i - internal
Origin codes: i - IGP, e - EGP, ? - incomplete

   Network          Next Hop            Metric LocPrf Weight Path
*> 144.223.8.0/24   0.0.0.0                  0           32768 i
```

With the primary route gone, the secondary route should be advertised to Router B:

```
rtrB#show ip bgp
BGP table version is 23, local router ID is 10.1.1.2
Status codes: s suppressed, d damped, h history, * valid, > best, i - internal
Origin codes: i - IGP, e - EGP, ? - incomplete

   Network          Next Hop            Metric LocPrf Weight Path
* i144.223.8.0/24   10.1.1.1                 0    100     0 i
```

The specific entries for the primary and secondary prefixes show the effect of **non-exist-map**:

```
rtrA#show ip bgp 144.223.8.0
BGP routing table entry for 144.223.8.0/24, version 31
Paths: (1 available, best #1)
  Advertised to non peer-group peers:
    10.1.1.2
```

```
(Continued)
  Local
    0.0.0.0 from 0.0.0.0 (156.26.32.1)
      Origin IGP, metric 0, localpref 100, weight 32768, valid, sourced, local,2

rtrA#show ip bgp 156.26.32.0
% Network not in table
```

Troubleshooting

1 Verify that the BGP neighbors are in the Established state using the **show ip bgp neighbors** command.

If the neighbor relationship is not in the Established state, see section 8-23.

2 Ensure that the primary and secondary prefixes are in the BGP table using the **show ip bgp** command.

3 If the primary and secondary routes are in the BGP table, go to Step 5.

4 If the primary and secondary routes are not in the BGP table, do the following:

(a) If the primary and secondary routes are directly connected, static, or redistributed from another protocol, check either the **network** commands or **redistribute** commands under router BGP. If you are using the **network** command, there must be an exact match between the **network** command (prefix/mask) and the IP routing table entry (prefix/mask). Go to Step 2.

(b) If the primary and secondary routes are learned from a BGP neighbor, check to see if the routes are in the neighbor's BGP table. If the routes are in the neighbor's BGP table and the BGP neighbors are in the Established state, check for any filters that might be blocking the routes. Go to Step 2.

5 Verify that *route-map-name1* is associated with the secondary route and that *route-map-name2* is associated with the primary route.

6 Verify that the route maps exist and are using the proper syntax.

7 Verify that the access lists referenced by the route maps exist and are using the proper syntax.

8 Check for any filters that might be blocking the advertisement of the primary route or secondary route if the primary is down.

9 Debug the BGP updates between the neighbors.

(a) Use the **debug ip bgp updates** command to verify that the primary is up and is being advertised.

```
rtrA#
1w6d: BGP: route up 156.26.32.0/24
1w6d: BGP: nettable_walker 156.26.32.0/24 route sourced locally
```

```
1w6d: BGP: 10.1.1.2 computing updates, neighbor version 27, table version 28,
starting at 0.0.0.0
1w6d: BGP: 10.1.1.2 send UPDATE 156.26.32.0/24, next 10.1.1.1, metric 0, path
1w6d: BGP: 10.1.1.2 1 updates enqueued (average=55, maximum=55)
1w6d: BGP: 10.1.1.2 update run completed, ran for 8ms, neighbor version 27, start
version 28, throttled to 28, check point net
1w6d: BGP: scanning routing tables
1w6d: BGP: Condition primary changes to Withdraw
1w6d: BGP: net 144.223.8.0 255.255.255.0 matches ADV MAP secondary: bump version to
29
1w6d: BGP: nettable_walker 144.223.8.0/24 route sourced locally
1w6d: BGP: 10.1.1.2 computing updates, neighbor version 28, table version 29,
starting at 0.0.0.0
1w6d: BGP: 144.223.8.0 255.255.255.0 matches advertise map secondary, state:
Withdraw
1w6d: BGP: 10.1.1.2 send UPDATE 144.223.8.0/24 - unreachable
```

(b) Use the **debug ip bgp updates** command to verify that the primary is down.

```
1w6d: BGP: route down 156.26.32.0/24
1w6d: BGP: no valid path for 156.26.32.0/24
1w6d: BGP: nettable_walker 156.26.32.0/24 no best path
1w6d: BGP: 10.1.1.2 computing updates, neighbor version 25, table version 26,
starting at 0.0.0.0
1w6d: BGP: 10.1.1.2 send UPDATE 156.26.32.0/24 -- unreachable
1w6d: BGP: 10.1.1.2 1 updates enqueued (average=27, maximum=27)
1w6d: BGP: 10.1.1.2 update run completed, ran for 8ms, neighbor version 25, start
version 26, throttled to 26, check point net
1w6d: BGP: scanning routing tables
1w6d: BGP: Condition secondary changes to Advertise
1w6d: BGP: net 144.223.8.0 255.255.255.0 matches ADV MAP secondary: bump version to
27
1w6d: BGP: nettable_walker 144.223.8.0/24 route sourced locally
1w6d: BGP: 10.1.1.2 computing updates, neighbor version 26, table version 27,
starting at 0.0.0.0
1w6d: BGP: 144.223.8.0 255.255.255.0 matches advertise map secondary, state:
Advertise
1w6d: BGP: 10.1.1.2 send UPDATE 144.223.8.0/24, next 10.1.1.1, metric 0, path
```

8-2: neighbor {*ip-address* | *peer-group-name*} advertisement-interval *seconds*

Syntax Description:

- *ip-address*—Neighbor's IP address.
- *peer-group-name*—Name of the peer group. See section 8-19.
- *seconds*—0 to 600.

Defaults: IBGP 5 seconds. EBGP 30 seconds.

Purpose: To set the minimum interval between the sending of Border Gateway Protocol (BGP) routing updates. To restore the default setting, use the **no** form of this command. When a route that is being advertised by BGP changes, BGP sends either an UPDATE or WITHDRAWN message. If an advertised route is flapping, usually caused when an interface is unstable, a flood of UPDATE and WITHDRAWN messages occurs. One method to control the flooding of BGP messages is to set a minimum advertisement interval. With the default value of 30 seconds for EBGP neighbors, BGP routing updates are sent only every 30 seconds, even if a route is flapping many times during this 30-second interval. BGP dampening can also be used to control the effects of flapping routes (see sections 3-7, 3-8, and 3-9).

Cisco IOS Software Release: 10.0. Peer group support was added in Release 11.0.

Configuration Example 1: Default Advertisement Interval

Figure 8-2 illustrates the default advertisement interval for IBGP and EBGP connections. The default advertisement interval is automatically set when the initial neighbor relationship is established.

Figure 8-2   *Default BGP Advertisement Intervals for IBGP and EBGP*

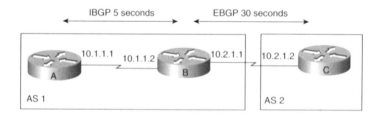

```
Router A
router bgp 1
 neighbor 10.1.1.2 remote-as 1
Router B
router bgp 1
 neighbor 10.1.1.1 remote-as 1
 neighbor 10.2.1.2 remote-as 2
Router C
router bgp 2
 neighbor 10.2.1.1 remote-as 1
```

Verification

The default advertisement value can be verified by examining the BGP neighbor information. Using the **show ip bgp neighbors** command on Router B, you can see the default advertisement interval for both the IBGP and EBGP neighbors, as shown in the following output:

```
RtrB#show ip bgp neighbors
BGP neighbor is 10.1.1.1, remote AS 1, internal link
  Index 0, Offset 0, Mask 0x0
  BGP version 4, remote router ID 10.1.1.1
  BGP state = Established, table version = 2, up for 00:10:19
  Last read 00:00:20, hold time is 180, keepalive interval is 60 seconds
  Minimum time between advertisement runs is 5 seconds
  Received 331 messages, 0 notifications, 0 in queue
  Sent 331 messages, 0 notifications, 0 in queue
  Connections established 2; dropped 1
Connection state is ESTAB, I/O status: 1, unread input bytes: 0
Local host: 10.1.1.2, Local port: 179
Foreign host: 10.1.1.1, Foreign port: 11013

BGP neighbor is 10.2.1.2, remote AS 2, external link
  Index 0, Offset 0, Mask 0x0
  BGP version 4, remote router ID 10.2.1.2
  BGP state = Established, table version = 2, up for 00:10:19
  Last read 00:00:15, hold time is 180, keepalive interval is 60 seconds
  Minimum time between advertisement runs is 30 seconds
  Received 229 messages, 0 notifications, 0 in queue
  Sent 229 messages, 0 notifications, 0 in queue
  Connections established 2; dropped 1
Connection state is ESTAB, I/O status: 1, unread input bytes: 0
Local host: 10.1.1.2, Local port: 179
Foreign host: 10.2.1.2, Foreign port: 11013
```

Configuration Example 2: Modifying the Advertisement Interval

In this example, we will change the advertisement interval on Router B for the IBGP neighbor to 15 seconds and for the EBGP neighbor to 45 seconds. The advertisement intervals on Routers A and C will remain set to the default values, as shown in Figure 8-3.

Figure 8-3 *Configuring BGP Advertisement Intervals for IBGP and EBGP*

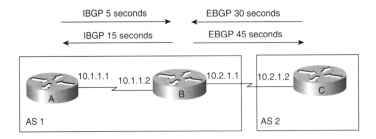

```
Router A
router bgp 1
 neighbor 10.1.1.2 remote-as 1
Router B
router bgp 1
 neighbor 10.1.1.1 remote-as 1
 neighbor 10.2.1.2 remote-as 2
 neighbor 10.1.1.1 advertisement-interval 15
 neighbor 10.2.1.2 advertisement-interval 45
Router C
router bgp 2
 neighbor 10.2.1.1 remote-as 1
```

Verification

The preceding configuration of the advertisement intervals on Router B can be verified by using the **show ip bgp neighbors** command:

```
RtrB#show ip bgp neighbors
BGP neighbor is 10.1.1.1,  remote AS 1, internal link
 Index 0, Offset 0, Mask 0x0
  BGP version 4, remote router ID 10.1.1.1
  BGP state = Established, table version = 2, up for 00:10:19
  Last read 00:00:20, hold time is 180, keepalive interval is 60 seconds
  Minimum time between advertisement runs is 15 seconds
  Received 331 messages, 0 notifications, 0 in queue
  Sent 331 messages, 0 notifications, 0 in queue
  Connections established 2; dropped 1
Connection state is ESTAB, I/O status: 1, unread input bytes: 0
Local host: 10.1.1.2, Local port: 179
Foreign host: 10.1.1.1, Foreign port: 11013

BGP neighbor is 10.2.1.2,  remote AS 2, external link
 Index 0, Offset 0, Mask 0x0
  BGP version 4, remote router ID 10.2.1.2
  BGP state = Established, table version = 2, up for 00:10:19
  Last read 00:00:15, hold time is 180, keepalive interval is 60 seconds
  Minimum time between advertisement runs is 45 seconds
  Received 229 messages, 0 notifications, 0 in queue
  Sent 229 messages, 0 notifications, 0 in queue
  Connections established 2; dropped 1
Connection state is ESTAB, I/O status: 1, unread input bytes: 0
Local host: 10.1.1.2, Local port: 179
Foreign host: 10.2.1.2, Foreign port: 11013
```

Troubleshooting

1 Verify that the BGP neighbors are in the Established state using the **show ip bgp neighbors** command.

   If the neighbor relationship is not in the Established state, see section 8-23.

2   Verify that you have used the correct IP address for the neighbor or the correct name for the peer group.

3   Verify the default or configured advertisement interval using the **show ip bgp neighbors** command.

8-3: neighbor {*ip-address* | *peer-group-name*} default-originate

Syntax Description:

- *ip-address*—Neighbor's IP address.

- *peer-group-name*—Name of the peer group. See section 8-19.

Purpose: Every router should have a default route that is used to forward packets to networks that are not in the local IP routing table. One method for ensuring that every router has a default route is to configure a static route on every router to establish the default route. Another method is to create one default route and advertise this route to the BGP neighbors. The router owning the default route can advertise it through BGP using the **default-originate** form of the **neighbor** command. Using this form is not recommended, because the router always advertises the default route, even if the router does not have a default route or if the network to the default route is down.

Cisco IOS Software Release: 11.0. Extended access lists are permitted in Release 12.0.

Configuration Example 1: Single Default Route

Figure 8-4 shows an autonomous system that has a connection to the Internet from Router B. The network directly connected to the Internet is to be used as the default route for the autonomous system. A static default route could be used on every router in the AS, but this is not the preferred method. These static routes require a high degree of maintenance. If the default route on Router B changes, every static route on every router in the AS needs to be changed. The preferred method is to dynamically propagate the default route attached to Router B throughout the AS. The following configuration contains the necessary instructions to enable Router B to propagate the default route.

Figure 8-4   *Single Default Route Advertisement*

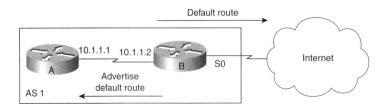

```
Router A
router bgp 1
 neighbor 10.1.1.2 remote-as 1
Router B
router bgp 1
 neighbor 10.1.1.1 remote-as 1
 neighbor 10.1.1.1 default-originate
!
ip route 0.0.0.0 0.0.0.0 serial 0
```

Verification

As always, verify that Routers A and B have established a BGP connection before configuring the default route. After configuring the default route advertisement, check the BGP routing table on Router A to ensure that the default is being advertised using the **show ip bgp** command. The following output verifies that the route is being advertised by Router B:

```
rtrA#show ip bgp
BGP table version is 1, local router ID is 10.1.1.1
Status codes: s suppressed, d damped, h history, * valid, > best, i - internal
Origin codes: i - IGP, e - EGP, ? - incomplete

   Network          Next Hop          Metric LocPrf Weight Path
* i0.0.0.0          10.1.1.2                  100      0 i
```

The preceding output verifies that Router A is receiving the default route advertisement from Router B. The next step in the verification process is to check the IP routing table of Router A to verify that the default route is being transferred via the **show ip route** command:

```
rtrA#show ip route
Codes: C - connected, S - static, I - IGRP, R - RIP, M - mobile, B - BGP
       D - EIGRP, EX - EIGRP external, O - OSPF, IA - OSPF inter area
       N1 - OSPF NSSA external type 1, N2 - OSPF NSSA external type 2
       E1 - OSPF external type 1, E2 - OSPF external type 2, E - EGP
       i - IS-IS, L1 - IS-IS level-1, L2 - IS-IS level-2, ia - IS-IS inter area
       * - candidate default, U - per-user static route, o - ODR
       P - periodic downloaded static route
Gateway of last resort is not set
10.0.0.0/24 is subnetted, 1 subnets
C        10.1.1.0 is directly connected, Serial0
```

The default route has not been transferred to the IP routing table, as shown in the preceding output. The reason for this is a property of IBGP called *synchronization* (see section 12-1). IBGP will not install a route learned from another IBGP speaker unless the route was learned through an Interior Gateway Protocol (IGP). For this example, we will disable synchronization on Router A, as shown in the following configuration. Disable synchronization only if Router A has a route to the next hop advertised with the default route:

```
Router A
router bgp 1
 neighbor 10.1.1.2 remote-as 1
 no synchronization
```

With synchronization disabled, recheck the IP routing table on Router A:

```
RtrA#show ip route
Codes: C - connected, S - static, I - IGRP, R - RIP, M - mobile, B - BGP
       D - EIGRP, EX - EIGRP external, O - OSPF, IA - OSPF inter area
       N1 - OSPF NSSA external type 1, N2 - OSPF NSSA external type 2
       E1 - OSPF external type 1, E2 - OSPF external type 2, E - EGP
       i - IS-IS, L1 - IS-IS level-1, L2 - IS-IS level-2, ia - IS-IS inter area
       * - candidate default, U - per-user static route, o - ODR
       P - periodic downloaded static route

Gateway of last resort is 10.1.1.2 to network 0.0.0.0

10.0.0.0/24 is subnetted, 1 subnets
C       10.1.1.0 is directly connected, Serial0
B*   0.0.0.0/0 [200/0] via 10.1.1.2, 00:00:05
```

The default route has been successfully installed in the IP routing table of Router A. This route will be installed regardless of whether Router B actually has a default route or if the network that is being used as the default route is functional. If the serial interface on Router B is shut down, Router B continues to advertise the default route. The next form of this instruction (see section 8-4) demonstrates how to conditionally advertise the default route based on the existence of a functional default network.

Configuration Example 2: Multiple Default Routes

In Figure 8-5, Router B is receiving a default route advertisement from both Routers A and C.

Figure 8-5   *Multiple Default BGP Route Advertisements*

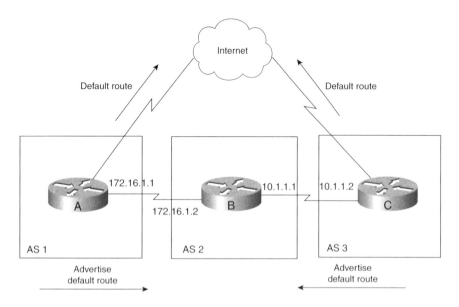

```
Router A
router bgp 1
 neighbor 172.16.1.2 remote-as 2
 neighbor 172.16.1.2 default-originate
 !
ip route 0.0.0.0 0.0.0.0 serial 1
Router B
router bgp 2
 neighbor 10.1.1.2 remote-as 3
 neighbor 172.16.1.1 remote-as 1
 !
Router C
router bgp 3
 neighbor 10.1.1.1 remote-as 2
 neighbor 10.1.1.1 default-originate
 !
ip route 0.0.0.0 0.0.0.0 serial 1
```

Verification

The default routes advertised to Router B can be examined by showing the BGP routing table:

```
rtrB#show ip bgp
BGP table version is 2, local router ID is 172.16.1.2
Status codes: s suppressed, d damped, h history, * valid, > best, i - internal
Origin codes: i - IGP, e - EGP, ? - incomplete

   Network          Next Hop          Metric LocPrf Weight Path
*  0.0.0.0          172.16.1.1                         0 3 i
*>                  10.0.0.2                            0 1 i
```

Router B installs the "best" default route into the IP routing table. Which default route is the best? All things being equal, BGP selects the route advertised by the router that has the lowest router ID. In this case, Router C has the lower router ID, and the default route advertised by Router C is installed in the IP routing table, as shown. Because this example uses EBGP, we do not need to worry about synchronization.

```
rtrB#show ip route
Codes: C - connected, S - static, I - IGRP, R - RIP, M - mobile, B - BGP
       D - EIGRP, EX - EIGRP external, O - OSPF, IA - OSPF inter area
       N1 - OSPF NSSA external type 1, N2 - OSPF NSSA external type 2
       E1 - OSPF external type 1, E2 - OSPF external type 2, E - EGP
       i - IS-IS, L1 - IS-IS level-1, L2 - IS-IS level-2, * - candidate default
       U - per-user static route, o - ODR
       T - traffic engineered route

Gateway of last resort is 10.1.1.2 to network 0.0.0.0

     172.16.0.0/24 is subnetted, 1 subnets
C       172.16.1.0 is directly connected, FastEthernet0/0
     10.0.0.0/30 is subnetted, 1 subnets
C       10.0.0.0 is directly connected, Serial3/0
B*   0.0.0.0/0 [20/0] via 10.1.1.2, 03:16:53
```

Troubleshooting

1 Verify that the BGP neighbors are in the Established state using the **show ip bgp neighbors** command.

   If the neighbor relationship is not in the Established state, see section 8-23.

2 Verify that the originating router is advertising the default route using the **show ip bgp** command.

   If the default route is being advertised, go to Step 3. If the route is not being advertised, verify the configuration of the **default-originate** command on the originating router. Also ensure that no filters are blocking the default route.

3 Verify that the default route is in the IP routing table using the **show ip route** command.

If the default route is not in the IP routing table, turn synchronization off if the next hop associated with the default route can be reached. This applies only to IBGP connections.

8-4: neighbor {*ip-address* | *peer-group-name*} default-originate route-map *route-map-name*

Syntax Description:

- *ip-address*—Neighbor's IP address.

- *peer-group-name*—Name of the peer group. See section 8-19.

- *route-map-name*—Name of the route map.

Purpose: Every router should have a default route that is used to forward packets to networks that are not in the local IP routing table. One method for ensuring that every router has a default route is to configure a static route on every router to establish the default route. Another method is to create one default route and advertise this route to the BGP neighbors. The router owning the default route can advertise it through BGP using the **default-originate route-map** form of the **neighbor** command. Using this form is recommended, because the router advertises the default route only if the condition of the specified route map is satisfied. The condition that is typically used is whether or not the default network is up.

Cisco IOS Software Release: 11.0. Extended access lists are permitted in Release 12.0.

Configuration Example: Conditional Default Route Advertisement

Figure 8-6 shows an autonomous system that has a connection to the Internet through Router B. The network directly connected to the Internet, 10.1.2.0/30, is to be used as the default route for the autonomous system. A static default route could be used on every router in the AS, but this is not the preferred method. These static routes require a high degree of maintenance. If the default route on Router B changes, every static route on every router in the AS needs to be changed. The preferred method is to dynamically propagate the default route attached to Router B throughout the AS. The following configuration contains the necessary instructions to enable Router B to propagate the default route only if the default route exists.

Section 8-4

Figure 8-6 *Conditionally Advertising a Default Route*

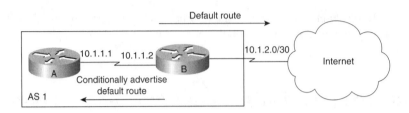

```
Router A
router bgp 1
 neighbor 10.1.1.2 remote-as 1
 no sync
Router B
router bgp 1
 neighbor 10.1.1.1 remote-as 1
 neighbor 10.1.1.1 default-originate route-map exists
!
access-list 1 permit 10.1.2.0 0.0.0.3
!
route-map exists permit 10
 match ip address 1
```

Verification

As always, verify that Routers A and B have established a BGP connection before configuring the default route. After configuring the default route advertisement, check the BGP routing table on Router A to ensure that the default is being advertised using the **show ip bgp** command. The following output verifies that the default route is being advertised by Router B.

```
rtrA#show ip bgp
BGP table version is 3, local router ID is 172.17.1.1
Status codes: s suppressed, d damped, h history, * valid, > best, i - internal
Origin codes: i - IGP, e - EGP, ? - incomplete

   Network          Next Hop         Metric LocPrf Weight Path
*>i0.0.0.0          10.1.1.2                 100      0 i
*>i10.1.2.0/30      10.1.1.2            0    100      0 i
```

The preceding output verifies that Router A is receiving the default route advertisement from Router B. The next step in the verification process is to check the IP routing table of Router A to verify that the default route is being transferred:

```
rtrA#show ip route
Codes: C - connected, S - static, I - IGRP, R - RIP, M - mobile, B - BGP
       D - EIGRP, EX - EIGRP external, O - OSPF, IA - OSPF inter area
       N1 - OSPF NSSA external type 1, N2 - OSPF NSSA external type 2
       E1 - OSPF external type 1, E2 - OSPF external type 2, E - EGP
       i - IS-IS, L1 - IS-IS level-1, L2 - IS-IS level-2, * - candidate default
       U - per-user static route, o - ODR, P - periodic downloaded static route
       T - traffic engineered route

Gateway of last resort is 10.1.1.2 to network 0.0.0.0

10.0.0.0/30 is subnetted, 2 subnets
B        10.1.2.0 [200/0] via 10.1.1.2
C        10.1.1.0 is directly connected, Serial0
B*   0.0.0.0/0 [200/0] via 10.1.1.2
```

The default route has been successfully installed in the IP routing table of Router A. This route is installed only if network 10.1.2.0 is up. If the serial interface on Router B that is connected to network 10.1.2.0 is shut down, Router B discontinues advertising the default route.

Troubleshooting

1 Verify that the BGP neighbors are in the Established state using the **show ip bgp neighbors** command.

If the neighbor relationship is not in the Established state, see section 8-23.

2 Verify that the originating router is advertising the default route using the **show ip bgp** command.

If the default route is being advertised, go to Step 3. If the route is not being advertised, verify the configuration of the **default-originate** command on the originating router. Also ensure that no filters are blocking the default route. Finally, check the syntax of the route map on the originating router.

3 Verify that the default route is in the IP routing table using the **show ip route** command.

If the default route is not in the IP routing table, turn synchronization off if the next hop associated with the default route can be reached. This applies only to IBGP connections.

8-5: neighbor {*ip-address* | *peer-group-name*} **description** *text*

Syntax Description:

- *ip-address*—Neighbor's IP address.
- *peer-group-name*—Name of the peer group. See section 8-19.
- *text*—Line describing the neighbor (1 to 80 characters).

Purpose: The **description** option performs a function that is similar to a comment in a software program. This function simply helps the reader determine the purpose of the code or, in the BGP case, the identification of the neighbor. Adding a neighbor description to a BGP configuration does not affect the operation of BGP. The description should convey useful information that can be quickly used to identify neighbors. For simple scenarios that have few neighbors, the **description** option has limited usefulness. For an ISP that has multiple neighbor relationships, however, you can use the **description** command to identify a neighbor without having to memorize its IP address.

Cisco IOS Software Release: 11.3

Configuration Example: Identifying a BGP Neighbor

Figure 8-7 shows an ISP and one of its neighbor connections. The ISP uses the **description** option to quickly identify the customers associated with each BGP connection.

Figure 8-7 *Using the Description Option to Identify a BGP Neighbor*

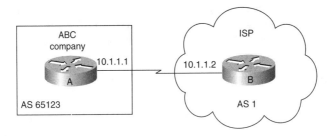

```
Router A
router bgp 65123
 neighbor 10.1.1.2 remote-as 1
Router B
router bgp 1
 neighbor 10.1.1.1 remote-as 65123
 neighbor 10.1.1.1 description ABC Company
```

Verification

Use the **show ip bgp neighbors** command to verify the description, as shown in the following output.

```
r3r1#show  ip bgp neighbors
BGP neighbor is 10.1.1.2,  remote AS 1, external link
 Description: ABC Company
 Index 1, Offset 0, Mask 0x2
  BGP version 4, remote router ID 10.1.1.2
  BGP state = Established, table version = 4, up for 00:08:56
  Last read 00:00:56, hold time is 180, keepalive interval is 60 seconds
  Minimum time between advertisement runs is 30 seconds
  Received 60 messages, 0 notifications, 0 in queue
  Sent 58 messages, 0 notifications, 0 in queue
  Prefix advertised 0, suppressed 0, withdrawn 0
 Connections established 2; dropped 1
  Last reset 00:09:27, due to User reset
  3 accepted prefixes consume 96 bytes
  0 history paths consume 0 bytes
 Connection state is ESTAB, I/O status: 1, unread input bytes: 0
 Local host: 10.1.1.1, Local port: 11000
 Foreign host: 10.1.1.2, Foreign port: 179
```

Troubleshooting

1   Verify that the BGP neighbors are in the Established state using the **show ip bgp neighbors** command.

    If the neighbor relationship is not in the Established state, see section 8-23.

2   If the description is not contained in the output from the **show ip bgp neighbors** command, the wrong neighbor IP address was used with the **neighbor** command containing the description.

8-6: neighbor {*ip-address* | *peer-group-name*} distribute-list *ip-access-list-number-or-name* in

Syntax Description:

*   *ip-address*—Neighbor's IP address.

*   *peer-group-name*—Name of the peer group. See section 8-19.

*   *ip-access-list-number-or-name*—Standard, extended, or named IP access list number.

Purpose: To filter incoming route updates from a particular BGP neighbor. Only one distribute list can be used per neighbor. The operation of the input distribute list is identical for both IBGP and EBGP neighbors.

Cisco IOS Software Release: 10.0. Peer group support was added in Release 11.0, support for named access lists was added in Release 11.2, and prefix list support was added in Release 12.0.

Configuration Example 1: Block a Particular Route

In Figure 8-8, Router B is advertising four network prefixes to Router A. Router A filters the route update from Router B in order to reject the 172.16.2.0 network. Loopbacks are used on Router B to simulate the advertised networks, as shown in the configuration.

Figure 8-8   *Scenario for the Use of the* **neighbor distribute-list in** *Command*

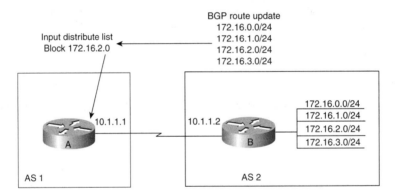

```
Router A
!
interface Serial0
 ip address 10.1.1.1 255.255.255.252
!
router bgp 1
 neighbor 10.1.1.2 remote-as 2
```
```
Router B
ip subnet-zero
!
interface Loopback0
 ip address 172.16.0.1 255.255.255.0
!
interface Loopback1
 ip address 172.16.1.1 255.255.255.0
!
```

(Continued)

```
interface Loopback2
 ip address 172.16.2.1 255.255.255.0
 !
interface Loopback3
 ip address 172.16.3.1 255.255.255.0
 !
interface Serial0
 ip address 10.1.1.2 255.255.255.252
 clockrate 64000
 !
router bgp 2
 network 172.16.0.0 mask 255.255.255.0
 network 172.16.1.0 mask 255.255.255.0
 network 172.16.2.0 mask 255.255.255.0
 network 172.16.3.0 mask 255.255.255.0
 neighbor 10.1.1.1 remote-as 1
```

Before proceeding to the distribute list example, you need to verify that Router A is receiving the routes from Router B:

```
rtrA#show ip bgp
BGP table version is 5, local router ID is 172.17.1.1
Status codes: s suppressed, d damped, h history, * valid, > best, i - internal
Origin codes: i - IGP, e - EGP, ? - incomplete

   Network          Next Hop            Metric LocPrf Weight Path
*> 172.16.0.0/24    10.1.1.2                 0             0 2 i
*> 172.16.1.0/24    10.1.1.2                 0             0 2 i
*> 172.16.2.0/24    10.1.1.2                 0             0 2 i
*> 172.16.3.0/24    10.1.1.2                 0             0 2 i
```

Modify the BGP configuration on Router A to filter the 172.16.2.0 prefix that is being received from Router B:

```
Router A
router bgp 1
 neighbor 10.1.1.2 remote-as 2
 neighbor 10.1.1.2 distribute-list 1 in
 !
access-list 1 deny   172.16.2.0 0.0.0.255
access-list 1 permit any
```

The distribute list always references an IP access list. For this example, the access list number is 1. The first statement in access list 1 rejects the 172.16.2.0/24 network. The second line in the access list is necessary because there is an implicit **deny any** at the end of every IP access list. Without the **permit any** statement, all routes from Router B would be rejected.

Verification

Verify that Router A is using the access list:

```
rtrA#show ip bgp neighbors
BGP neighbor is 10.1.1.2,  remote AS 2, external link
 Index 1, Offset 0, Mask 0x2
  BGP version 4, remote router ID 172.16.3.1
  BGP state = Established, table version = 5, up for 00:10:08
  Last read 00:00:08, hold time is 180, keepalive interval is 60 seconds
  Minimum time between advertisement runs is 30 seconds
  Received 14 messages, 0 notifications, 0 in queue
  Sent 13 messages, 0 notifications, 0 in queue
  Prefix advertised 0, suppressed 0, withdrawn 0
  Incoming update network filter list is 1
  Connections established 1; dropped 0
  Last reset never
  4 accepted prefixes consume 128 bytes
  0 history paths consume 0 bytes
 Connection state is ESTAB, I/O status: 1, unread input bytes: 0
 Local host: 10.1.1.1, Local port: 11028
 Foreign host: 10.1.1.2, Foreign port: 179
```

Finally, check the BGP routing table on Router A to ensure that the 172.16.2.0/24 network has been filtered:

```
rtrA#show ip bgp
 BGP table version is 4, local router ID is 172.17.1.1
 Status codes: s suppressed, d damped, h history, * valid, > best, i - internal
 Origin codes: i - IGP, e - EGP, ? - incomplete

    Network          Next Hop          Metric LocPrf Weight Path
 *> 172.16.0.0/24    10.1.1.2               0            0 2 i
 *> 172.16.1.0/24    10.1.1.2               0            0 2 i
 *> 172.16.3.0/24    10.1.1.2               0            0 2 i
```

Configuration Example 2: Allow a Particular Route and Block All Others

For this example, we will allow network 172.16.2.0/24 and block all other route advertisements from Router B. The access list required on Router A is

```
access-list 1 permit 172.16.2.0 0.0.0.255
```

The BGP router configuration on Router A remains unchanged. Because there is an implicit **deny any** at the end of every access list, we will let this implicit statement block the remaining routes.

Verification

As in the previous example, check the BGP table on Router A to verify that only network 172.16.2.0/24 is in the BGP table:

```
rtrA#show ip bgp
BGP table version is 2, local router ID is 172.17.1.1
Status codes: s suppressed, d damped, h history, * valid, > best, i - internal
Origin codes: i - IGP, e - EGP, ? - incomplete

   Network          Next Hop          Metric LocPrf Weight Path
*> 172.16.2.0/24    10.1.1.2               0             0 2 I
```

Configuration Example 3: Allow an Aggregate Route and Block the More-Specific Routes

Assume that Router B is advertising an aggregate advertisement for 172.16.0.0/22 and the four more-specific routes 172.16.0.0/24, 172.16.1.0/24, 172.16.2.0/24, and 172.16.3.0/24. The BGP configuration for Router B would become

```
router bgp 2
 network 172.16.0.0 mask 255.255.255.0
 network 172.16.1.0 mask 255.255.255.0
 network 172.16.2.0 mask 255.255.255.0
 network 172.16.3.0 mask 255.255.255.0
 aggregate-address 172.16.0.0 255.255.252.0
 neighbor 10.1.1.1 remote-as 1
```

The BGP table on Router A would contain

```
rtrA#show ip bgp
BGP table version is 10, local router ID is 172.17.1.1
Status codes: s suppressed, d damped, h history, * valid, > best, i - internal
Origin codes: i - IGP, e - EGP, ? - incomplete

   Network          Next Hop          Metric LocPrf Weight Path
*> 172.16.0.0/24    10.1.1.2               0             0 2 i
*> 172.16.0.0/22    10.1.1.2                             0 2 i
*> 172.16.1.0/24    10.1.1.2               0             0 2 i
*> 172.16.2.0/24    10.1.1.2               0             0 2 i
*> 172.16.3.0/24    10.1.1.2               0             0 2 i
```

If we want to allow only the aggregate route and block the more-specific routes, a standard IP access won't work. To allow the aggregate using a standard IP access list while blocking the more-specific routes, we could try the access list:

```
access-list 1 deny 172.16.0.0 0.0.0.255
access-list 1 deny 172.16.1.0 0.0.0.255
```

continues

```
(Continued)
access-list 1 deny 172.16.2.0 0.0.0.255
access-list 1 deny 172.16.3.0 0.0.0.255
access-list 1 permit 172.16.0.0 0.0.3.255
```

Unfortunately, the first statement also blocks the aggregate route. If we rearrange the statements, we could try this:

```
access-list 1 permit 172.16.0.0 0.0.3.255
access-list 1 deny 172.16.0.0 0.0.0.255
access-list 1 deny 172.16.1.0 0.0.0.255
access-list 1 deny 172.16.2.0 0.0.0.255
access-list 1 deny 172.16.3.0 0.0.0.255
```

Now the first statement allows all the routes. The only way to permit the aggregate and reject the specific routes is to use an extended IP access list. Normally, the second address/mask pair in an extended IP access list signifies the destination address and mask. For a distribute list, the second address/mask pair indicates the mask size. Therefore, we can use the following:

```
Router A
router bgp 1
 neighbor 10.1.1.2 distribute-list 100 in
 !
 access-list 100 permit 172.16.0.0 0.0.3.255 255.255.252.0 0.0.0.0
```

Verification

By examining the BGP table on Router A, we can verify that the extended access list has permitted only the aggregate address:

```
rtrA#show ip bgp
BGP table version is 2, local router ID is 172.17.1.1
Status codes: s suppressed, d damped, h history, * valid, > best, i - internal
Origin codes: i - IGP, e - EGP, ? - incomplete

   Network          Next Hop            Metric LocPrf Weight Path
*> 172.16.0.0/22    10.1.1.2                           0 2 i
```

Troubleshooting

1 Verify that the BGP neighbors are in the Established state using the **show ip bgp neighbors** command.

   If the neighbor relationship is not in the Established state, see section 8-23.

2 Verify that the advertising router has the routes in the BGP table using the **show ip bgp** command. If the routes are not in the BGP table, see sections 9-1 and 9-2 for the proper use of the **network** command.

3 Verify that the routes are in the receiving router's BGP table. If they are not, check the syntax of the access list associated with the distribute list.

4 If the routes are not in the BGP table on Router A, and you are sure that there are no errors in the configuration for Router B, clear and restart the BGP connection using **clear ip bgp** *. This command can be used on either Router A or B. This command clears all BGP connections. To clear a particular neighbor, use the neighbor's IP address in place of the *. After clearing the connection, you can monitor the BGP route exchange using **debug ip bgp updates**, which should produce output similar to the following for the first configuration:

```
rtrA#debug ip bgp updates
6d15h: BGP: 10.1.1.2 rcv UPDATE w/ attr: nexthop 10.1.1.2, origin i, metric 0, path 2
6d15h: BGP: 10.1.1.2 rcv UPDATE about 172.16.0.0/24
6d15h: BGP: 10.1.1.2 rcv UPDATE about 172.16.1.0/24
6d15h: BGP: 10.1.1.2 rcv UPDATE about 172.16.2.0/2424 -
  DENIED due to: distribute/prefix-list;
6d15h: BGP: 10.1.1.2 rcv UPDATE about 172.16.3.0/24
```

For the second configuration, the **debug** output will be similar to this:

```
rtr A#debug ip bgp updates
6d15h: BGP: 10.1.1.2 rcv UPDATE w/ attr: nexthop 10.1.1.2, origin i, metric 0, path 2
6d15h: BGP: 10.1.1.2 rcv UPDATE about 172.16.0.0/24 -
  DENIED due to: distribute/prefix-list;
6d15h: BGP: 10.1.1.2 rcv UPDATE about 172.16.1.0/24 -
  DENIED due to: distribute/prefix-list;
6d15h: BGP: 10.1.1.2 rcv UPDATE about 172.16.2.0/24
6d15h: BGP: 10.1.1.2 rcv UPDATE about 172.16.3.0/24 -
  DENIED due to: distribute/prefix-list;
```

8-7: **neighbor** *{ip-address | peer-group-name}* **distribute-list** *ip-access-list-number-or-name* **out**

Syntax Description:

- *ip-address*—Neighbor's IP address.

- *peer-group-name*—Name of the peer group. See section 8-19.

- *ip-access-list-number-or-name*—Standard, extended, or named IP access list number.

Purpose: To filter outgoing route updates to a particular BGP neighbor. Only one distribute list can be used per neighbor. The operation of the output distribute list is identical for both IBGP and EBGP neighbors.

Cisco IOS Software Release: 10.0. Peer group support was added in Release 11.0, support for named access lists was added in Release 11.2, and prefix list support was added in Release 12.0.

Configuration Example 1: Block a Particular Route

In Figure 8-9, Router B is advertising four network prefixes to Router A. Router B filters the route update to Router A in order to reject the 172.16.2.0 network. Loopbacks are used on Router B to simulate the advertised networks, as shown in the following configuration.

Figure 8-9 *Scenario for the Use of the* **neighbor distribute-list out** *Command*

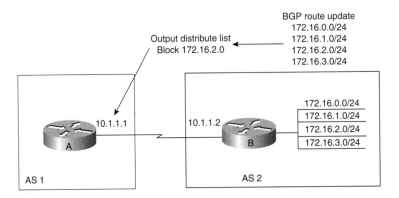

```
Router A
!
interface Serial0
 ip address 10.1.1.1 255.255.255.252
!
router bgp 1
 neighbor 10.1.1.2 remote-as 2
Router B
ip subnet-zero
!
interface Loopback0
 ip address 172.16.0.1 255.255.255.0
!
interface Loopback1
 ip address 172.16.1.1 255.255.255.0
!
interface Loopback2
 ip address 172.16.2.1 255.255.255.0
!
interface Loopback3
 ip address 172.16.3.1 255.255.255.0
!
```

```
(Continued)
interface Serial0
 ip address 10.1.1.2 255.255.255.252
 clockrate 64000
!
router bgp 2
 network 172.16.0.0 mask 255.255.255.0
 network 172.16.1.0 mask 255.255.255.0
 network 172.16.2.0 mask 255.255.255.0
 network 172.16.3.0 mask 255.255.255.0
 neighbor 10.1.1.1 remote-as 1
```

Before proceeding to the distribute list example, verify that Router A is receiving the routes from Router B:

```
rtrA#show ip bgp
BGP table version is 5, local router ID is 172.17.1.1
Status codes: s suppressed, d damped, h history, * valid, > best, i - internal
Origin codes: i - IGP, e - EGP, ? - incomplete

   Network          Next Hop          Metric LocPrf Weight Path
*> 172.16.0.0/24    10.1.1.2               0             0 2 i
*> 172.16.1.0/24    10.1.1.2               0             0 2 i
*> 172.16.2.0/24    10.1.1.2               0             0 2 i
*> 172.16.3.0/24    10.1.1.2               0             0 2 i
```

Modify the BGP configuration on Router B to filter the 172.16.2.0 prefix that is being sent on Router A:

```
Router B
router bgp 2
 neighbor 10.1.1.1 remote-as 2
 neighbor 10.1.1.1 distribute-list 1 out
access-list 1 deny    172.16.2.0 0.0.0.255
access-list 1 permit any
```

The distribute list always references an IP access list. For this example, the access list number is 1. The first statement in access list 1 rejects the 172.16.2.0/24 network. The second line in the access list is necessary because there is an implicit **deny any** at the end of every IP access list. Without the **permit any** statement, all routes to Router A would be rejected.

Verification

Verify that Router B is using the access list:

```
rtrB#show ip bgp n
BGP neighbor is 10.1.1.1,   remote AS 1, external link
 Index 1, Offset 0, Mask 0x2
```

continues

Section 8-7

```
(Continued)
  BGP version 4, remote router ID 172.17.1.1
  BGP state = Established, table version = 6, up for 00:00:25
  Last read 00:00:25, hold time is 180, keepalive interval is 60 seconds
  Minimum time between advertisement runs is 30 seconds
  Received 47 messages, 3 notifications, 0 in queue
  Sent 63 messages, 0 notifications, 0 in queue
  Prefix advertised 32, suppressed 0, withdrawn 1
  Outgoing update network filter list is 1
  Connections established 7; dropped 6
  Last reset 00:00:50, due to User reset
  0 accepted prefixes consume 0 bytes
  0 history paths consume 0 bytes
Connection state is ESTAB, I/O status: 1, unread input bytes: 0
Local host: 10.1.1.2, Local port: 11054
Foreign host: 10.1.1.1, Foreign port: 179
```

Check the BGP routing table on Router A to ensure that the 172.16.2.0/24 network has been filtered:

```
rtrA#show ip bgp
BGP table version is 4, local router ID is 172.17.1.1
Status codes: s suppressed, d damped, h history, * valid, > best, i - internal
Origin codes: i - IGP, e - EGP, ? - incomplete

   Network          Next Hop          Metric LocPrf Weight Path
*> 172.16.0.0/24    10.1.1.2               0             0 2 i
*> 172.16.1.0/24    10.1.1.2               0             0 2 i
*> 172.16.3.0/24    10.1.1.2               0             0 2 i
```

Configuration Example 2: Allow a Particular Route and Block All Others

For this example, we will allow network 172.16.2.0/24 and block all other route advertisements to Router A. The access list required on Router B is

```
access-list 1 permit 172.16.2.0 0.0.0.255
```

The BGP router configuration on Router B remains unchanged. Because there is an implicit **deny any** at the end of every access list, we will let this implicit statement block the remaining routes.

Verification

As in the previous example, check the BGP table on Router A to verify that only network 172.16.2.0/24 is in the BGP table:

```
rtrA#show ip bgp
BGP table version is 2, local router ID is 172.17.1.1
Status codes: s suppressed, d damped, h history, * valid, > best, i - internal
Origin codes: i - IGP, e - EGP, ? - incomplete
```

(Continued)

```
   Network            Next Hop          Metric LocPrf Weight Path
*> 172.16.2.0/24      10.1.1.2               0              0 2 I
```

Configuration Example 3: Allow an Aggregate Route and Block the More-Specific Routes

Assume that Router B is advertising an aggregate advertisement for 172.16.0.0/22 and the four more-specific routes 172.16.0.0/24, 172.16.1.0/24, 172.16.2.0/24, and 172.16.3.0/24. The BGP configuration for Router B would become

```
router bgp 2
 network 172.16.0.0 mask 255.255.255.0
 network 172.16.1.0 mask 255.255.255.0
 network 172.16.2.0 mask 255.255.255.0
 network 172.16.3.0 mask 255.255.255.0
 aggregate-address 172.16.0.0 255.255.252.0
 neighbor 10.1.1.1 remote-as 1
```

The BGP table on Router A would contain

```
rtrA#show ip bgp
BGP table version is 5, local router ID is 172.17.1.1
Status codes: s suppressed, d damped, h history, * valid, > best, i - internal
Origin codes: i - IGP, e - EGP, ? - incomplete

   Network            Next Hop          Metric LocPrf Weight Path
*> 172.16.0.0/24      10.1.1.2               0              0 2 i
*> 172.16.1.0/24      10.1.1.2               0              0 2 i
*> 172.16.2.0/24      10.1.1.2               0              0 2 i
*> 172.16.3.0/24      10.1.1.2               0              0 2 i
*> 172.16.0.0/22      10.1.1.2               0              0 2 i
```

If we want to allow only the aggregate route and block the more-specific routes, a standard IP access won't work. To allow the aggregate using a standard IP access list while blocking the more-specific routes, we could try the following access list:

```
access-list 1 deny 172.16.0.0 0.0.0.255
access-list 1 deny 172.16.1.0 0.0.0.255
access-list 1 deny 172.16.2.0 0.0.0.255
access-list 1 deny 172.16.3.0 0.0.0.255
access-list 1 permit 172.16.0.0 0.0.255.255
```

Section 8-7

Unfortunately, the first statement also blocks the aggregate route. If we rearrange the statements, we could try this:

```
access-list 1 permit 172.16.0.0 0.0.255.255.
access-list 1 deny 172.16.0.0 0.0.0.255
access-list 1 deny 172.16.1.0 0.0.0.255
access-list 1 deny 172.16.2.0 0.0.0.255
access-list 1 deny 172.16.3.0 0.0.0.255
```

Now the first statement allows all the routes. The only way to permit the aggregate and reject the specific routes is to use an extended IP access list. Normally, the second address/mask pair in an extended IP access list signifies the destination address and mask. For a distribute list, the second address/mask pair indicates the mask size. Therefore, we can use this:

```
Router B
router bgp 2
  neighbor 10.1.1.1 distribute-list 100 out
  access-list 100 permit 172.16.0.0 0.0.3.255 255.255.252.0 0.0.0.0
```

Verification

By examining the BGP table on Router A, we can verify that the extended access list has permitted only the aggregate address.

```
rtrA#show ip bgp
BGP table version is 2, local router ID is 172.17.1.1
Status codes: s suppressed, d damped, h history, * valid, > best, i - internal
Origin codes: i - IGP, e - EGP, ? - incomplete

   Network          Next Hop          Metric LocPrf Weight Path
*> 172.16.0.0/22    10.1.1.2                            0 2 i
```

Troubleshooting

1 Verify that the BGP neighbors are in the Established state using the **show ip bgp neighbors** command.

   If the neighbor relationship is not in the Established state, see section 8-23.

2 Verify that the advertising router has the routes in the BGP table using the **show ip bgp** command. If the routes are not in the BGP table, see sections 9-1 and 9-2 for the proper use of the **network** command.

3 Verify that the routes are in the receiving router's BGP table. If they are not, check the syntax of the access list associated with the distribute list.

4 If the routes are not in the BGP table on Router A, and you are sure that there are no errors in the configuration for Router B, clear and restart the BGP connection using **clear ip bgp** *. This command can be used on either Router A or B. This command clears all BGP connections. To clear a particular neighbor, use the neighbor's IP address in place of the *. After clearing the connection, you can monitor the BGP route exchange using **debug ip bgp updates**, which should produce output similar to the following for the first configuration:

```
6d15h: BGP: 10.1.1.1 computing updates, neighbor version 1, table version 5,
starting at 0.0.0.0
6d15h: BGP: 10.1.1.1 send UPDATE 172.16.0.0/24, next 10.1.1.2, metric 0, path 2
6d15h: BGP: 10.1.1.1 send UPDATE 172.16.1.0/24 (chgflags: 0x8), next 10.1.1.2, path
(before routemap/aspath update)
6d15h: BGP: 10.1.1.1 send UPDATE 172.16.3.0/24 (chgflags: 0x8), next 10.1.1.2, path
(before routemap/aspath update)
```

For the second configuration, the **debug** output will be similar to this:

```
6d15h: BGP: 10.1.1.1 computing updates, neighbor version 1, table version 5,
starting at 0.0.0.0
6d15h: BGP: 10.1.1.1 send UPDATE 172.16.2.0/24, next 10.1.1.2, metric 0, path 2
```

8-8: neighbor {*ip-address* | *peer-group-name*} **ebgp-multihop**

8-9: neighbor {*ip-address* | *peer-group-name*} **ebgp-multihop** *maximum-hop-count*

Syntax Description:

- *ip-address*—Neighbor's IP address.

- *peer-group-name*—Name of the peer group. See section 8-19.

- *maximum-hop-count*—Optional parameter with a value of 1 to 255. The default hop count is 255.

Purpose: EBGP neighbors are typically directly connected. In situations in which EBGP neighbors are not directly connected, the **ebgp-multihop** option must be used in order to form a neighbor relationship.

Cisco IOS Software Release: 10.0. Peer group support was added in Release 11.0.

Configuration Example: Nonconnected EBGP Neighbors

Figure 8-10 shows a situation in which we are trying to establish an EBGP connection between two routers that are not directly connected. BGP uses TCP, and Routers A and C must have routes to each other. The static routes on Routers A and C are necessary in order for BGP to establish the connection. On Router A, the default hop count of 255 is used. On Router C, a maximum hop count of 2 is used. A maximum hop count of 1 is interpreted as directly connected and therefore has no effect.

Figure 8-10   **ebgp-multihop** *Is Used to Form an EBGP Connection Between Peers That Are Not Directly Connected*

```
Router A
router bgp 1
 neighbor 10.1.2.2 remote-as 2
 neighbor 10.1.2.2 ebgp-multihop 255
!
ip route 10.1.2.0 255.255.255.252 serial0
```
```
Router C
router bgp 2
 neighbor 10.1.1.1 remote-as 1
 neighbor 10.1.1.1 ebgp-multihop 2
!
ip route 10.1.1.0 255.255.255.252 serial 0
```

Verification

Verification is the same as with directly connected EBGP neighbors. Use the **show ip bgp neighbors** command to verify that the relationship has been established:

```
rtrA#show ip bgp neighbors
BGP neighbor is 10.1.2.2,  remote AS 2, external link
  Index 1, Offset 0, Mask 0x2
   BGP version 4, remote router ID 172.17.1.2
   BGP state = Established, table version = 1, up for 00:07:52
   Last read 00:00:52, hold time is 180, keepalive interval is 60 seconds
   Minimum time between advertisement runs is 30 seconds
   Received 10 messages, 0 notifications, 0 in queue
   Sent 10 messages, 0 notifications, 0 in queue
   Prefix advertised 0, suppressed 0, withdrawn 0
   Connections established 1; dropped 0
   Last reset never
   0 accepted prefixes consume 0 bytes
   0 history paths consume 0 bytes
```

(Continued)

```
   External BGP neighbor may be up to 255 hops away.
Connection state is ESTAB, I/O status: 1, unread input bytes: 0
Local host: 10.1.1.1, Local port: 179
Foreign host: 10.1.2.2, Foreign port: 11048
rtrC#show ip bgp neighbors
BGP neighbor is 10.1.1.1,  remote AS 1, external link
 Index 1, Offset 0, Mask 0x2
   BGP version 4, remote router ID 172.17.1.1
   BGP state = Established, table version = 1, up for 00:02:01
   Last read 00:00:01, hold time is 180, keepalive interval is 60 seconds
   Minimum time between advertisement runs is 30 seconds
   Received 20 messages, 0 notifications, 0 in queue
   Sent 20 messages, 0 notifications, 0 in queue
   Prefix advertised 0, suppressed 0, withdrawn 0
   Connections established 2; dropped 1
   Last reset 00:03:37, due to User reset
   0 accepted prefixes consume 0 bytes
   0 history paths consume 0 bytes
   External BGP neighbor may be up to 2 hops away.
Connection state is ESTAB, I/O status: 1, unread input bytes: 0
Local host: 10.1.2.2, Local port: 179
Foreign host: 10.1.1.1, Foreign port: 11011
```

Troubleshooting

1 If the neighbors are not in the Established state, make sure each neighbor can ping the address used in the **neighbor** command.

2 If the ping is successful, ensure that you are using the correct neighbor IP address, remote AS number, and hop count in the respective BGP configurations.

3 If the ping is unsuccessful, trace the route to the EBGP neighbor to determine where your IP routing breaks down.

8-10: neighbor {*ip-address* | *peer-group-name*} filter-list *as-path-list-number* in

Syntax Description:

- *ip-address*—Neighbor's IP address.

- *peer-group-name*—Name of the peer group. See section 8-19.

- *as-path-list-number*—IP AS path list number.

Purpose: To filter incoming route updates from a particular BGP neighbor. Filtering is based on AS path information. Only one filter list can be used per neighbor. The operation of the input filter list is identical for both IBGP and EBGP neighbors.

Cisco IOS Software Release: 10.0. Peer group support was added in Release 11.0.

Configuration Example 1: Block Routes Originating from a Particular AS

In Figure 8-11, Routers B and C are advertising four network prefixes. Router A filters the route update from Router B in order to reject networks originating from AS 3. The last AS listed in the AS path list is the originating AS. Loopbacks are used on Routers B and C to simulate the advertised networks, as shown in the configuration.

Figure 8-11 *Scenario for the Use of the* **neighbor filter-list in** *Command*

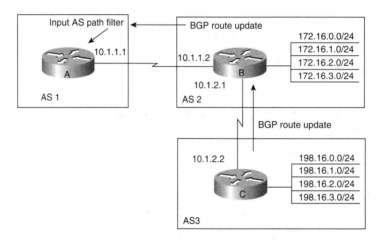

```
Router A
interface Serial0
 ip address 10.1.1.1 255.255.255.252
!
router bgp 1
 neighbor 10.1.1.2 remote-as 2
```
```
Router B
ip subnet-zero
!
interface Loopback0
 ip address 172.16.0.1 255.255.255.0
!
interface Loopback1
 ip address 172.16.1.1 255.255.255.0
!
interface Loopback2
 ip address 172.16.2.1 255.255.255.0
!
interface Loopback3
 ip address 172.16.3.1 255.255.255.0
!
```

```
(Continued)
interface Serial0
 ip address 10.1.1.2 255.255.255.252
 clockrate 64000
!
router bgp 2
 network 172.16.0.0 mask 255.255.255.0
 network 172.16.1.0 mask 255.255.255.0
 network 172.16.2.0 mask 255.255.255.0
 network 172.16.3.0 mask 255.255.255.0
 neighbor 10.1.1.1 remote-as 1
 neighbor 10.1.2.2 remote-as 3
```
```
Router C
ip subnet-zero
!
interface Loopback0
 ip address 198.16.0.1 255.255.255.0
!
interface Loopback1
 ip address 198.16.1.1 255.255.255.0
!
interface Loopback2
 ip address 198.16.2.1 255.255.255.0
!
interface Loopback3
 ip address 198.16.3.1 255.255.255.0
!
interface Serial0
 ip address 10.1.2.2 255.255.255.252
!
router bgp 3
 network 198.16.0.0
 network 198.16.1.0
 network 198.16.2.0
 network 198.16.3.0
 neighbor 10.1.2.1 remote-as 2
```

Before proceeding to the filter list example, verify that BGP is propagating the routes:

```
rtrA#show ip bgp
BGP table version is 22, local router ID is 172.17.1.1
Status codes: s suppressed, d damped, h history, * valid, > best, i - internal
Origin codes: i - IGP, e - EGP, ? - incomplete

   Network          Next Hop          Metric LocPrf Weight Path
*> 172.16.0.0/24    10.1.1.2               0             0 2 i
*> 172.16.1.0/24    10.1.1.2               0             0 2 i
*> 172.16.2.0/24    10.1.1.2               0             0 2 i
*> 172.16.3.0/24    10.1.1.2               0             0 2 i
*> 198.16.0.0       10.1.1.2                             0 2 3 i
*> 198.16.1.0       10.1.1.2                             0 2 3 i
*> 198.16.2.0       10.1.1.2                             0 2 3 i
*> 198.16.3.0       10.1.1.2                             0 2 3 i
```

continues

Section 8-10

(Continued)

```
rtrB#show ip bgp
BGP table version is 9, local router ID is 172.16.3.1
Status codes: s suppressed, d damped, h history, * valid, > best, i - internal
Origin codes: i - IGP, e - EGP, ? - incomplete

   Network          Next Hop          Metric LocPrf Weight Path
*> 172.16.0.0/24    0.0.0.0                0             32768 i
*> 172.16.1.0/24    0.0.0.0                0             32768 i
*> 172.16.2.0/24    0.0.0.0                0             32768 i
*> 172.16.3.0/24    0.0.0.0                0             32768 i
*> 198.16.0.0       10.1.2.2               0                 0 3 i
*> 198.16.1.0       10.1.2.2               0                 0 3 i
*> 198.16.2.0       10.1.2.2               0                 0 3 i
*> 198.16.3.0       10.1.2.2               0                 0 3 i
rtrC#show ip bgp
BGP table version is 18, local router ID is 198.16.3.1
Status codes: s suppressed, d damped, h history, * valid, > best, i - internal
Origin codes: i - IGP, e - EGP, ? - incomplete

   Network          Next Hop          Metric LocPrf Weight Path
*> 172.16.0.0/24    10.1.2.1               0                 0 2 i
*> 172.16.1.0/24    10.1.2.1               0                 0 2 i
*> 172.16.2.0/24    10.1.2.1               0                 0 2 i
*> 172.16.3.0/24    10.1.2.1               0                 0 2 i
*> 198.16.0.0       0.0.0.0                0             32768 i
*> 198.16.1.0       0.0.0.0                0             32768 i
*> 198.16.2.0       0.0.0.0                0             32768 i
*> 198.16.3.0       0.0.0.0                0             32768 i
```

Notice the AS path information contained in the BGP tables of the three routers. Before a router sends an update to another router in a different AS, the advertising router prepends its AS number to the update. This information is used to filter the updates. For this example, we want to filter the route update that Router A is receiving from Router B and block the routes that originate in AS 3. We can identify the routes originating in AS 3 by looking at the last AS number in the AS path information. If the last AS number is 3, these routes originated in AS 3. We don't care how many AS numbers are listed in the path as long as the last AS number is 3.

In order to filter routes based on AS path information, we need to use an AS path filter in conjunction with the BGP **filter-list** command. An AS path filter utilizes regular expressions to match patterns in the AS path list. Refer to Appendix B for a discussion of regular expressions. The regular expression used to match any prefix originating from AS 3 is _3$. Two of the characters that an underscore matches are a space and the beginning-of-string character. There is always a space between the AS numbers listed in an AS path. The **3$** must match a 3 and then the end-of-string character. So, the regular expression _3$ matches any path originating from AS 3, regardless of the length of the AS path. Now modify the BGP configuration on Router A to filter routes originating in AS 3:

```
Router A
router bgp 1
 neighbor 10.1.1.2 remote-as 2
 neighbor 10.1.1.2 filter-list 1 in
!
ip as-path access-list 1 deny _3$
ip as-path access-list 1 permit .*
```

The filter list always references an IP AS path access list. For this example, the AS path access list number is 1. The first statement in access list 1 rejects any routes originating in AS 3. The second line in the AS path access list is necessary because there is an implicit **deny any** at the end of every AS path access list. Without the **permit .*** statement, all routes from Router B would be rejected.

Verification

Verify that the routes originating in AS 3 are being blocked on Router A:

```
rtrA#show ip bgp
BGP table version is 5, local router ID is 172.17.1.1
Status codes: s suppressed, d damped, h history, * valid, > best, i - internal
Origin codes: i - IGP, e - EGP, ? - incomplete

   Network          Next Hop          Metric LocPrf Weight Path
*> 172.16.0.0/24    10.1.1.2               0            0 2 i
*> 172.16.1.0/24    10.1.1.2               0            0 2 i
*> 172.16.2.0/24    10.1.1.2               0            0 2 i
*> 172.16.3.0/24    10.1.1.2               0            0 2 I
```

Configuration Example 2: Block Routes Originating in AS 3 But Allow Routes That Pass Through AS 3

Remove the AS path filter on Router A using the **no** form of the **filter-list** command:

```
Router A
router bgp 1
 no neighbor 10.1.1.2 filter-list 1 in
```

For this example, we will modify the AS path information associated with networks 198.16.0.0/24 and 198.16.1.0/24. The modification makes these routes look like they originated in AS 4. This is accomplished by using a route map on Router C.

```
Router C
router bgp 3
 network 198.16.0.0
 network 198.16.1.0
 network 198.16.2.0
```

continues

Section 8-10

(Continued)
```
 network 198.16.3.0
 neighbor 10.1.2.1 remote-as 2
 neighbor 10.1.2.1 route-map adjust out
!
access-list 1 permit 198.16.0.0 0.0.1.255
route-map adjust permit 10
 match ip address 1
 set as-path prepend 4
!
route-map adjust permit 20
```

The route map on Router C prepends AS number 4 onto the 198.16.0.0/24 and 198.16.1.0/24 prefixes in order to demonstrate the AS path filter used in this example. Before installing the new AS path filter on Router A, check the BGP tables on Routers A and B to see if the AS path information has been modified:

```
rtrB#show ip bgp
BGP table version is 30, local router ID is 172.16.3.1
Status codes: s suppressed, d damped, h history, * valid, > best, i - internal
Origin codes: i - IGP, e - EGP, ? - incomplete

   Network          Next Hop         Metric LocPrf Weight Path
*> 172.16.0.0/24    0.0.0.0               0         32768 i
*> 172.16.1.0/24    0.0.0.0               0         32768 i
*> 172.16.2.0/24    0.0.0.0               0         32768 i
*> 172.16.3.0/24    0.0.0.0               0         32768 i
*> 198.16.0.0       10.1.2.2              0             0 3 4 i
*> 198.16.1.0       10.1.2.2              0             0 3 4 i
*> 198.16.2.0       10.1.2.2              0             0 3 i
*> 198.16.3.0       10.1.2.2              0             0 3 i
rtrA#show ip bgp
BGP table version is 9, local router ID is 172.17.1.1
Status codes: s suppressed, d damped, h history, * valid, > best, i - internal
Origin codes: i - IGP, e - EGP, ? - incomplete

   Network          Next Hop         Metric LocPrf Weight Path
*> 172.16.0.0/24    10.1.1.2              0             0 2 i
*> 172.16.1.0/24    10.1.1.2              0             0 2 i
*> 172.16.2.0/24    10.1.1.2              0             0 2 i
*> 172.16.3.0/24    10.1.1.2              0             0 2 i
*> 198.16.0.0       10.1.1.2                            0 2 3 4 i
*> 198.16.1.0       10.1.1.2                            0 2 3 4 i
*> 198.16.2.0       10.1.1.2                            0 2 3 i
*> 198.16.3.0       10.1.1.2                            0 2 3 i
```

The AS path filter that we will use is the same one used in Configuration Example 1. It demonstrates that the filter blocks only routes originating in AS 3 but allows routes that have passed through AS 3. Of course, all the 198.16.*x.x* routes originated in AS 3, but Routers A and B now think that two of the routes originated in AS 4:

```
Router A
router bgp 1
 neighbor 10.1.1.2 remote-as 2
 neighbor 10.1.1.2 filter-list 1 in
 !
ip as-path access-list 1 deny _3$
ip as-path access-list 1 permit .*
```

Verification

As in the previous example, check the BGP table on Router A to verify that only the networks whose AS path information ends in 3 are being blocked:

```
rtrA#show ip bgp
BGP table version is 7, local router ID is 172.17.1.1
Status codes: s suppressed, d damped, h history, * valid, > best, i - internal
Origin codes: i - IGP, e - EGP, ? - incomplete

   Network          Next Hop          Metric LocPrf Weight Path
*> 172.16.0.0/24    10.1.1.2               0            0 2 i
*> 172.16.1.0/24    10.1.1.2               0            0 2 i
*> 172.16.2.0/24    10.1.1.2               0            0 2 i
*> 172.16.3.0/24    10.1.1.2               0            0 2 i
*> 198.16.0.0       10.1.1.2                            0 2 3 4 i
*> 198.16.2.0       10.1.1.2                            0 2 3 4 I
```

Configuration Example 3: Block All Routes Containing AS Path Number 3

For this configuration example, we want to block any route whose AS path contains a 3. Remove the AS path list on Router A using the **no** form of the command:

```
Router A
router bgp 1
 no neighbor 10.1.1.2 filter-list 1 in
 !
no ip as-path acess-list 1
```

Because we have changed a neighbor policy, we need to use the **clear ip bgp *** command in order for the new policy to take effect. The BGP table on Router A should again contain all the routes being advertised by Router B:

```
rtrA#show ip bgp
BGP table version is 9, local router ID is 172.17.1.1
Status codes: s suppressed, d damped, h history, * valid, > best, i - internal
Origin codes: i - IGP, e - EGP, ? - incomplete
```

continues

Section 8-10

(Continued)

```
   Network          Next Hop          Metric LocPrf Weight Path
*> 172.16.0.0/24    10.1.1.2               0              0 2 i
*> 172.16.1.0/24    10.1.1.2               0              0 2 i
*> 172.16.2.0/24    10.1.1.2               0              0 2 i
*> 172.16.3.0/24    10.1.1.2.              0              0 2 i
*> 198.16.0.0       10.1.1.2                              0 2 3 4 i
*> 198.16.1.0       10.1.1.2                              0 2 3 4 i
*> 198.16.2.0       10.1.1.2                              0 2 3 i
*> 198.16.3.0       10.1.1.2                              0 2 3 i
```

The filter we want to use for this example should match any AS path containing a 3. Four patterns will match a 3 anywhere in the AS path:

<beginning of string>3<space>
<beginning of string>3<end of string>
<space>3<end of string>
<space>3<space>

Because an underscore matches a space, beginning of string, or end of string, we can use the regular expression _3_ to match all four patterns. Configure the AS path filter list on Router A:

```
Router A
router bgp 1
 neighbor 10.1.1.2 remote-as 2
 neighbor 10.1.1.2 filter-list 1 out
!
ip as-path access-list 1 deny _3_
ip as-path access-list 1 permit .*
```

Verification

Check the BGP table on Router A to verify that any route containing a 3 in the AS path has been blocked:

```
rtrA#show ip bgp
BGP table version is 5, local router ID is 172.17.1.1
Status codes: s suppressed, d damped, h history, * valid, > best, i - internal
Origin codes: i - IGP, e - EGP, ? - incomplete

   Network          Next Hop          Metric LocPrf Weight Path
*> 172.16.0.0/24    10.1.1.2               0              0 2 i
*> 172.16.1.0/24    10.1.1.2               0              0 2 i
*> 172.16.2.0/24    10.1.1.2               0              0 2 i
*> 172.16.3.0/24    10.1.1.2               0              0 2 i
```

Configuration Example 4: Block All Routes Originating from a Directly Connected EBGP Neighbor

Routes originating from a directly connected EBGP neighbor contain one AS number in the AS path. The form of the AS path is

<beginning of string>AS number<end of string>

The regular expression that matches routes from a directly connected EBGP neighbor is **^AS-number$**. For this example, we use a filter list on Router A to block routes originating from AS 2. Configure the following filter on Router A. Remember to remove any existing AS path filters:

```
Router A
router bgp 1
 neighbor 10.1.1.2 remote-as 2
 neighbor 10.1.1.2 filter-list 1 in
 !
ip as-path access-list 1 deny ^2$
ip as-path access-list 1 permit .*
```

Verification

Before you apply the filter, the BGP table on Router A should contain the routes from AS 2:

```
rtrA#show ip bgp
BGP table version is 9, local router ID is 172.17.1.1
Status codes: s suppressed, d damped, h history, * valid, > best, i - internal
Origin codes: i - IGP, e - EGP, ? - incomplete

   Network          Next Hop          Metric LocPrf Weight Path
*> 172.16.0.0/24    10.1.1.2               0             0 2 i
*> 172.16.1.0/24    10.1.1.2               0             0 2 i
*> 172.16.2.0/24    10.1.1.2               0             0 2 i
*> 172.16.3.0/24    10.1.1.2               0             0 2 i
*> 198.16.0.0       10.1.1.2                             0 2 3 4 i
*> 198.16.1.0       10.1.1.2                             0 2 3 4 i
*> 198.16.2.0       10.1.1.2                             0 2 3 i
*> 198.16.3.0       10.1.1.2                             0 2 3 i
```

After you apply the AS path filter, the routes originated by AS 2 should be gone:

```
rtrA#show ip bgp
BGP table version is 9, local router ID is 172.17.1.1
Status codes: s suppressed, d damped, h history, * valid, > best, i - internal
Origin codes: i - IGP, e - EGP, ? - incomplete
```

continues

Section 8-10

```
(Continued)
   Network          Next Hop           Metric LocPrf Weight Path
*> 198.16.0.0       10.1.1.2                            0 2 3 4 i
*> 198.16.1.0       10.1.1.2                            0 2 3 4 i
*> 198.16.2.0       10.1.1.2                            0 2 3 i
*> 198.16.3.0       10.1.1.2                            0 2 3 i
```

Troubleshooting

1 Verify that the BGP neighbors are in the Established state using the **show ip bgp neighbors** command.

If the neighbor relationship is not in the Established state, see section 8-23.

2 Verify that the routes to be filtered are being advertised using the **show ip bgp** command.

3 In some cases, there might not be any routes to filter. Your filter might be used to block future advertisements from a particular AS. In this case, the routes will not be in the BGP table.

4 If routes that you think should be filtered are showing up in the BGP table, check the syntax of your AS path filter and your regular expressions. You can check the operation of the filters by debugging the BGP updates. For the third example, the **debug** output would be similar to this:

```
Router A
6d16h: BGP: 10.1.1.2 rcv UPDATE about 198.16.0.0/24 -- DENIED due to: filter-list;
6d16h: BGP: 10.1.1.2 rcv UPDATE about 198.16.1.0/24 -- DENIED due to: filter-list;
6d16h: BGP: 10.1.1.2 rcv UPDATE about 198.16.0.0/24 -- DENIED due to: filter-list;
6d16h: BGP: 10.1.1.2 rcv UPDATE about 198.16.2.0/24 -- DENIED due to: filter-list;
6d16h: BGP: 10.1.1.2 rcv UPDATE w/ attr: nexthop 10.1.1.2, origin i, metric 0,
  path 2
6d16h: BGP: 10.1.1.2 rcv UPDATE about 172.16.0.0/24
6d16h: BGP: 10.1.1.2 rcv UPDATE about 172.16.1.0/24
6d16h: BGP: 10.1.1.2 rcv UPDATE about 172.16.2.0/24
6d16h: BGP: 10.1.1.2 rcv UPDATE about 172.16.3.0/24
6d16h: BGP: 10.1.1.2 rcv UPDATE w/ attr: nexthop 10.1.1.2, origin i, path 2 3 4
```

For the fourth example, the **debug** output would be similar to this:

```
Router A
6d16h: BGP: 10.1.1.2 rcv UPDATE w/ attr: nexthop 10.1.1.2, origin i, path 2 3
6d16h: BGP: 10.1.1.2 rcv UPDATE about 198.16.2.0/24
6d16h: BGP: 10.1.1.2 rcv UPDATE about 198.16.3.0/24
6d16h: BGP: 10.1.1.2 rcv UPDATE w/ attr: nexthop 10.1.1.2, origin i, metric 0,
  path 2
6d16h: BGP: 10.1.1.2 rcv UPDATE about 172.16.0.0/24 -- DENIED due to: filter-list;
6d16h: BGP: 10.1.1.2 rcv UPDATE about 172.16.1.0/24 -- DENIED due to: filter-list;
6d16h: BGP: 10.1.1.2 rcv UPDATE about 172.16.2.0/24 -- DENIED due to: filter-list;
6d16h: BGP: 10.1.1.2 rcv UPDATE about 172.16.3.0/24 -- DENIED due to: filter-list;
6d16h: BGP: 10.1.1.2 rcv UPDATE w/ attr: nexthop 10.1.1.2, origin i, path 2 3 4
6d16h: BGP: 10.1.1.2 rcv UPDATE about 198.16.0.0/24
6d16h: BGP: 10.1.1.2 rcv UPDATE about 198.16.1.0/24
```

8-11: **neighbor** {*ip-address* | *peer-group-name*} **filter-list** *as-path-list-number* **out**

Syntax Description:

- *ip-address*—Neighbor's IP address.
- *peer-group-name*—Name of the peer group. See section 8-19.
- *as-path-list-number*—IP AS path list number.

Purpose: To filter outgoing route updates to a particular BGP neighbor. Filtering is based on AS path information. Only one filter list can be used per neighbor. The operation of the output filter list is identical for both IBGP and EBGP neighbors.

Cisco IOS Software Release: 10.0. Peer group support was added in Release 11.0.

Configuration Example 1: Block Routes Originating from a Particular AS

In Figure 8-12, Routers B and C are advertising four network prefixes. Router B filters the route update to Router A in order to reject networks originating from AS 3. The last AS listed in the AS path list is the originating AS. Loopbacks are used on Routers B and C to simulate the advertised networks, as shown in the configuration.

Figure 8-12 *Scenario for the Use of the* **neighbor filter-list out** *Command*

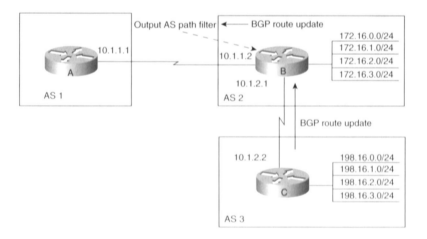

```
Router A
interface Serial0
 ip address 10.1.1.1 255.255.255.252
 !
```

continues

(Continued)

```
router bgp 1
 neighbor 10.1.1.2 remote-as 2
```

```
Router B
ip subnet-zero
!
interface Loopback0
 ip address 172.16.0.1 255.255.255.0
!
interface Loopback1
 ip address 172.16.1.1 255.255.255.0
!
interface Loopback2
 ip address 172.16.2.1 255.255.255.0
!
interface Loopback3
 ip address 172.16.3.1 255.255.255.0
!
interface Serial0
 ip address 10.1.1.2 255.255.255.252
 clockrate 64000
!
router bgp 2
 network 172.16.0.0 mask 255.255.255.0
 network 172.16.1.0 mask 255.255.255.0
 network 172.16.2.0 mask 255.255.255.0
 network 172.16.3.0 mask 255.255.255.0
 neighbor 10.1.1.1 remote-as 1
 neighbor 10.1.2.2 remote-as 3
```

```
Router C
ip subnet-zero
!
interface Loopback0
 ip address 198.16.0.1 255.255.255.0
!
interface Loopback1
 ip address 198.16.1.1 255.255.255.0
!
interface Loopback2
 ip address 198.16.2.1 255.255.255.0
!
interface Loopback3
 ip address 198.16.3.1 255.255.255.0
!
interface Serial0
 ip address 10.1.2.2 255.255.255.252
!
router bgp 3
 network 198.16.0.0
 network 198.16.1.0
 network 198.16.2.0
 network 198.16.3.0
 neighbor 10.1.2.1 remote-as 2
```

Before proceeding to the filter list example, verify that BGP is propagating the routes:

```
rtrA#show ip bgp
BGP table version is 22, local router ID is 172.17.1.1
Status codes: s suppressed, d damped, h history, * valid, > best, i - internal
Origin codes: i - IGP, e - EGP, ? - incomplete

 Network          Next Hop          Metric LocPrf Weight Path
*> 172.16.0.0/24    10.1.1.2              0              0 2 i
*> 172.16.1.0/24    10.1.1.2              0              0 2 i
*> 172.16.2.0/24    10.1.1.2              0              0 2 i
*> 172.16.3.0/24    10.1.1.2              0              0 2 i
*> 198.16.0.0       10.1.1.2                             0 2 3 i
*> 198.16.1.0       10.1.1.2                             0 2 3 i
*> 198.16.2.0       10.1.1.2                             0 2 3 i
*> 198.16.3.0       10.1.1.2                             0 2 3 i
```
```
rtrB#show ip bgp
BGP table version is 9, local router ID is 172.16.3.1
Status codes: s suppressed, d damped, h history, * valid, > best, i - internal
Origin codes: i - IGP, e - EGP, ? - incomplete

 Network          Next Hop          Metric LocPrf Weight Path
*> 172.16.0.0/24    0.0.0.0               0          32768 i
*> 172.16.1.0/24    0.0.0.0               0          32768 i
*> 172.16.2.0/24    0.0.0.0               0          32768 i
*> 172.16.3.0/24    0.0.0.0               0          32768 i
*> 198.16.0.0       10.1.2.2              0              0 3 i
*> 198.16.1.0       10.1.2.2              0              0 3 i
*> 198.16.2.0       10.1.2.2              0              0 3 i
*> 198.16.3.0       10.1.2.2              0              0 3 i
```
```
rtrC#show ip bgp
BGP table version is 18, local router ID is 198.16.3.1
Status codes: s suppressed, d damped, h history, * valid, > best, i - internal
Origin codes: i - IGP, e - EGP, ? - incomplete

 Network          Next Hop          Metric LocPrf Weight Path
*> 172.16.0.0/24    10.1.2.1              0              0 2 i
*> 172.16.1.0/24    10.1.2.1              0              0 2 i
*> 172.16.2.0/24    10.1.2.1              0              0 2 i
*> 172.16.3.0/24    10.1.2.1              0              0 2 i
*> 198.16.0.0       0.0.0.0               0          32768 i
*> 198.16.1.0       0.0.0.0               0          32768 i
*> 198.16.2.0       0.0.0.0               0          32768 i
*> 198.16.3.0       0.0.0.0               0          32768 i
```

Notice the AS path information contained in the BGP tables of the three routers. Before a router sends an update to another router in a different AS, the advertising router prepends its AS number to the update. This information is used to filter the updates. For this example, we want to filter the route update that Router B is sending to Router A and block routes that originate in AS 3. We can identify the routes originating in AS 3 by looking at the last AS number in the AS path information. If the last AS number is 3, these routes originated in AS 3. We don't care how many AS numbers are listed in the path, as long as the last AS number is 3. In order to filter routes based on AS path information, we need to use an AS path filter in conjunction with the BGP **filter-list** command. An AS path filter utilizes regular expressions to match patterns in the AS path list. Refer to Appendix B for a discussion of regular expressions. The regular expression used to match any prefix originating from AS 3 is _3$. Two of the characters that an underscore matches are a space and the beginning-of-string character. There is always a space between the AS numbers listed in an AS path. The **3$** must match a 3 and then the end-of-string character. So, the regular expression _3$ matches any path originating from AS 3, regardless of the length of the AS path. Now modify the BGP configuration on Router B to filter routes originating in AS 3:

```
Router B
router bgp 2
 neighbor 10.1.1.1 remote-as 1
 neighbor 10.1.2.2 remote-as 3
 neighbor 10.1.1.1 filter-list 1 out
 !
ip as-path access-list 1 deny _3$
ip as-path access-list 1 permit .*
```

The filter list always references an IP AS path access list. For this example, the AS path access list number is 1. The first statement in access list 1 rejects any routes originating in AS 3. The second line in the AS path access list is necessary because there is an implicit **deny any** at the end of every AS path access list. Without the **permit .*** statement, all routes from Router B would be rejected.

Verification

Verify that the routes originating in AS 3 are being blocked on Router A:

```
rtrA#show ip bgp
BGP table version is 5, local router ID is 172.17.1.1
Status codes: s suppressed, d damped, h history, * valid, > best, i - internal
Origin codes: i - IGP, e - EGP, ? - incomplete

   Network          Next Hop         Metric LocPrf Weight Path
*> 172.16.0.0/24    10.1.1.2              0             0 2 i
*> 172.16.1.0/24    10.1.1.2              0             0 2 i
*> 172.16.2.0/24    10.1.1.2              0             0 2 i
*> 172.16.3.0/24    10.1.1.2              0             0 2 I
```

Configuration Example 2: Block Routes Originating in AS 3 But Allow Routes That Pass Through AS 3

Remove the AS path filter on Router B using the **no** form of the **filter-list** command:

```
Router B
router bgp 2
 no neighbor 10.1.1.1 filter-list 1 out
```

For this example, we will modify the AS path information associated with networks 198.16.0.0/24 and 198.16.1.0/24. This modification makes these routes look like they originated in AS 4. This is accomplished by using a route map on Router C:

```
Router C
router bgp 3
 network 198.16.0.0
 network 198.16.1.0
 network 198.16.2.0
 network 198.16.3.0
 neighbor 10.1.2.1 remote-as 2
 neighbor 10.1.2.1 route-map adjust out
 !
access-list 1 permit 198.16.0.0 0.0.1.255
route-map adjust permit 10
 match ip address 1
 set as-path prepend 4
 !
route-map adjust permit 20
```

The route map on Router C prepends AS number 4 onto the 198.16.0.0/24 and 198.16.1.0/24 prefixes in order to demonstrate the AS path filter used in this example. Before installing the new AS path filter on Router B, check the BGP tables on Routers A and B to see if the AS path information has been modified:

```
rtrB#show ip bgp
BGP table version is 30, local router ID is 172.16.3.1
Status codes: s suppressed, d damped, h history, * valid, > best, i - internal
Origin codes: i - IGP, e - EGP, ? - incomplete

   Network          Next Hop         Metric LocPrf Weight Path
*> 172.16.0.0/24    0.0.0.0               0          32768 i
*> 172.16.1.0/24    0.0.0.0               0          32768 i
*> 172.16.2.0/24    0.0.0.0               0          32768 i
*> 172.16.3.0/24    0.0.0.0               0          32768 i
*> 198.16.0.0       10.1.2.2              0              0 3 4 i
*> 198.16.1.0       10.1.2.2              0              0 3 4 i
*> 198.16.2.0       10.1.2.2              0              0 3 i
*> 198.16.3.0       10.1.2.2              0              0 3 i
```

continues

(Continued)

```
rtrA#show ip bgp
BGP table version is 9, local router ID is 172.17.1.1
Status codes: s suppressed, d damped, h history, * valid, > best, i - internal
Origin codes: i - IGP, e - EGP, ? - incomplete

   Network          Next Hop         Metric LocPrf Weight Path
*> 172.16.0.0/24    10.1.1.2              0            0 2 i
*> 172.16.1.0/24    10.1.1.2              0            0 2 i
*> 172.16.2.0/24    10.1.1.2              0            0 2 i
*> 172.16.3.0/24    10.1.1.2              0            0 2 i
*> 198.16.0.0       10.1.1.2                           0 2 3 4 i
*> 198.16.1.0       10.1.1.2                           0 2 3 4 i
*> 198.16.2.0       10.1.1.2                           0 2 3 i
*> 198.16.3.0       10.1.1.2                           0 2 3 i
```

The AS path filter that we will use is the same one used in Configuration Example 1. It demonstrates that the filter blocks only routes originating in AS 3 but allows routes that have passed through AS 3. Of course, all the 198.16.*x.x* routes originated in AS 3, but Routers A and B now think that two of the routes originated in AS 4:

```
Router B
router bgp 2
 neighbor 10.1.1.1 remote-as 1
 neighbor 10.1.2.2 remote-as 3
 neighbor 10.1.1.1 filter-list 1 out
!
ip as-path access-list 1 deny _3$
ip as-path access-list 1 permit .*
```

Verification

As in the previous example, check the BGP table on Router A to verify that only the networks whose AS path information ends in 3 are being blocked:

```
rtrA#show ip bgp
BGP table version is 7, local router ID is 172.17.1.1
Status codes: s suppressed, d damped, h history, * valid, > best, i - internal
Origin codes: i - IGP, e - EGP, ? - incomplete

   Network          Next Hop         Metric LocPrf Weight Path
*> 172.16.0.0/24    10.1.1.2              0            0 2 i
*> 172.16.1.0/24    10.1.1.2              0            0 2 i
*> 172.16.2.0/24    10.1.1.2              0            0 2 i
*> 172.16.3.0/24    10.1.1.2              0            0 2 i
*> 198.16.0.0       10.1.1.2                           0 2 3 4 i
*> 198.16.2.0       10.1.1.2                           0 2 3 4 I
```

Configuration Example 3: Block All Routes Containing AS Path Number 3

For this configuration example, we want to block any route whose AS path contains a 3. Remove the AS path list on Router B using the **no** form of the command:

```
Router B
router bgp 2
 no neighbor 10.1.1.1 filter-list 1 out
 !
no ip as-path acess-list 1
```

The BGP table on Router A should again contain all the routes being advertised by Router B:

```
rtrA#show ip bgp
BGP table version is 9, local router ID is 172.17.1.1
Status codes: s suppressed, d damped, h history, * valid, > best, i - internal
Origin codes: i - IGP, e - EGP, ? - incomplete

   Network          Next Hop          Metric LocPrf Weight Path
*> 172.16.0.0/24    10.1.1.2               0             0 2 i
*> 172.16.1.0/24    10.1.1.2               0             0 2 i
*> 172.16.2.0/24    10.1.1.2               0             0 2 i
*> 172.16.3.0/24    10.1.1.2               0             0 2 i
*> 198.16.0.0       10.1.1.2                             0 2 3 4 i
*> 198.16.1.0       10.1.1.2                             0 2 3 4 i
*> 198.16.2.0       10.1.1.2                             0 2 3 i
*> 198.16.3.0       10.1.1.2                             0 2 3 i
```

The filter we want to use for this example should match any AS path containing a 3. Four patterns match a 3 anywhere in the AS path:

> <beginning of string>3<space>
> <beginning of string>3<end of string>
> <space>3<end of string>
> <space>3<space>

Because an underscore matches a space, beginning of string, or end of string, we can use the regular expression _3_ to match all four patterns. Configure the AS path filter list on Router B:

```
Router B
router bgp 2
 neighbor 10.1.1.1 remote-as 1
 neighbor 10.1.2.2 remote-as 3
 neighbor 10.1.1.1 filter-list 1 out
 !
ip as-path access-list 1 deny _3_
ip as-path access-list 1 permit .*
```

Verification

Check the BGP table on Router A to verify that any route containing a 3 in the AS path has been blocked:

```
rtrA#show ip bgp
BGP table version is 5, local router ID is 172.17.1.1
Status codes: s suppressed, d damped, h history, * valid, > best, i - internal
Origin codes: i - IGP, e - EGP, ? - incomplete

   Network          Next Hop          Metric LocPrf Weight Path
*> 172.16.0.0/24    10.1.1.2               0             0 2 i
*> 172.16.1.0/24    10.1.1.2               0             0 2 i
*> 172.16.2.0/24    10.1.1.2               0             0 2 i
*> 172.16.3.0/24    10.1.1.2               0             0 2 i
```

Configuration Example 4: Block All Routes Originating from a Directly Connected EBGP Neighbor

Routes originating from a directly connected EBGP neighbor contain one AS number in the AS path. The form of the AS path is

<beginning of string>AS number<end of string>

The regular expression that matches routes from a directly connected EBGP neighbor is **^AS-number$**. For this example, we use a filter list on Router A to block routes originating from AS 2. Configure the following filter on Router B, remembering to remove any existing AS path filters:

```
Router B
router bgp 2
 neighbor 10.1.1.1 remote-as 1
 neighbor 10.1.2.2 remote-as 3
 neighbor 10.1.1.2 filter-list 1 out
!
ip as-path access-list 1 deny ^2$
ip as-path access-list 1 permit .*
```

Verification

Before you apply the filter, the BGP table on Router A should contain the routes from AS 2:

```
rtrA#show ip bgp
BGP table version is 9, local router ID is 172.17.1.1
Status codes: s suppressed, d damped, h history, * valid, > best, i - internal
Origin codes: i - IGP, e - EGP, ? - incomplete
```

(Continued)

```
    Network              Next Hop            Metric LocPrf Weight Path
*>  172.16.0.0/24        10.1.1.2                 0               0 2 i
*>  172.16.1.0/24        10.1.1.2                 0               0 2 i
*>  172.16.2.0/24        10.1.1.2                 0               0 2 i
*>  172.16.3.0/24        10.1.1.2                 0               0 2 i
*>  198.16.0.0           10.1.1.2                                 0 2 3 4 i
*>  198.16.1.0           10.1.1.2                                 0 2 3 4 i
*>  198.16.2.0           10.1.1.2                                 0 2 3 i
*>  198.16.3.0           10.1.1.2                                 0 2 3 i
```

After you apply the AS path filter, the routes originated by AS 2 should be gone:

```
rtrA#show ip bgp
BGP table version is 9, local router ID is 172.17.1.1
Status codes: s suppressed, d damped, h history, * valid, > best, i - internal
Origin codes: i - IGP, e - EGP, ? - incomplete

    Network              Next Hop            Metric LocPrf Weight Path
*>  198.16.0.0           10.1.1.2                                 0 2 3 4 i
*>  198.16.1.0           10.1.1.2                                 0 2 3 4 i
*>  198.16.2.0           10.1.1.2                                 0 2 3 i
*>  198.16.3.0           10.1.1.2                                 0 2 3 i
```

Troubleshooting

1 Verify that the BGP neighbors are in the Established state using the **show ip bgp
   neighbors** command.

   If the neighbor relationship is not in the Established state, see section 8-23.

2 Verify that the routes to be filtered are being advertised using the **show ip bgp**
   command.

3 In some cases, there might not be routes to filter. Your filter might be used to block
   future advertisements from a particular AS. In this case, the routes are not in the BGP
   table.

4 If routes that you think should be filtered are showing up in the BGP table, check the
   syntax of your AS path filter and your regular expressions. You can check the
   operation of the filters by debugging the BGP updates. For the second example, the
   debug output would be similar to this:

```
Router B
6d17h: BGP: 10.1.1.1 send UPDATE 172.16.0.0/24, next 10.1.1.2, metric 0, path 2
6d17h: BGP: 10.1.1.1 send UPDATE 172.16.1.0/24 (chgflags: 0x0), next 10.1.1.2,
   path  (before routemap/aspath update)
6d17h: BGP: 10.1.1.1 send UPDATE 172.16.2.0/24 (chgflags: 0x0), next 10.1.1.2,
   path  (before routemap/aspath update)
```

continues

```
(Continued)
6d17h: BGP: 10.1.1.1 send UPDATE 172.16.3.0/24 (chgflags: 0x0), next 10.1.1.2,
  path (before routemap/aspath update)
6d17h: BGP: 10.1.1.1 send UPDATE 198.16.2.0/24, next 10.1.1.2, metric 0,
  path 2 3 4
6d17h: BGP: 10.1.1.1 send UPDATE 198.16.3.0/24 (chgflags: 0x0), next 10.1.1.2,
  path 3 4 (before routemap/aspath update).
```

Notice that the preceding debug output doesn't indicate routes that are blocked. Because the routes you intended to block are not being sent in the update, the AS path filter is working. If you see routes that you intended to block in the update, there is a problem with the AS path filter.

8-12: neighbor {*ip-address* | *peer-group-name*} filter-list *as-path-list-number* weight *weight*

Syntax Description:

- *ip-address*—Neighbor's IP address.

- *peer-group-name*—Name of the peer group. See section 8-19.

- *as-path-list-number*—IP AS path list number.

- *weight*—1 to 65535. This value is applied to the **weight** attribute of incoming routes matching the conditions in the AS path filter list.

Purpose: Routes learned from BGP neighbors have the **weight** attribute set to 0. This form of the **filter-list** command allows you to set the **weight** attribute of selected routes received from a particular neighbor. This command applies only to incoming route updates. The operation of the filter list is identical for both IBGP and EBGP neighbors.

Cisco IOS Software Release: 10.0. Peer group support was added in Release 11.0, and the **weight** keyword was removed in Release 12.1.

Configuration Example: Set the Weight of Routes Originating from a Particular AS

In Figure 8-13, Routers B and C are advertising four network prefixes. Router A inspects the route update coming from Router B and sets the weight of networks originating from AS 3 to 850. The last AS listed in the AS path list is the originating AS. Loopbacks are used on Routers B and C to simulate the advertised networks, as shown in the configuration.

Figure 8-13 *Scenario for the Use of the* **neighbor filter-list weight** *Command*

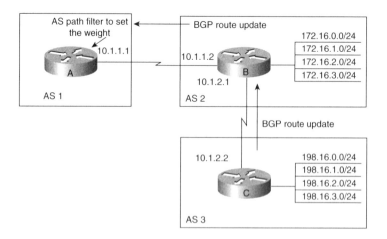

```
Router A
interface Serial0
 ip address 10.1.1.1 255.255.255.252
 !
router bgp 1
 neighbor 10.1.1.2 remote-as 2
```
```
Router B
ip subnet-zero
 !
interface Loopback0
 ip address 172.16.0.1 255.255.255.0
 !
interface Loopback1
 ip address 172.16.1.1 255.255.255.0
 !
interface Loopback2
 ip address 172.16.2.1 255.255.255.0
 !
interface Loopback3
 ip address 172.16.3.1 255.255.255.0
 !
interface Serial0
 ip address 10.1.1.2 255.255.255.252
 clockrate 64000
 !
router bgp 2
 network 172.16.0.0 mask 255.255.255.0
 network 172.16.1.0 mask 255.255.255.0
 network 172.16.2.0 mask 255.255.255.0
 network 172.16.3.0 mask 255.255.255.0
 neighbor 10.1.1.1 remote-as 1
 neighbor 10.1.2.2 remote-as 3
```

continues

(Continued)

```
Router C
ip subnet-zero
!
interface Loopback0
 ip address 198.16.0.1 255.255.255.0
!
interface Loopback1
 ip address 198.16.1.1 255.255.255.0
!
interface Loopback2
 ip address 198.16.2.1 255.255.255.0
!
interface Loopback3
 ip address 198.16.3.1 255.255.255.0
!
interface Serial0
 ip address 10.1.2.2 255.255.255.252
!
router bgp 3
 network 198.16.0.0
 network 198.16.1.0
 network 198.16.2.0
 network 198.16.3.0
 neighbor 10.1.2.1 remote-as 2
```

Before proceeding to the filter list weight example, verify that BGP is propagating the routes:

```
rtrA#show ip bgp
BGP table version is 22, local router ID is 172.17.1.1
Status codes: s suppressed, d damped, h history, * valid, > best, i - internal
Origin codes: i - IGP, e - EGP, ? - incomplete

   Network          Next Hop          Metric LocPrf Weight Path
*> 172.16.0.0/24    10.1.1.2               0             0 2 i
*> 172.16.1.0/24    10.1.1.2               0             0 2 i
*> 172.16.2.0/24    10.1.1.2               0             0 2 i
*> 172.16.3.0/24    10.1.1.2               0             0 2 i
*> 198.16.0.0       10.1.1.2                             0 2 3 i
*> 198.16.1.0       10.1.1.2                             0 2 3 i
*> 198.16.2.0       10.1.1.2                             0 2 3 i
*> 198.16.3.0       10.1.1.2                             0 2 3 i
rtrB#show ip bgp
BGP table version is 9, local router ID is 172.16.3.1
Status codes: s suppressed, d damped, h history, * valid, > best, i - internal
Origin codes: i - IGP, e - EGP, ? - incomplete

   Network          Next Hop          Metric LocPrf Weight Path
*> 172.16.0.0/24    0.0.0.0                0         32768 i
*> 172.16.1.0/24    0.0.0.0                0         32768 i
*> 172.16.2.0/24    0.0.0.0                0         32768 i
*> 172.16.3.0/24    0.0.0.0                0         32768 i
```

```
(Continued)
*> 198.16.0.0        10.1.2.2                    0             0 3 i
*> 198.16.1.0        10.1.2.2                    0             0 3 i
*> 198.16.2.0        10.1.2.2                    0             0 3 i
*> 198.16.3.0        10.1.2.2                    0             0 3 i
rtrC#show ip bgp
BGP table version is 18, local router ID is 198.16.3.1
Status codes: s suppressed, d damped, h history, * valid, > best, i - internal
Origin codes: i - IGP, e - EGP, ? - incomplete

    Network            Next Hop          Metric LocPrf Weight Path
*> 172.16.0.0/24      10.1.2.1               0             0 2 i
*> 172.16.1.0/24      10.1.2.1               0             0 2 i
*> 172.16.2.0/24      10.1.2.1               0             0 2 i
*> 172.16.3.0/24      10.1.2.1               0             0 2 i
*> 198.16.0.0         0.0.0.0                0         32768 i
*> 198.16.1.0         0.0.0.0                0         32768 i
*> 198.16.2.0         0.0.0.0                0         32768 i
*> 198.16.3.0         0.0.0.0                0         32768 i
```

Notice the AS path information contained in the BGP tables of the three routers. Before a router sends an update to another router in a different AS, the advertising router prepends its AS number to the update. This information is used to inspect the updates. For this example, we want to inspect the route update that Router B is sending to Router A and set the weight of routes that originate in AS 3 to 850. We can identify the routes originating in AS 3 by looking at the last AS number in the AS path information. If the last AS number is 3, these routes originated in AS 3. We don't care how many AS numbers are listed in the path, as long as the last AS number is 3. In order to set the weight of routes based on AS path information, we need to use an AS path filter in conjunction with the BGP **filter-list** command. An AS path filter utilizes regular expressions to match patterns in the AS path list. Refer to Appendix B for a discussion of regular expressions. The regular expression used to match any prefix originating from AS 3 is _3$. Two of the characters an underscore matches are a space and the beginning-of-string character. There is always a space between the AS numbers listed in an AS path. The **3$** must match a 3 and then the end-of-string character. So, the regular expression _3$ matches any path originating from AS 3, regardless of the length of the AS path. Now modify the BGP configuration on Router A to set the weight of routes originating in AS 3 to 850:

```
Router A
router bgp 1
 neighbor 10.1.1.2 remote-as 2
 neighbor 10.1.1.2 filter-list 1 weight 850
!
ip as-path access-list 1 permit _3$
```

The filter list always references an IP AS path access list. For this example, the AS path access list number is 1. The first statement in access list 1 matches any routes originating in AS 3 and allows their weights to be set to 850.

Verification

Verify that the routes originating in AS 3 have a weight of 850 on Router A:

```
rtrA#show ip bgp
BGP table version is 9, local router ID is 172.17.1.1
Status codes: s suppressed, d damped, h history, * valid, > best, i - internal
Origin codes: i - IGP, e - EGP, ? - incomplete

   Network          Next Hop          Metric LocPrf Weight Path
*> 172.16.0.0/24    10.1.1.2               0             0 2 i
*> 172.16.1.0/24    10.1.1.2               0             0 2 i
*> 172.16.2.0/24    10.1.1.2               0             0 2 i
*> 172.16.3.0/24    10.1.1.2               0             0 2 i
*> 198.16.0.0       10.1.1.2                           850 2 3 i
*> 198.16.1.0       10.1.1.2                           850 2 3 i
*> 198.16.2.0       10.1.1.2                           850 2 3 i
*> 198.16.3.0       10.1.1.2                           850 2 3 I
```

Troubleshooting

1 Verify that the BGP neighbors are in the Established state using the **show ip bgp neighbors** command.

   If the neighbor relationship is not in the Established state, see section 8-23.

2 Verify that the routes to be adjusted are being advertised using the **show ip bgp** command.

3 In some cases, there might not be routes to adjust. Your filter might be used to adjust future advertisements from a particular AS. In this case, the routes will not be in the BGP table.

   If routes that you think should be adjusted are showing up in the BGP table with a weight of 0, check the syntax of your AS path filter and your regular expressions.

8-13: neighbor {*ip-address* | *peer-group-name*} maximum-prefix *prefix-limit*

8-14: neighbor {*ip-address* | *peer-group-name*} maximum-prefix *prefix-limit* **warning-only**

8-15: neighbor *{ip-address | peer-group-name}* maximum-prefix *prefix-limit threshold-value*

8-16: neighbor *{ip-address | peer-group-name}* maximum-prefix *prefix-limit threshold-value* warning-only

Syntax Description:

- *ip-address*—Neighbor's IP address.

- *peer-group-name*—Name of the peer group. See section 8-19.

- *prefix-limit*—1 to 4294967295.

- *threshold-value*—1 to 100 percent. If this isn't explicitly set, the default value is 75 percent.

Purpose: To limit the number of prefixes learned from a specific neighbor. The *threshold-value* determines the value that causes the router to generate a warning. For example, if the *prefix-limit* is set to 1000 and the *threshold-value* is set to 75 percent, the router generates a warning when 751 prefixes are received from the neighbor. When the number of prefixes received from the neighbor exceeds the *prefix-limit,* the BGP connection between the neighbors is terminated. If the **warning-only** option is used, the router issues a warning when the prefix limit has been exceeded, but the connection is not terminated.

Cisco IOS Software Release: 11.3

Configuration Example: Controlling the Maximum Prefixes Learned from a BGP Neighbor

The configuration shown in Figure 8-14 demonstrates the **maximum-prefix** commands. Router A is configured with a *prefix-limit* of 8. The nine loopback interfaces on Router B are used to generate the prefixes that are advertised to Router A.

Sections 8-13 – 8-16

Figure 8-14 *Configuration Used to Demonstrate the* **maximum-prefix** *Commands*

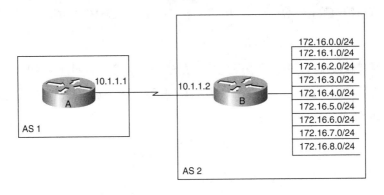

```
Router A
router bgp 1
 neighbor 10.1.1.2 remote-as 2
 neighbor 10.1.1.2 maximum-prefix 8
```
```
Router B
interface loopback 0
 ip address 172.16.0.1 255.255.255.0
!
interface loopback 1
 ip address 172.16.1.1 255.255.255.0
!
interface loopback 2
 ip address 172.16.2.1 255.255.255.0
!
interface loopback 3
 ip address 172.16.3.1 255.255.255.0
!
interface loopback 4
 ip address 172.16.4.1 255.255.255.0
!
interface loopback 5
 ip address 172.16.5.1 255.255.255.0
!
interface loopback 6
 ip address 172.16.6.1 255.255.255.0
!
interface loopback 7
 ip address 172.16.7.1 255.255.255.0
!
interface loopback 8
 ip address 172.16.8.1 255.255.255.0
!
router bgp 2
 neighbor 10.1.1.1 remote-as 2
 network 172.16.0.0 mask 255.255.255.0
```

(Continued)
```
network 172.16.1.0 mask 255.255.255.0
network 172.16.2.0 mask 255.255.255.0
network 172.16.3.0 mask 255.255.255.0
network 172.16.4.0 mask 255.255.255.0
network 172.16.5.0 mask 255.255.255.0
```

For this initial configuration, the default threshold value of 75 percent is used on Router A. This should cause a warning on Router A when seven routes ([%75 percent of 8] + 1) are received from Router B.

Verification

Verify the **maximum-prefix** parameters by using the **show ip bgp neighbors** command on Router A:

```
rtrA#show ip bgp neighbors
BGP neighbor is 10.1.1.2,  remote AS 2, external link
 Index 1, Offset 0, Mask 0x2
  BGP version 4, remote router ID 10.1.1.2
  BGP state = Established, table version = 7, up for 00:53:07
  Last read 00:00:08, hold time is 180, keepalive interval is 60 seconds
  Minimum time between advertisement runs is 30 seconds
  Received 375 messages, 0 notifications, 0 in queue
  Sent 343 messages, 0 notifications, 0 in queue
  Prefix advertised 0, suppressed 0, withdrawn 0
 Connections established 20; dropped 19
  Last reset 00:53:28, due to User reset
  6 accepted prefixes consume 192 bytes, maximum limit 8
  Threshold for warning message 75%
  0 history paths consume 0 bytes
 Connection state is ESTAB, I/O status: 1, unread input bytes: 0
 Local host: 10.1.1.1, Local port: 11015
 Foreign host: 10.1.1.2, Foreign port: 179
```

In order to test the **maximum-prefix** command, add a **network** statement to the BGP configuration on Router B. This will cause the number of received prefixes to exceed the threshold value of 75 percent:

```
Router B
router bgp 2
 neighbor 10.1.1.1 remote-as 2
 network 172.16.0.0 mask 255.255.255.0
 network 172.16.1.0 mask 255.255.255.0
 network 172.16.2.0 mask 255.255.255.0
 network 172.16.3.0 mask 255.255.255.0
 network 172.16.4.0 mask 255.255.255.0
 network 172.16.5.0 mask 255.255.255.0
 network 172.16.6.0 mask 255.255.255.0
```

Sections 8-13 – 8-16

Router A should generate the following warning:

```
rtrA#
05:04:45: %BGP-4-MAXPFX: No. of prefix received from 10.1.1.2 reaches 7, max 8
```

If we add one more **network** statement to the BGP configuration on Router B, the prefix limit will be reached on Router A:

```
Router B
router bgp 2
 neighbor 10.1.1.1 remote-as 2
 network 172.16.0.0 mask 255.255.255.0
 network 172.16.1.0 mask 255.255.255.0
 network 172.16.2.0 mask 255.255.255.0
 network 172.16.3.0 mask 255.255.255.0
 network 172.16.4.0 mask 255.255.255.0
 network 172.16.5.0 mask 255.255.255.0
 network 172.16.6.0 mask 255.255.255.0
 network 172.16.7.0 mask 255.255.255.0
```

Router A will generate the following message:

```
rtrA#
05:10:58: %BGP-4-MAXPFX: No. of prefix received from 10.1.1.2 reaches 8, max 8
```

If we add one more network statement to the BGP configuration on Router B, the prefix limit set on Router A will be exceeded. Because we did not use the **warning-only** option, the BGP connection will be terminated:

```
Router B
router bgp 2
 neighbor 10.1.1.1 remote-as 2
 network 172.16.0.0 mask 255.255.255.0
 network 172.16.1.0 mask 255.255.255.0
 network 172.16.2.0 mask 255.255.255.0
 network 172.16.3.0 mask 255.255.255.0
 network 172.16.4.0 mask 255.255.255.0
 network 172.16.5.0 mask 255.255.255.0
 network 172.16.6.0 mask 255.255.255.0
 network 172.16.7.0 mask 255.255.255.0
 network 172.16.8.0 mask 255.255.255.0
```

The BGP connection should terminate. Verify this claim by using the **show ip bgp neighbors** command:

```
rtrA#show ip bgp neighbors
BGP neighbor is 10.1.1.2,  remote AS 2, external link
Index 1, Offset 0, Mask 0x2
  BGP version 4, remote router ID 0.0.0.0
  BGP state = Idle, table version = 0
```

(Continued)

```
 Last read 00:00:45, hold time is 180, keepalive interval is 60 seconds
 Minimum time between advertisement runs is 30 seconds
 Received 402 messages, 0 notifications, 0 in queue
 Sent 360 messages, 0 notifications, 0 in queue
 Prefix advertised 0, suppressed 0, withdrawn 0
 Connections established 22; dropped 22
 Last reset 00:00:46, due to Peer over prefix limit
 Peer had exceeded the max. no. of prefixes configured.
 Reduce the no. of prefix and clear ip bgp 10.1.1.2 to restore peering
 No active TCP connection
```

The BGP connection has been terminated, as indicated by the Idle state. If we had used the **warning-only** option on Router A, only a warning would be generated, as shown:

```
rtrA#
05:12:59: %BGP-3-MAXPFXEXCEED: No. of prefix received from 10.1.1.2: 9 exceed 8
```

With the **warning-only** option, the BGP connection is not terminated if the prefix limit is exceeded. This can be seen by using the **show ip bgp neighbors** command on Router A:

```
rtrA#show ip bgp neighbors
 BGP neighbor is 10.1.1.2,  remote AS 2, external link
 Index 1, Offset 0, Mask 0x2
  BGP version 4, remote router ID 10.1.1.2
  BGP state = Established, table version = 7, up for 00:53:07
  Last read 00:00:08, hold time is 180, keepalive interval is 60 seconds
  Minimum time between advertisement runs is 30 seconds
  Received 375 messages, 0 notifications, 0 in queue
  Sent 343 messages, 0 notifications, 0 in queue
  Prefix advertised 0, suppressed 0, withdrawn 0
  Connections established 20; dropped 19
  Last reset 00:53:28, due to User reset
  6 accepted prefixes consume 192 bytes, maximum limit 8 (warning-only)
  Threshold for warning message 75%
  0 history paths consume 0 bytes
 Connection state is ESTAB, I/O status: 1, unread input bytes: 0
 Local host: 10.1.1.1, Local port: 11015
 Foreign host: 10.1.1.2, Foreign port: 179
```

Troubleshooting

1 Verify that the BGP neighbors are in the Established state using the **show ip bgp neighbors** command.

   If the neighbor relationship is not in the Established state, see section 8-23.

2 Verify that the maximum prefix limit and threshold value parameters are set using the **show ip bgp neighbors** command.

8-17: neighbor {*ip-address* | *peer-group-name*} next-hop-self

Syntax Description:

- *ip-address*—Neighbor's IP address.

- *peer-group-name*—Name of the peer group. See section 8-19.

Purpose: When a BGP router learns routes via EBGP, and those routes are advertised to an IBGP neighbor, the next-hop information is sent unchanged. This command allows a BGP router to change the next-hop information that is sent to IBGP peers. The next-hop information is set to the IP address of the interface used to communicate with the neighbor.

Cisco IOS Software Release: 10.0. Peer group support was added in Release 11.0.

Configuration Example: Setting Next-Hop Information for Advertised Prefixes

Every prefix that is advertised using BGP contains next-hop information. Figure 8-15 shows the next-hop behavior for EBGP and IBGP. The advertisement for network 198.16.1.0/24 from Router B to Router A contains a next hop of 172.16.1.1. EBGP next-hop information is preserved when the prefix is advertised via IBGP. Router B advertises network 198.16.1.0/24 to Router C, with the next-hop information received from Router A.

Figure 8-15 *Next Hop for EBGP and IBGP Connections*

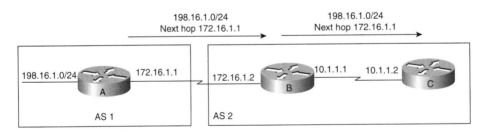

On a multiaccess network, such as Ethernet or Token Ring, the next-hop behavior is as shown in Figure 8-16. Router B learns about network 198.16.1.0/24 from Router A via IGP. Router B advertises 198.16.1.0/24 to Router C via EBGP with the next-hop information set to the address of Router A. This is done to avoid the extra hop of sending packets destined to network 198.16.1.0/24 to Router B.

Figure 8-16 *Next Hop for Multiaccess Networks*

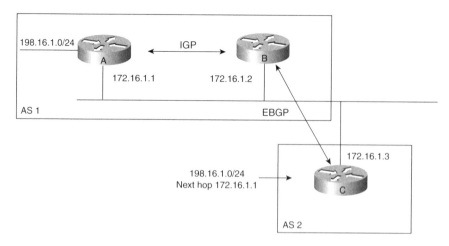

The next-hop behavior for a nonbroadcast multiaccess (NBMA) network is similar to that of a multiaccess network. Figure 8-17 shows a partially meshed NBMA network using a hub-and-spoke configuration. PVCs have been configured between the hub (Router B) and the spokes (Routers A and C). There is no PVC from Router A to C. Both PVCs are assigned to the same IP subnet, 172.16.1.0/24. Because the PVCs are on the same IP subnet, Router B sets the next-hop information for 198.16.1.0/24 to 172.16.1.1 when sending an update to Router C. Because Router C does not have a PVC to Router A, routing for this network will fail. In this situation, Router B needs to set the next hop for 198.16.1.0/24 to 172.16.1.2, as shown in the following configuration:

```
Router B
router bgp 1
 neighbor 172.16.1.3 remote-as 2
 neighbor 172.16.1.3 next-hop-self
```

Figure 8-17 *Next Hop for NBMA Networks*

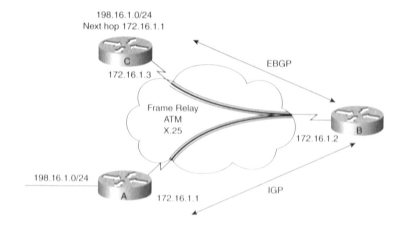

Verification

Verify the next hop for network 198.16.1.0/24 on Router C by using the **show ip bgp** command on Router C:

```
rtrC#show ip bgp
BGP table version is 22, local router ID is 172.16.1.13
Status codes: s suppressed, d damped, h history, * valid, > best, i - internal
Origin codes: i - IGP, e - EGP, ? - incomplete

   Network          Next Hop          Metric LocPrf Weight Path
*> 198.16.1.0/24    172.16.1.2             0             0 2 i
```

Troubleshooting

1   Verify that the BGP neighbors are in the Established state using the **show ip bgp neighbors** command.

   If the neighbor relationship is not in the Established state, see section 8-23.

2   Verify the next-hop setting using **show ip bgp**.

8-18: neighbor {*ip-address* | *peer-group-name*} password *password*

Syntax Description:

- *ip-address*—Neighbor's IP address.

- *peer-group-name*—Name of the peer group. See section 8-19.

- *password*—Case-sensitive password. The length of the password can be up to 80 characters. The first character of the password cannot be a number. The password can contain any alphanumeric characters, including spaces. For operational reasons, do not use a space after a number.

Purpose: To enable Message Digest 5 (MD5) authentication on a TCP connection between two BGP peers.

Cisco IOS Software Release: 11.0

Configuration Example: Enabling MD5 Authentication on a TCP Connection Between BGP Peers

The network shown in Figure 8-18 is used to demonstrate password configuration between neighbors.

Figure 8-18 *Authentication of a BGP Connection*

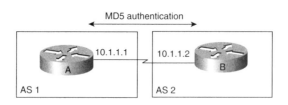

```
Router A
router bgp 1
 neighbor 10.1.1.2 remote-as 2
 neighbor 10.1.1.2 password cisco
Router B
router bgp 2
 neighbor 10.1.1.1 remote-as 1
 neighbor 10.1.1.1 password cisco
```

When a password is configured on the first neighbor, the BGP connection is terminated. When the password on the second neighbor is configured, the BGP session is reestablished.

Verification

Verification is easy. If the neighbors are in the Established state, authentication is working.

Troubleshooting

1 Verify that the BGP neighbors are in the Established state using the **show ip bgp neighbors** command.

   If the neighbor relationship is not in the Established state, see section 8-23.

2 If the neighbors are not in the Established state, there are two possibilities. Either one neighbor has not been configured with a password, or there is a password mismatch between the neighbors.

   If only one neighbor has a password configured, you see a message similar to the following:

   ```
   1d15h: %TCP-6-BADAUTH: No MD5 digest from 10.1.1.1:179 to 10.1.1.2:11028
   ```

   If there is a password mismatch, the following message is generated:

   ```
   1d15h: %TCP-6-BADAUTH: Invalid MD5 digest from 10.1.1.1:11018 to
   10.1.1.2:179
   ```

8-19: neighbor *peer-group-name* **peer-group**

8-20: neighbor *ip-address* **peer-group** *peer-group-name*

Syntax Description:

- *peer-group-name*—Name of the peer group to create or the name of the peer group to which the neighbor will be added.

- *ip-address*—IP address of the neighbor to be placed in the peer group with the name *peer-group-name*.

Purpose: Use the **neighbor** *peer-group-name* **peer-group** command to create a BGP peer group. The **neighbor** *ip-address* **peer-group** *peer-group-name* command adds a neighbor to an existing peer group. Assume that a router has multiple BGP neighbors and that it has identical update policies with those neighbors. The update policy could be configured for each neighbor. In this case, BGP would calculate a separate update for each neighbor even though the updates are identical. If the update policy is applied to a peer group and the neighbors are members of the peer group, the update is calculated once and then sent to all the neighbors in the peer group.

Cisco IOS Software Release: 11.0

Configuration Example: Creating Peer Groups

Router A in Figure 8-19 has two IBGP peers and two EBGP peers. Assume that Router A has the same update policy for the IBGP peers and the EBGP peers. The IBGP peers could be configured in one peer group and the EBGP peers in another. The first configuration is without using peer groups. The second configuration uses peer groups so that you can compare the syntax.

Figure 8-19 *BGP Peer Groups*

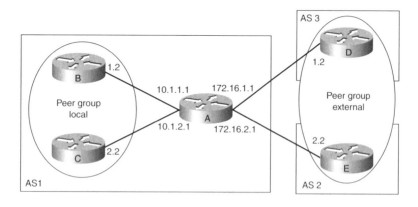

```
Router A (without using peer groups)
router bgp 1
 neighbor 10.1.1.2 remote-as 1
 neighbor 10.1.1.2 distribute-list 1 out
 neighbor 10.1.2.2 remote-as 1
 neighbor 10.1.2.2 distribute-list 1 out
 neighbor 172.16.1.2 remote-as 2
 neighbor 172.16.1.2 distribute-list 2 out
 neighbor 172.16.2.2 remote-as 3
 neighbor 172.16.2.2 distribute-list 2 out
Router A (Using peer groups)
router bgp 1
 neighbor local peer-group
 neighbor local remote-as 1
 neighbor 10.1.1.2 peer-group local
 neighbor 10.1.2.2 peer-group local
 neighbor local distribute-list 1 out
 neighbor 10.1.2.2 peer-group local
 neighbor external peer-group
 neighbor 172.16.1.2 remote-as 2
 neighbor 172.16.2.2 remote-as 3
 neighbor 172.16.1.2 peer-group external
 neighbor 172.16.2.2 peer-group external
 neighbor external distribute-list 2 out
```

The sequence of events in configuring peer groups is as follows:

Step 1   Create the peer group.

Step 2   Assign neighbors to the peer group.

Step 3   If all members of a peer group are in the same AS, assign the peer group to the AS.

Step 4   Assign update policies to the peer group.

The commands **neighbor local peer-group** and **neighbor external peer-group** create the peer groups local and external. Routers B and C are in the same AS, so we can place the peer group local in AS 1 using **neighbor local remote-as 1**. Routers D and E are in different autonomous systems, so the peer group external cannot be put in an AS. In this case, the individual neighbors are placed in their respective autonomous systems.

The update policy for neighbors B and C uses **distribute list 1 out**. Applying **distribute list** to the peer group applies the policy to each member of the peer group. The same is true for the external peer group. Incoming policies can also be assigned to a peer group. For example, we can apply an incoming filter list to peer group local:

```
neighbor local filter-list 1 in
```

If another incoming policy is applied to a specific neighbor, this policy overrides the peer group policy:

```
neighbor local filter-list 1 in
neighbor 10.1.1.2 filter-list 2 in
```

Filter list 2 is applied to neighbor 10.1.1.2 instead of filter list 1. You can override only incoming policies.

Verification

Verify that a neighbor is a member of the peer group. For example, check the status of the relationship between Routers A and B:

```
rtrA#show ip bgp neighbors
BGP neighbor is 10.1.1.2, remote AS 1, internal link
 Index 1, Offset 0, Mask 0x2
   local peer-group member
   BGP version 4, remote router ID 10.1.1.2
   BGP state = Established, table version = 41, up for 00:00:08
   Last read 00:00:07, hold time is 180, keepalive interval is 60 seconds
   Minimum time between advertisement runs is 5 seconds
   Received 14126 messages, 0 notifications, 0 in queue
   Sent 14138 messages, 0 notifications, 0 in queue
   Prefix advertised 15, suppressed 0, withdrawn 12
   Outgoing update network filter list is 1
   Connections established 5; dropped 3
   Last reset 00:00:17, due to Member added to peergroup
   2 accepted prefixes consume 64 bytes
   0 history paths consume 0 bytes
 Connection state is ESTAB, I/O status: 1, unread input bytes: 0
 Local host: 10.1.1.1, Local port: 11010
 Foreign host: 10.1.1.2, Foreign port: 179
```

Troubleshooting

1 Verify that the BGP neighbors are in the Established state using the **show ip bgp neighbors** command.

If the neighbor relationship is not in the Established state, see section 8-23.

2 If the neighbors are in the Established state, check the following:

- The spelling of the peer group name in the **neighbor** *peer-group-name* **peer-group** command.

- The spelling of the peer group name in the **neighbor** *ip-address* **peer-group** *peer-group-name* command.

- The IP address of the neighbor in the **neighbor** *ip-address* **peer-group** *peer-group-name* command.

8-21: neighbor {*ip-address* | *peer-group-name*} prefix-list *prefix-list-name* in

Syntax Description:

- *ip-address*—Neighbor's IP address.

- *peer-group-name*—Name of the peer group. See section 8-19.

- *prefix-list-name*—Name of the input IP prefix list.

Purpose: To filter incoming route updates from a particular BGP neighbor based on the IP address and mask length. Only one prefix list can be used per neighbor. The operation of the input prefix list is identical for both IBGP and EBGP neighbors. Using a prefix list is an alternative to using an extended IP access list and a distribute list.

Cisco IOS Software Release: 12.0

Configuration Example 1: Allow an Aggregate Route While Blocking the More-Specific Routes

In Figure 8-20, Router B is advertising four network prefixes and the aggregate of the prefixes to Router A. Router A filters the route update from Router B in order to reject the more-specific routes. Loopbacks are used on Router B to simulate the advertised networks, as shown in the configuration.

Figure 8-20 *Scenario for Use of the* **neighbor prefix-list in** *Command*

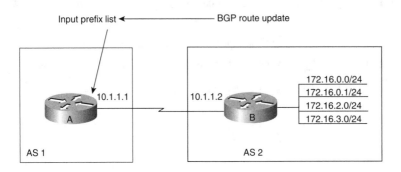

```
Router A
!
interface Serial0
 ip address 10.1.1.1 255.255.255.252
!
router bgp 1
 neighbor 10.1.1.2 remote-as 2
```
```
Router B
ip subnet-zero
!
interface Loopback0
 ip address 172.16.0.1 255.255.255.0
!
interface Loopback1
 ip address 172.16.1.1 255.255.255.0
!
interface Loopback2
 ip address 172.16.2.1 255.255.255.0
!
interface Loopback3
 ip address 172.16.3.1 255.255.255.0
!
interface Serial0
 ip address 10.1.1.2 255.255.255.252
 clockrate 64000
!
router bgp 2
 network 172.16.0.0 mask 255.255.255.0
 network 172.16.1.0 mask 255.255.255.0
 network 172.16.2.0 mask 255.255.255.0
 network 172.16.3.0 mask 255.255.255.0
 aggregate-address 172.16.0.0 255.255.252.0
 neighbor 10.1.1.1 remote-as 1
```

Before proceeding to the prefix list example, verify that Router A is receiving the routes from Router B:

```
rtrA#show ip bgp
BGP table version is 5, local router ID is 172.17.1.1
Status codes: s suppressed, d damped, h history, * valid, > best, i - internal
Origin codes: i - IGP, e - EGP, ? - incomplete

   Network          Next Hop          Metric LocPrf Weight Path
*> 172.16.0.0/24    10.1.1.2               0          0 2 i
*> 172.16.0.0/22    10.1.1.2                          0 2 i
*> 172.16.1.0/24    10.1.1.2               0          0 2 i
*> 172.16.2.0/24    10.1.1.2               0          0 2 i
*> 172.16.3.0/24    10.1.1.2               0          0 2 i
```

Modify the BGP configuration on Router A to allow only the aggregate prefix 172.16.0.0/22:

```
Router A
router bgp 1
 neighbor 10.1.1.2 remote-as 2
 neighbor 10.1.1.2 prefix-list aggregate in
!
 ip prefix-list aggregate seq 5 permit 172.16.0.0/22
```

The prefix list is similar to a route map. Prefix lists are named, and each statement in a prefix list has a sequence number. Elements in a prefix list are executed in numerical order, and processing stops when a match occurs. Before proceeding, we will discuss the commands available with an IP prefix list:

```
ip prefix-list sequence-number (default)
no ip prefix-list sequence-number
```

The default form includes the sequence numbers in the configuration. Using the **no** form of this command excludes the sequence numbers. If we list our configuration on Router A, we see that the sequence numbers are included in the configuration. By default, the sequence numbers start at 5 and increment by 5:

```
ip prefix-list aggregate seq 5 permit 172.16.0.0/22
```

Using the **no** form produces this:

```
ip prefix-list aggregate permit 172.16.0.0/22
```

If the **no** form is used, the sequence numbers can be seen using the **show ip prefix-list** command:

```
rtrA#show ip prefix-list
ip prefix-list aggregate: 2 entries
   seq 5 permit 172.16.0.0/22
```

Here is the general form of the command:

```
rtrA(config)#ip prefix-list ?
  WORD             Name of a prefix list
  sequence-number  Include/exclude sequence numbers in NVGEN

rtrA(config)#ip prefix-list aggregate ?
  deny         Specify packets to reject
  description  Prefix-list specific description
  permit       Specify packets to forward
  seq          sequence number of an entry
```

The **permit** and **deny** statements are used to determine if a prefix is allowed or prevented when received from a neighbor. The **description** option is useful if you have many prefix lists. We can add a description to our configuration using this:

```
ip prefix-list aggregate description filter specific routes of 172.16.0.0/22
```

The **seq** (sequence number) option allows us to apply our own sequence number to each **permit** or **deny** statement. If it is not used, the default sequence numbers are applied.

After the **permit** or **deny** option comes the prefix/length entry:

```
rtrA(config)#ip prefix-list aggregate permit ?
  A.B.C.D  IP prefix <network>/<length>, e.g., 35.0.0.0/8
```

For our example we used this:

```
ip prefix-list aggregate seq 5 permit 172.16.0.0/22
```

This permits the aggregate advertisement received from Router B. Finally, we can further specify a range for the number of bits to match in the prefix length by using the optional parameters greater than or equal to (**ge**) or less than or equal to (**le**):

```
rtrA(config)#ip prefix-list aggregate permit 172.16.0.0/22 ?
  ge  Minimum prefix length to be matched
  le  Maximum prefix length to be matched
  <cr>
```

The possibilities are to match the following:

- Less than or equal to a number of bits:

  ip prefix-list aggregate permit 172.16.0.0 /22 le 23

- Greater than a number of bits:

  ip prefix-list aggregate permit 172.16.0.0 /22 ge 23

- Greater than one value and less than or equal to another value:

  ip prefix-list aggregate permit 172.16.0.0 /22 ge 23 le 24

The last form allows the more-specific routes and blocks the aggregate prefix.

Verification

Verify that Router A is using the prefix list:

```
rtrA#show ip bgp
BGP neighbor is 10.1.1.2,  remote AS 2, external link
 Index 1, Offset 0, Mask 0x2
  BGP version 4, remote router ID 172.16.3.1
  BGP state = Established, table version = 2, up for 01:01:10
  Last read 00:00:09, hold time is 180, keepalive interval is 60 seconds
  Minimum time between advertisement runs is 30 seconds
  Received 172 messages, 0 notifications, 0 in queue
  Sent 150 messages, 0 notifications, 0 in queue
  Prefix advertised 0, suppressed 0, withdrawn 0
  Incoming update prefix filter list is aggregate
  Connections established 10; dropped 9
  Last reset 01:01:27, due to User reset
  1 accepted prefixes consume 32 bytes
  0 history paths consume 0 bytes
Connection state is ESTAB, I/O status: 1, unread input bytes: 0
Local host: 10.1.1.1, Local port: 11052
Foreign host: 10.1.1.2, Foreign port: 179
```

The prefix list can be examined by using the **show ip prefix- list** or **show ip prefix-list detail** commands:

```
rtrA#show ip prefix-list
ip prefix-list aggregate: 1 entries
   seq 5 permit 172.16.0.0/22

rtrA#show ip prefix-list detail
Prefix-list with the last deletion/insertion: aggregate
ip prefix-list aggregate:
   Description: filter specific routes of 172.16.0.0/22
   count: 1, range entries: 0, sequences: 5 - 5, refcount: 3
   seq 5 permit 172.16.0.0/22 (hit count: 1, refcount: 1)
```

Finally, check the BGP routing table on Router A to ensure that the 172.16.0.0/22 prefix has been allowed and that the more-specific prefixes have been filtered:

```
rtrA#show ip bgp
BGP table version is 2, local router ID is 172.17.1.1
Status codes: s suppressed, d damped, h history, * valid, > best, i - internal
Origin codes: i - IGP, e - EGP, ? - incomplete

   Network          Next Hop          Metric LocPrf Weight Path
*> 172.16.0.0/22    10.1.1.2                           0 2 i
```

Configuration Example 2: Allow the More-Specific Prefixes and Block the Aggregate

For this example, we will allow the more-specific prefixes and block the aggregate. The first method uses the following prefix list:

```
ip prefix-list aggregate permit 172.16.0.0/24
ip prefix-list aggregate permit 172.16.1.0/24
ip prefix-list aggregate permit 172.16.2.0/24
ip prefix-list aggregate permit 172.16.3.0/24
```

Here is a more compact form to achieve the same results:

```
ip prefix-list aggregate permit 172.16.0.0/22 ge 23
```

The BGP router configuration on Router A remains unchanged. Because there is an implicit **deny any** at the end of every prefix list, we will let this implicit statement block the aggregate.

Verification

As in the previous example, check the BGP table on Router A to verify that only the more-specific prefixes of 172.16.0.0 are being allowed:

```
rtrA#show ip bgp
BGP table version is 5, local router ID is 172.17.1.1
Status codes: s suppressed, d damped, h history, * valid, > best, i - internal
Origin codes: i - IGP, e - EGP, ? - incomplete

   Network          Next Hop          Metric LocPrf Weight Path
*> 172.16.0.0/24    10.1.1.2               0             0 2 i
*> 172.16.1.0/24    10.1.1.2               0             0 2 i
*> 172.16.2.0/24    10.1.1.2               0             0 2 i
*> 172.16.3.0/24    10.1.1.2               0             0 2 i
```

Troubleshooting

1 Verify that the BGP neighbors are in the Established state using the **show ip bgp neighbors** command.

   If the neighbor relationship is not in the Established state, see section 8-23.

2 Check the syntax of your prefix list.

   You can monitor the BGP route exchange using **debug ip bgp updates**, which should produce output similar to the following for the second configuration:

```
1w0d: BGP: 10.1.1.2 rcv UPDATE w/ attr: nexthop 10.1.1.2, origin i,
   aggregated by 2 172.16.3.1, path 2
1w0d: BGP: 10.1.1.2 rcv UPDATE about 172.16.0.0/22 -- DENIED due to: distribute/
prefix-list;
```

```
(Continued)
1w0d: BGP: 10.1.1.2 rcv UPDATE w/ attr: nexthop 10.1.1.2, origin i, metric 0,
  path 2
1w0d: BGP: 10.1.1.2 rcv UPDATE about 172.16.0.0/24
1w0d: BGP: 10.1.1.2 rcv UPDATE about 172.16.1.0/24
1w0d: BGP: 10.1.1.2 rcv UPDATE about 172.16.2.0/24
1w0d: BGP: 10.1.1.2 rcv UPDATE about 172.16.3.0/24
```

8-22: neighbor {*ip-address* | *peer-group-name*} prefix-list *prefix-list-name* out

Syntax Description:

- *ip-address*—Neighbor's IP address.

- *peer-group-name*—Name of the peer group. See section 8-19.

- *prefix-list-name*—Name of the output IP prefix list.

Purpose: To filter outgoing route updates to a particular BGP neighbor based on the IP address and mask length. Only one prefix list can be used per neighbor. The operation of the output prefix list is identical for both IBGP and EBGP neighbors. Using a prefix list is an alternative to using an extended IP access list and a distribution list.

Cisco IOS Software Release: 12.0

Configuration Example 1: Allow an Aggregate Route While Blocking the More-Specific Routes

In Figure 8-21, Router B is advertising four network prefixes and the aggregate of the prefixes to Router A. Router B filters the route update to Router A in order to reject the more-specific routes. Loopbacks are used on Router B to simulate the advertised networks, as shown in the configuration.

Figure 8-21 *Scenario for Using the* **neighbor prefix-list out** *Command*

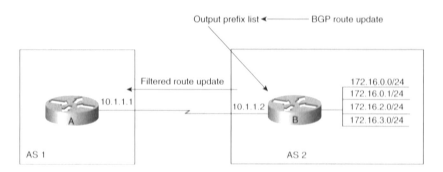

```
Router A
!
interface Serial0
 ip address 10.1.1.1 255.255.255.252
!
!
router bgp 1
 neighbor 10.1.1.2 remote-as 2
```
```
Router B
ip subnet-zero
!
interface Loopback0
 ip address 172.16.0.1 255.255.255.0
!
interface Loopback1
 ip address 172.16.1.1 255.255.255.0
!
interface Loopback2
 ip address 172.16.2.1 255.255.255.0
!
interface Loopback3
 ip address 172.16.3.1 255.255.255.0
!
interface Serial0
 ip address 10.1.1.2 255.255.255.252
 clockrate 64000
!
router bgp 2
 network 172.16.0.0 mask 255.255.255.0
 network 172.16.1.0 mask 255.255.255.0
 network 172.16.2.0 mask 255.255.255.0
 network 172.16.3.0 mask 255.255.255.0
 aggregate-address 172.16.0.0 255.255.252.0
 neighbor 10.1.1.1 remote-as 1
```

Before proceeding to the prefix list example, verify that Router A is receiving the routes from Router B:

```
rtrA#show ip bgp
BGP table version is 5, local router ID is 172.17.1.1
Status codes: s suppressed, d damped, h history, * valid, > best, i - internal
Origin codes: i - IGP, e - EGP, ? - incomplete

   Network          Next Hop            Metric LocPrf Weight Path
*> 172.16.0.0/24    10.1.1.2                 0             0 2 i
*> 172.16.0.0/22    10.1.1.2                               0 2 i
*> 172.16.1.0/24    10.1.1.2                 0             0 2 i
*> 172.16.2.0/24    10.1.1.2                 0             0 2 i
*> 172.16.3.0/24    10.1.1.2                 0             0 2 i
```

Modify the BGP configuration on Router B to allow only the aggregate prefix 172.16.0.0/22:

```
Router B
router bgp 2
 neighbor 10.1.1.1 remote-as 1
 neighbor 10.1.1.1 prefix-list aggregate out
 !
 ip prefix-list aggregate seq 5 permit 172.16.0.0/22
```

The prefix list is similar to a route map. Prefix lists are named, and each statement in a prefix list has a sequence number. Elements in a prefix list are executed in numerical order, and processing stops when a match occurs. Before proceeding, we will discuss the commands available with an IP prefix list:

```
ip prefix-list sequence-number (default)
no ip prefix-list sequence-number
```

The default form includes the sequence numbers in the configuration. Using the **no** form of this command excludes the sequence numbers. If we list our configuration on Router A, we see that the sequence numbers are included in the configuration. By default, the sequence numbers start at 5 and increment by 5:

```
ip prefix-list aggregate seq 5 permit 172.16.0.0/22
```

Using the **no** form produces this:

```
ip prefix-list aggregate permit 172.16.0.0/22
```

If the **no** form is used, the sequence numbers can be seen using the **show ip prefix-list** command:

```
rtrA#show ip prefix-list
ip prefix-list aggregate: 2 entries
   seq 5 permit 172.16.0.0/22
```

The general form of the command is:

```
rtrA(config)#ip prefix-list ?
  WORD             Name of a prefix list
  sequence-number  Include/exclude sequence numbers in NVGEN

rtrA(config)#ip prefix-list aggregate ?
  deny         Specify packets to reject
  description  Prefix-list specific description
  permit       Specify packets to forward
  seq          sequence number of an entry
```

The **permit** and **deny** statements are used to determine if a prefix is allowed or prevented when received from a neighbor. The **description** option is useful if you have many prefix lists. We can add a description to our configuration using this:

```
ip prefix-list aggregate description filter specific routes of 172.16.0.0/22
```

Section 8-22

The **seq** (sequence number) option allows us to apply our own sequence number to each **permit** or **deny** statement. If it is not used, the default sequence numbers are applied.

After the **permit** or **deny** option comes the prefix/length entry:

```
rtrB(config)#ip prefix-list aggregate permit ?
  A.B.C.D  IP prefix <network>/<length>, e.g., 35.0.0.0/8
```

For our example we used:

```
ip prefix-list aggregate seq 5 permit 172.16.0.0/22
```

This permits the aggregate advertisement to be sent to Router A. Finally, we can further specify a range for the number of bits to match in the prefix length by using the optional parameters greater than or equal to (**ge**) or less than or equal to (**le**):

```
rtrA(config)#ip prefix-list aggregate permit 172.16.0.0/22 ?
  ge  Minimum prefix length to be matched
  le  Maximum prefix length to be matched
  <cr>
```

The possibilities are to match the following:

- Less than or equal to a number of bits:

```
ip prefix-list aggregate permit 172.16.0.0 /22 le 23
```

- Greater than a number of bits:

```
ip prefix-list aggregate permit 172.16.0.0 /22 ge 23
```

- Greater than one value and less than or equal to another value:

```
ip prefix-list aggregate permit 172.16.0.0 /22 ge 23 le 24
```

The last form allows the more-specific routes and blocks the aggregate prefix.

Verification

The prefix list can be examined by using the **show ip prefix- list** or **show ip prefix-list detail** commands:

```
rtrB#show ip prefix-list
ip prefix-list aggregate: 1 entries
   seq 5 permit 172.16.0.0/22

rtrB#sh ip prefix-list  detail
Prefix-list with the last deletion/insertion: aggregate
ip prefix-list aggregate:
   count: 1, range entries: 0, sequences: 5 - 5, refcount: 3
   seq 5 permit 172.16.0.0/22 (hit count: 1, refcount: 1)
```

Finally, check the BGP routing table on Router A to ensure that the 172.16.0.0/22 prefix has been allowed and that the more-specific prefixes have been filtered:

```
rtrA#show ip bgp
BGP table version is 2, local router ID is 172.17.1.1
Status codes: s suppressed, d damped, h history, * valid, > best, i - internal
Origin codes: i - IGP, e - EGP, ? - incomplete

   Network          Next Hop            Metric LocPrf Weight Path
*> 172.16.0.0/22    10.1.1.2                              0 2 i
```

Configuration Example 2: Allow the More-Specific Prefixes and Block the Aggregate

For this example, we will allow the more-specific prefixes and block the aggregate. The first method uses the following prefix list:

```
ip prefix-list aggregate permit 172.16.0.0/24
ip prefix-list aggregate permit 172.16.1.0/24
ip prefix-list aggregate permit 172.16.2.0/24
ip prefix-list aggregate permit 172.16.3.0/24
```

The following prefix list is a more compact form that achieves the same results:

```
ip prefix-list aggregate permit 172.16.0.0/22 ge 23
```

The BGP router configuration on Router B remains unchanged. Because there is an implicit **deny any** at the end of every prefix list, we will let this implicit statement block the aggregate.

Verification

As in the previous example, check the BGP table on Router A to verify that only the more-specific prefixes of 172.16.0.0 are being allowed:

```
rtrA#show ip bgp
BGP table version is 5, local router ID is 172.17.1.1
Status codes: s suppressed, d damped, h history, * valid, > best, i - internal
Origin codes: i - IGP, e - EGP, ? - incomplete

   Network          Next Hop            Metric LocPrf Weight Path
*> 172.16.0.0/24    10.1.1.2                 0            0 2 i
*> 172.16.1.0/24    10.1.1.2                 0            0 2 i
*> 172.16.2.0/24    10.1.1.2                 0            0 2 i
*> 172.16.3.0/24    10.1.1.2                 0            0 2 i
```

Troubleshooting

1 Verify that the BGP neighbors are in the Established state using the **show ip bgp neighbors** command.

   If the neighbor relationship is not in the Established state, see section 8-23.

2 Check the syntax of your prefix list.

8-23: neighbor {*ip-address* | *peer-group-name*} remote-as number

Syntax Description

- *ip-address*—Neighbor's IP address.

- *peer-group-name*—Name of the peer group. See section 8-19.

- *number*—Neighbor's autonomous system number (1 to 65534).

Purpose: This form of the **neighbor** command is the most important. This command is used to configure an internal BGP (IBGP) or external BGP (EBGP) TCP session with another router. Routing information cannot be exchanged without a proper neighbor configuration. When configuring BGP, either in a customer's network or on the CCIE exam, we suggest that you first establish and verify that the neighbor relationships have been established. A common mistake is to attempt to enter a complete BGP configuration, which might include route exchange, route filtering, attribute manipulation, and route redistribution. If the configuration does not produce the intended results, it is usually very difficult to debug due to the configuration complexity. The preferred method is to configure BGP in steps, with the **neighbor** command being the first step. If neighbors are properly configured, you can continue to satisfy the other requirements.

Cisco IOS Software Release: 10.0. Peer group support was added in Release 11.0.

Configuration Example 1: EBGP Neighbor

EBGP is used between neighbors in different autonomous systems. Typically, EBGP neighbors are directly connected, as shown in Figure 8-22. If the neighbors are not directly connected, **bgp multihop** can be used (see sections 8-8 and 8-9). For this example, the neighbors are directly connected. The following configuration illustrates the use of the **neighbor** command to establish an EBGP relationship.

Figure 8-22 *EBGP Neighbor Relationship*

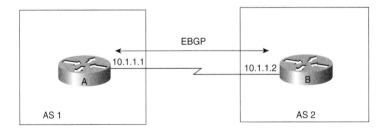

```
Router A
router bgp 1
 neighbor 10.1.1.2 remote-as 2
Router B
router bgp 2
 neighbor 10.1.1.1 remote-as 1
```

You need to set only two variables in order to establish a BGP session: the remote neighbor's IP address and the remote neighbor's autonomous system number, as shown in the preceding configuration. Therefore, you can make only two mistakes using this command.

Verification

To verify that the neighbor relationship has been established, use the **show ip bgp neighbors** command (see section 14-90):

```
RtrA#show ip bgp neighbors
BGP neighbor is 10.1.1.2,  remote AS 2, external link
 Index 0, Offset 0, Mask 0x0
  BGP version 4, remote router ID 10.1.1.2
  BGP state = Established, table version = 2, up for 00:17:01
  Last read 00:00:01, hold time is 180, keepalive interval is 60 seconds
  Minimum time between advertisement runs is 5 seconds
  Received 24 messages, 0 notifications, 0 in queue
  Sent 24 messages, 0 notifications, 0 in queue
  Connections established 2; dropped 1
Connection state is ESTAB, I/O status: 1, unread input bytes: 0
Local host: 172.16.1.3, Local port: 179
Foreign host: 172.16.1.7, Foreign port: 11001
```

The important elements that are illustrated are the BGP neighbor's IP address, autonomous system number, link type, and BGP state.

Troubleshooting

1 Ping the neighbor. If the ping is unsuccessful, you do not have a BGP problem.

2 If the ping is successful, you have improperly configured either the neighbor's IP address or autonomous system number.

If the neighbor relationship is not being established, only two things could be wrong, assuming that there are no physical layer problems. If you can ping the neighbor, you should be able to establish a BGP connection. Either the neighbor IP address or the **remote-as** number is incorrect. A correct configuration would produce the following debug output during the establishment of the BGP connection:

```
RtrB# debug ip bgp events
BGP: 10.1.1.1 went from Idle to Active
BGP: scanning routing tables
BGP: 10.1.1.1 went from Active to OpenSent
BGP: 10.1.1.1 went from OpenSent to OpenConfirm
BGP: 10.1.1.1 went from OpenConfirm to Established
BGP: 10.1.1.1 computing updates, neighbor version 0, table version 1, starting 0
BGP: 10.1.1.1 update run completed, ran for 0ms, neighbor version 0, start vers
```

Notice that the BGP state transitions from Idle to Active to OpenSent to OpenConfirm to Established.

If the wrong AS number is used but the neighbor's IP address is correct, the neighbors can establish a TCP session, but they will disagree on the AS number, and the connection will be closed. The following debug output is produced when the incorrect AS number is used for the neighbor:

```
BGP: 10.1.1.1 went from Idle to Active
BGP: 10.1.1.1 went from Active to Idle
BGP: 10.1.1.1 went from Idle to Connect
BGP: 10.1.1.1 went from Connect to OpenSent
BGP: 10.1.1.1 went from OpenSent to Closing
BGP: 10.1.1.1 went from Closing to Idle
```

If the neighbor IP address is incorrect, it really doesn't matter what AS number is used. The neighbors will never establish the TCP connection in order to exchange AS information. The following debug output is produced when an incorrect neighbor IP address is used:

```
BGP: 10.1.1.3 went from Idle to Active
BGP: scanning routing tables
BGP: 10.1.1.1 went from Active to OpenSent
BGP: 10.1.1.1 went from OpenSent to Closing
BGP: 10.1.1.1 went from Closing to Idle
```

Configuration Example 2: IBGP Neighbor

IBGP is used between neighbors in the same AS. IBGP neighbors do not need to be directly connected in order to establish a neighbor relationship. Also, the neighbor's IP address does not need to be the address assigned to a physical interface. We recommend that you use loopback addresses when establishing IBGP sessions. Section 8-33 examines techniques for using loopback addresses with IBGP. For this example, the objective is to demonstrate configuring IBGP neighbors and verifying the configuration. Figure 8-23 shows the scenario for two routers in the same AS. This example uses the IP address of a physical interface in the **neighbor** command.

Figure 8-23 *IBGP Neighbor Relationship*

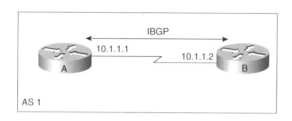

```
Router A
router bgp 1
 neighbor 10.1.1.2 remote-as 1
Router B
router bgp 1
 neighbor 10.1.1.1 remote-as 1
```

Notice that the only differences from the EBGP configuration are the remote AS number that is used on Router A and the BGP process number on Router B.

Verification

To verify that the neighbor relationship has been established, use the **show ip bgp neighbors** command (see section 14-90):

```
RtrA#show ip bgp neighbors
BGP neighbor is 10.1.1.2,  remote AS 1, internal link
  Index 0, Offset 0, Mask 0x0
  BGP version 4, remote router ID 10.1.1.2
  BGP state = Established, table version = 2, up for 00:17:01
  Last read 00:00:01, hold time is 180, keepalive interval is 60 seconds
  Minimum time between advertisement runs is 5 seconds
  Received 24 messages, 0 notifications, 0 in queue
  Sent 24 messages, 0 notifications, 0 in queue
  Connections established 2; dropped 1
Connection state is ESTAB, I/O status: 1, unread input bytes: 0
Local host: 172.16.1.3, Local port: 179
Foreign host: 172.16.1.7, Foreign port: 11001
```

The link type is now **internal** because we have established a BGP session between two routers in the same autonomous system. As with EBGP, the only errors that can occur are using the wrong neighbor IP address or using the wrong neighbor AS number.

Troubleshooting

Troubleshooting for IBGP neighbors is identical to troubleshooting EBGP neighbors. Remember, if you can ping the neighbor, you should be able to establish an IBGP connection if it's configured properly.

8-24: neighbor {*ip-address* | *peer-group-name*} remove-private-as

Syntax Description:

* *ip-address*—Neighbor's IP address.
* *peer-group-name*—Name of the peer group. See section 8-19.

Purpose: To remove private autonomous systems in updates to the neighbor or peer group. Private AS numbers are in the range 64512 to 65535. Private AS numbers should not be advertised to the Internet. The following conditions apply when using this command:

* Use only with EBGP peers.
* If the update has only private AS numbers in the AS path, BGP removes them.
* If the AS path includes both private and public AS numbers, BGP doesn't remove the private AS numbers. This situation is considered a configuration error.
* If the AS path contains the AS number of the EBGP neighbor, BGP doesn't remove the private AS number.
* If the AS path contains confederations, BGP removes the private AS numbers only if they come after the confederation portion of the AS path.

Cisco IOS Software Release: 12.0

Configuration Example: Removing a Private AS Number from Updates to Neighbors or Peer Groups

In Figure 8-24, an ISP is connected to a customer who is using a private AS number. The ISP is connected to another ISP for Internet connectivity. The ISP in AS 1 needs to remove the private AS number before advertising routes to the ISP in AS 2.

Figure 8-24 *Private AS Numbers Should Be Suppressed If Routes Are Advertised to the Internet*

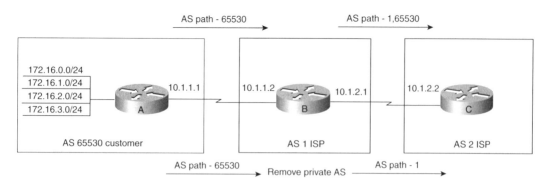

```
Router A
router bgp 65530
 network 172.16.0.0 mask 255.255.255.0
 network 172.16.1.0 mask 255.255.255.0
 network 172.16.2.0 mask 255.255.255.0
 network 172.16.3.0 mask 255.255.255.0
 neighbor 10.1.1.2 remote-as 1
Router B
router bgp 1
 neighbor 10.1.1.1 remote-as 65530
 neighbor 10.1.2.2 remote-as 2
 neighbor 10.1.2.2 remove-private-as
Router C
router bgp 2
 neighbor 10.1.2.1 remote-as 1
```

Verification

Before using the command **neighbor 10.1.2.2 remove-private-as**, check the BGP tables on Routers B and C to view the private AS number in the AS path:

```
rtrB#show ip bgp
BGP table version is 21, local router ID is 172.16.1.1
Status codes: s suppressed, d damped, h history, * valid, > best, i - internal
Origin codes: i - IGP, e - EGP, ? - incomplete

   Network          Next Hop          Metric LocPrf Weight Path
*> 172.16.0.0/24    10.1.1.1               0             0 65530 i
*> 172.16.1.0/24    10.1.1.1               0             0 65530 i
*> 172.16.2.0/24    10.1.1.1               0             0 65530 i
*> 172.16.3.0/24    10.1.1.1               0             0 65530 i
```

continues

(Continued)

```
rtrC#show ip bgp
BGP table version is 5, local router ID is 156.26.32.1
Status codes: s suppressed, d damped, h history, * valid, > best, i - internal
Origin codes: i - IGP, e - EGP, ? - incomplete

   Network          Next Hop         Metric LocPrf Weight Path
*> 172.16.0.0/24    10.1.2.1                        0 1 65530 i
*> 172.16.1.0/24    10.1.2.1                        0 1 65530 i
*> 172.16.2.0/24    10.1.2.1                        0 1 65530 i
*> 172.16.3.0/24    10.1.2.1                        0 1 65530 i
```

Now add the command **neighbor 10.1.2.2 remove-private-as** on Router B and recheck the BGP table on Router C:

```
rtrC#show ip bgp
BGP table version is 5, local router ID is 156.26.32.1
Status codes: s suppressed, d damped, h history, * valid, > best, i - internal
Origin codes: i - IGP, e - EGP, ? - incomplete

   Network          Next Hop         Metric LocPrf Weight Path
*> 172.16.0.0/24    10.1.2.1                        0 1 i
*> 172.16.1.0/24    10.1.2.1                        0 1 i
*> 172.16.2.0/24    10.1.2.1                        0 1 i
*> 172.16.3.0/24    10.1.2.1                        0 1 i
```

As you can see, the private AS number (65530) has been removed.

Troubleshooting

1   Verify that the BGP neighbors are in the Established state using the **show ip bgp neighbors** command.

   If the neighbor relationship is not in the Established state, see section 8-23.

2   Verify that the private AS numbers have been removed by using **show ip bgp**.

3   If the private AS numbers have not been removed, check the neighbor's IP address or peer group name in the **remove-private-as** command.

8-25: neighbor {*ip-address* | *peer-group-name*} **route-map** *route-map-name* **in**

Syntax Description:

- *ip-address*—Neighbor's IP address.

- *peer-group-name*—Name of the peer group. See section 8-19.

- *route-map-name*—Name of the route map used for incoming updates from the specified neighbor or peer group.

Purpose: A route map is an extremely powerful tool for route filtering and BGP attribute manipulation. Appendix C contains a complete discussion of route map logic. In this section, we will examine common uses of a route map for route filtering and BGP attribute manipulation.

Cisco IOS Software Release: 10.0. Peer group support was added in Release 11.0.

Configuration Example 1: Basic Route Filter Using an IP Standard Access List

The configuration in Figure 8-25 will be used for each route map example in this section.

Figure 8-25 *Configuration Used to Demonstrate the Use of an Input Route Map*

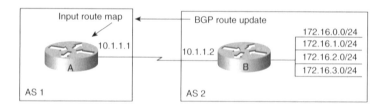

```
Router A
router bgp 1
 neighbor 10.1.1.2 remote-as 2
```
```
Router B
interface loopback 0
 ip address 172.16.0.1 255.255.255.0
!
interface loopback 1
 ip address 172.16.1.1 255.255.255.0
!
interface loopback 2
 ip address 172.16.2.1 255.255.255.0
!
interface loopback 3
 ip address 172.16.3.1 255.255.255.0
!
router bgp 2
 neighbor 10.1.1.1 remote-as 1
 network 172.16.0.0 mask 255.255.255.0
 network 172.16.1.0 mask 255.255.255.0
 network 172.16.2.0 mask 255.255.255.0
 network 172.16.3.0 mask 255.255.255.0
```

Before looking at the first route map example, verify that Router A is receiving the four 172.16 prefixes from Router B:

```
rtrA#show ip bgp
BGP table version is 5, local router ID is 172.17.1.1
Status codes: s suppressed, d damped, h history, * valid, > best, i - internal
Origin codes: i - IGP, e - EGP, ? - incomplete

   Network          Next Hop          Metric LocPrf Weight Path
*> 172.16.0.0/24    10.1.1.2               0            0 2 i
*> 172.16.1.0/24    10.1.1.2               0            0 2 i
*> 172.16.2.0/24    10.1.1.2               0            0 2 i
*> 172.16.3.0/24    10.1.1.2               0            0 2 i
```

We want to use an input route map on Router A to block network 172.16.2.0/24. We could use a neighbor distribute list (see section 8-6) or prefix list (see section 8-21) to accomplish this task, but because this section concerns route maps, we might as well use one. Configure the following route map on Router A.

Releases of Cisco IOS Software prior to 11.2 did not permit the use of an input route map that matched on the IP address. This restriction was removed in Release 11.2 and later versions.

```
Router A
router bgp 1
 neighbor 10.1.1.2 remote-as 2
 neighbor 10.1.1.2 route-map filter in
!
access-list 1 deny 172.16.2.0 0.0.0.255
access-list 1 permit any
!
route-map filter permit 10
 match ip address 1
```

Whenever you change a policy with a neighbor, you need to restart the BGP session by using **clear ip bgp *** or **clear ip bgp** *neighbor-address*. For this example, use **clear ip bgp 10.1.1.2**.

Because we are either denying or permitting a route, we do not need any **set** commands in the route map. Each route or prefix received from Router B is processed by the input route map with a name filter. The result of a route map is to either permit or deny an action. The action in this example is to permit routes received from a BGP neighbor to be installed in the BGP table.

Verification

Verify that the prefix 172.16.2.0/24 has been filtered:

```
rtrA#show ip bgp
BGP table version is 22, local router ID is 172.17.1.1
Status codes: s suppressed, d damped, h history, * valid, > best, i - internal
Origin codes: i - IGP, e - EGP, ? - incomplete

   Network          Next Hop         Metric LocPrf Weight Path
*> 172.16.0.0/24    10.1.1.2              0            0 2 i
*> 172.16.1.0/24    10.1.1.2              0            0 2 i
*> 172.16.3.0/24    10.1.1.2              0            0 2 i
```

Configuration Example 2: Basic Route Filter Using an IP Extended Access List

An extended IP access list can be used to match on the incoming prefix and mask. The second subnet/mask portion of the extended access list is used to match the mask length. Configure an aggregate address on Router B in order to generate a prefix with a 22-bit mask length:

```
Router B
router bgp 2
 network 172.16.0.0 mask 255.255.255.0
 network 172.16.1.0 mask 255.255.255.0
 network 172.16.2.0 mask 255.255.255.0
 network 172.16.3.0 mask 255.255.255.0
 aggregate-address 172.16.0.0 255.255.252.0
 neighbor 10.1.1.1 remote-as 1
```

Verify that the aggregate address is being advertised to Router A:

```
rtrA#show ip bgp
BGP table version is 10, local router ID is 192.16.2.1
Status codes: s suppressed, d damped, h history, * valid, > best, i - internal
Origin codes: i - IGP, e - EGP, ? - incomplete

   Network          Next Hop         Metric LocPrf Weight Path
*> 172.16.0.0/24    10.1.1.2              0            0 2 i
*> 172.16.0.0/22    10.1.1.2                           0 2 i
*> 172.16.1.0/24    10.1.1.2              0            0 2 i
*> 172.16.2.0/24    10.1.1.2              0            0 2 i
*> 172.16.3.0/24    10.1.1.2              0            0 2 i
```

Section 8-25

Now add the route map on Router A to filter the aggregate prefix 172.16.0.0/22:

```
Router A
router bgp 1
 neighbor 10.1.1.2 remote-as 2
 neighbor 10.1.1.2 route-map filter in
!
access-list 100 deny ip 172.16.0.0 0.0.3.255 255.255.252.0 0.0.0.0
access-list 100 permit ip any any
!
route-map filter permit 10
 match ip address 100
```

Verification

Verify that the 172.16.0.0/22 prefix has been filtered on Router A:

```
rtrA#show ip bgp
BGP table version is 5, local router ID is 192.16.2.1
Status codes: s suppressed, d damped, h history, * valid, > best, i - internal
Origin codes: i - IGP, e - EGP, ? - incomplete

   Network          Next Hop          Metric LocPrf Weight Path
*> 172.16.0.0/24    10.1.1.2               0             0 2 i
*> 172.16.1.0/24    10.1.1.2               0             0 2 i
*> 172.16.2.0/24    10.1.1.2               0             0 2 i
*> 172.16.3.0/24    10.1.1.2               0             0 2 i
```

Configuration Example 3: Basic BGP Attribute Manipulation

Assume that we do not want to block any routes received from a neighbor but we want to adjust one or more BGP attributes. For this example, we will set the weight of all routes received from Router B to 90 using a route map. Because we will apply this policy to all updates from Router B, we do not need a **match** clause, only a **set** clause, as shown in the following configuration for Router A:

```
Router A
router bgp 1
 neighbor 10.1.1.2 remote-as 2
 neighbor 10.1.1.2 route-map filter in
!
route-map filter permit 10
 set weight 90
```

The command **neighbor** *ip-address* **weight** (see section 8-35) would have accomplished the same objective.

Verification

Verify that the weight of all routes received from Router B has been set to 90:

```
rtrA#show ip bgp
BGP table version is 6, local router ID is 192.16.2.1
Status codes: s suppressed, d damped, h history, * valid, > best, i - internal
Origin codes: i - IGP, e - EGP, ? - incomplete

   Network          Next Hop         Metric LocPrf Weight Path
*> 172.16.0.0/24    10.1.1.2              0            90 2 i
*> 172.16.1.0/24    10.1.1.2              0            90 2 i
*> 172.16.2.0/24    10.1.1.2              0            90 2 i
*> 172.16.3.0/24    10.1.1.2              0            90 2 i
```

Configuration Example 4: Selective BGP Attribute Manipulation

In the preceding example, we set the weight of all routes learned from Router B to 90. In this example, we will set the weight of 172.16.2.0 to 90 and the rest of the weights to 45. This demonstrates the flexibility of using a route map. Modify the configuration on Route A to the following:

```
Router A
router bgp 1
 neighbor 10.1.1.2 remote-as 2
 neighbor 10.1.1.2 route-map filter in
!
access-list 1 permit 172.16.2.0 0.0.0.255
route-map filter permit 10
 match ip address 1
 set weight 90
route-map filter permit 20
 set weight 45
```

The second stanza of the route map is the default case. If we had not used a second route map stanza, all routes that did not match IP address 1 would have been blocked. Therefore, it is extremely important that you configure a default route map stanza if needed.

Verification

Verify the new weight settings on Router A:

```
rtrA#show ip bgp
BGP table version is 6, local router ID is 192.16.2.1
Status codes: s suppressed, d damped, h history, * valid, > best, i - internal
Origin codes: i - IGP, e - EGP, ? - incomplete
```

continues

```
(Continued)
   Network            Next Hop           Metric LocPrf Weight Path
*> 172.16.0.0/24      10.1.1.2                0            45 2 i
*> 172.16.1.0/24      10.1.1.2                0            45 2 i
*> 172.16.2.0/24      10.1.1.2                0            90 2 i
*> 172.16.3.0/24      10.1.1.2                0            45 2 i
```

Configuration Example 5: Filter Based on AS Path Information

The previous examples have made filtering decisions based on the route/prefix information in the neighbor updates. In this example, we will see how to filter routes based on the BGP AS PATH attribute. All the routes from Router B have the same AS path information, but this example demonstrates the required route map syntax. Again, the objective is to set the weight of the routes learned from Router B to 90, but the decision will be based on the AS path information. The decision is to set the weights only on routes originating from a directly connected BGP neighbor. For this case, the AS path to match is

<beginning of string>AS number<end of string>

The required regular expression is **^2$**, as shown in the following configuration for Router A:

```
Router A
router bgp 1
 neighbor 10.1.1.2 remote-as 2
 neighbor 10.1.1.2 route-map filter in
!
ip as-path access-list 1 permit ^2$
route-map filter permit 10
 match as_path 1
 set weight 90
route-map filter permit 20
```

Without the second route map stanza, all routes not matching AS path **^2$** would be denied. This might or might not be the result you intended.

Verification

Verify the weight settings on Router A:

```
rtrA#show ip bgp
BGP table version is 6, local router ID is 192.16.2.1
Status codes: s suppressed, d damped, h history, * valid, > best, i - internal
Origin codes: i - IGP, e - EGP, ? - incomplete

   Network            Next Hop           Metric LocPrf Weight Path
*> 172.16.0.0/24      10.1.1.2                0            90 2 i
*> 172.16.1.0/24      10.1.1.2                0            90 2 i
*> 172.16.2.0/24      10.1.1.2                0            90 2 i
*> 172.16.3.0/24      10.1.1.2                0            90 2 i
```

Troubleshooting

1 Verify that the BGP neighbors are in the Established state using the **show ip bgp neighbors** command.

If the neighbor relationship is not in the Established state, see section 8-23.

2 Verify that the input route map is being used with the BGP neighbor using the **show ip bgp neighbors** command:

```
rtrA#sh ip bgp n
BGP neighbor is 10.1.1.2,  remote AS 2, external link
 Index 1, Offset 0, Mask 0x2
  BGP version 4, remote router ID 172.16.3.1
  BGP state = Established, table version = 5, up for 00:02:51
  Last read 00:00:52, hold time is 180, keepalive interval is 60 seconds
  Minimum time between advertisement runs is 30 seconds
  Received 19097 messages, 0 notifications, 0 in queue
  Sent 19028 messages, 0 notifications, 0 in queue
  Prefix advertised 6, suppressed 0, withdrawn 2
  Inbound path policy configured
  Route map for incoming advertisements is filter
  Connections established 38; dropped 37
  Last reset 00:03:22, due to User reset
  4 accepted prefixes consume 128 bytes
  0 history paths consume 0 bytes
Connection state is ESTAB, I/O status: 1, unread input bytes: 0
Local host: 10.1.1.1, Local port: 11076
Foreign host: 10.1.1.2, Foreign port: 179
Enqueued packets for retransmit: 0, input: 0  mis-ordered: 0 (0 bytes)
```

3 Verify that the correct neighbor address is being used with the **neighbor** *ip-address* **route-map** *route-map-name* **in** command.

4 Verify that you are using the correct route map name.

5 Verify the logic of your route map (see Appendix C).

6 You can view the route map using the **show route-map** *route-map-name* command:

```
rtrA#show route-map filter
route-map filter, permit, sequence 10
  Match clauses:
    ip address (access-lists): 1
  Set clauses:
    weight 90
  Policy routing matches: 0 packets, 0 bytes
route-map filter, permit, sequence 20
  Match clauses:
  Set clauses:
    weight 45
  Policy routing matches: 0 packets, 0 bytes
```

8-26: neighbor {*ip-address* | *peer-group-name*} route-map *route-map-name* out

Syntax Description:

- *ip-address*—Neighbor's IP address.

- *peer-group-name*—Name of the peer group. See section 8-19.

- *route-map-name*—Name of the route map used for outgoing updates to a specified neighbor or peer group.

Purpose: A route map is an extremely powerful tool for route filtering and BGP attribute manipulation. Appendix C contains a complete discussion of route map logic. In this section, we will examine common uses of a route map for route filtering and BGP attribute manipulation.

Cisco IOS Software Release: 10.0. Peer group support was added in Release 11.0.

Configuration Example 1: Basic Route Filter Using an IP Standard Access List

The configuration shown in Figure 8-26 will be used for each route map example in this section.

Figure 8-26 *Configuration Used to Demonstrate the Use of an Output Route Map*

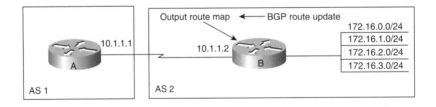

```
Router A
router bgp 1
 neighbor 10.1.1.2 remote-as 2
Router B
interface loopback 0
 ip address 172.16.0.1 255.255.255.0
!
interface loopback 1
 ip address 172.16.1.1 255.255.255.0
!
interface loopback 2
 ip address 172.16.2.1 255.255.255.0
!
```

(Continued)
```
interface loopback 3
 ip address 172.16.3.1 255.255.255.0
 !
router bgp 2
 neighbor 10.1.1.1 remote-as 1
 network 172.16.0.0 mask 255.255.255.0
 network 172.16.1.0 mask 255.255.255.0
 network 172.16.2.0 mask 255.255.255.0
 network 172.16.3.0 mask 255.255.255.0
```

Before looking at the first route map example, verify that Router A is receiving the four 172.16 prefixes from Router B:

```
rtrA#show ip bgp
BGP table version is 5, local router ID is 172.17.1.1
Status codes: s suppressed, d damped, h history, * valid, > best, i - internal
Origin codes: i - IGP, e - EGP, ? - incomplete

   Network          Next Hop          Metric LocPrf Weight Path
*> 172.16.0.0/24    10.1.1.2               0          0 2 i
*> 172.16.1.0/24    10.1.1.2               0          0 2 i
*> 172.16.2.0/24    10.1.1.2               0          0 2 i
*> 172.16.3.0/24    10.1.1.2               0          0 2 i
```

We want to use an output route map on Router B to block network 172.16.1.0/24. We could use a neighbor distribute list (see section 8-7) or prefix list (see section 8-21) to accomplish this task, but because this section concerns route maps, we might as well use one. Configure the following route map on Router B:

```
Router B
router bgp 2
 neighbor 10.1.1.1 remote-as 1
 neighbor 10.1.1.1 route-map filter out
 !
access-list 1 deny 172.16.1.0 0.0.0.255
access-list 1 permit any
 !
route-map filter permit 10
 match ip address 1
```

Whenever you change a policy with a neighbor, you need to restart the BGP session by using **clear ip bgp *** or **clear ip bgp** *neighbor-address*. For this example, use **clear ip bgp 10.1.1.1** on Router B.

Because we are either denying or permitting a route, we do not need any **set** commands in the route map. Each route or prefix advertised to Router A will be processed by the output route map with a name filter. The result of a route map is to either permit or deny an action. The action in this example is to permit routes to be advertised to a BGP neighbor.

Verification

Verify that the prefix 172.16.1.0/24 has been filtered:

```
rrtA#show ip bgp
BGP table version is 22, local router ID is 172.17.1.1
Status codes: s suppressed, d damped, h history, * valid, > best, i - internal
Origin codes: i - IGP, e - EGP, ? - incomplete

   Network         Next Hop        Metric LocPrf Weight Path
*> 172.16.0.0/24   10.1.1.2             0            0 2 i
*> 172.16.2.0/24   10.1.1.2             0            0 2 i
*> 172.16.3.0/24   10.1.1.2             0            0 2 i
```

Configuration Example 2: Manipulate AS Path Information

A route map will be used on Router B to adjust the AS path information sent to Router A. Normally, Router B would append only its AS number to the updates sent to Router A. For this example, we will prepend an additional AS number to the routes. The route map required to accomplish this is shown in the following configuration:

```
Router B
router bgp 2
 neighbor 10.1.1.1 remote-as 1
 neighbor 10.1.1.1 route-map filter out
!
route-map filter permit 10
 set as-path prepend 6
```

Verification

Verify that the routes received by Router A have the AS number 6 prepended to the AS path information:

```
rtrA#show ip bgp
BGP table version is 17, local router ID is 192.16.2.1
Status codes: s suppressed, d damped, h history, * valid, > best, i - internal
Origin codes: i - IGP, e - EGP, ? - incomplete

   Network         Next Hop        Metric LocPrf Weight Path
*> 172.16.0.0/24   10.1.1.2             0            0 2 6 i
*> 172.16.1.0/24   10.1.1.2             0            0 2 6 i
*> 172.16.2.0/24   10.1.1.2             0            0 2 6 i
*> 172.16.3.0/24   10.1.1.2             0            0 2 6 i
```

Configuration Example 3: Append AS Information to Selected Routes

In the preceding example, the AS number 6 was prepended to all routes advertised by Router B. In this example, we want to prepend this AS number only to the route 172.16.2.0/24. This requires a match condition in the route map, as shown in the following configuration:

```
Router B
router bgp 2
 neighbor 10.1.1.1 remote-as 1
 neighbor 10.1.1.1 route-map filter out
 !
access-list 1 permit 172.16.2.0 0.0.0.255
 !
route-map filter permit 10
 match ip add 1
 set as-path prepend 6
route-map filter permit 20
```

The **route-map filter permit 20** statement is the default case. Without it, routes not matching access list 1 would be denied.

Verification

Verify that the AS number 6 has been applied to only the 172.16.2.0/24 prefix:

```
rtrA#show ip bgp
BGP table version is 28, local router ID is 192.16.2.1
Status codes: s suppressed, d damped, h history, * valid, > best, i - internal
Origin codes: i - IGP, e - EGP, ? - incomplete

   Network          Next Hop          Metric LocPrf Weight Path
*> 172.16.0.0/24    10.1.1.2               0            0 2 i
*> 172.16.1.0/24    10.1.1.2               0            0 2 i
*> 172.16.2.0/24    10.1.1.2               0            0 2 6 i
*> 172.16.3.0/24    10.1.1.2               0            0 2 i
```

Configuration Example 4: Modify the COMMUNITY Attribute

The COMMUNITY attribute can be used to group prefixes, and then policies can be applied to the community as a whole. In this example, we will set the community value for prefixes 172.16.0.0/24 through 172.16.3.0/24 to 1, 2, 3, and 4, respectively:

```
router bgp 2
 network 172.16.0.0 mask 255.255.255.0
 network 172.16.1.0 mask 255.255.255.0
 network 172.16.2.0 mask 255.255.255.0
 network 172.16.3.0 mask 255.255.255.0
 neighbor 10.1.1.1 send-community
 neighbor 10.1.1.1 route-map filter out
!
access-list 1 permit 172.16.0.0 0.0.0.255
access-list 2 permit 172.16.1.0 0.0.0.255
access-list 3 permit 172.16.2.0 0.0.0.255
access-list 4 permit 172.16.3.0 0.0.0.255
!
route-map filter permit 10
 match ip address 1
 set community 1
!
route-map filter permit 20
 match ip address 2
 set community 2
!
route-map filter permit 30
 match ip address 3
 set community 3
!
route-map filter permit 40
 match ip address 4
 set community 4
!
route-map filter permit 50
```

Don't forget to use the **neighbor send-community** command. Without it, the community values we are setting will not be advertised. The last stanza in the route map is the default case. We will pass all routes unmodified that don't match the first four route map stanzas.

Verification

Verify the new community settings on Router A:

```
rtrA#show ip bgp community 1
BGP table version is 50, local router ID is 192.16.2.1
Status codes: s suppressed, d damped, h history, * valid, > best, i - internal
Origin codes: i - IGP, e - EGP, ? - incomplete

   Network          Next Hop          Metric LocPrf Weight Path
*> 172.16.0.0/24    10.1.1.2               0             0 2 I

rtrA#show ip bgp community 2
BGP table version is 50, local router ID is 192.16.2.1
Status codes: s suppressed, d damped, h history, * valid, > best, i - internal
Origin codes: i - IGP, e - EGP, ? - incomplete
```

```
(Continued)
   Network          Next Hop              Metric LocPrf Weight Path
*> 172.16.1.0/24    10.1.1.2                 0              0 2 I


rtrA#show ip bgp community 3
BGP table version is 50, local router ID is 192.16.2.1
Status codes: s suppressed, d damped, h history, * valid, > best, i - internal
Origin codes: i - IGP, e - EGP, ? - incomplete

   Network          Next Hop              Metric LocPrf Weight Path
*> 172.16.2.0/24    10.1.1.2                 0              0 2 I


rtrA#show ip bgp community 4
BGP table version is 50, local router ID is 192.16.2.1
Status codes: s suppressed, d damped, h history, * valid, > best, i - internal
Origin codes: i - IGP, e - EGP, ? - incomplete

   Network          Next Hop              Metric LocPrf Weight Path
*> 172.16.3.0/24    10.1.1.2                 0              0 2 I
```

Troubleshooting

1 Verify that the BGP neighbors are in the Established state using the **show ip bgp neighbors** command.

   If the neighbor relationship is not in the Established state, see section 8-23.

2 Verify that the input route map is being used with the BGP neighbor using the **show ip bgp neighbors** command:

```
rtrB#show ip bgp n
BGP neighbor is 10.1.1.1,  remote AS 1, external link
 Index 1, Offset 0, Mask 0x2
  Community attribute sent to this neighbor
  BGP version 4, remote router ID 192.16.2.1
  BGP state = Established, table version = 6, up for 00:04:28
  Last read 00:00:27, hold time is 180, keepalive interval is 60 seconds
  Minimum time between advertisement runs is 30 seconds
  Received 19132 messages, 3 notifications, 0 in queue
  Sent 19248 messages, 0 notifications, 0 in queue
  Prefix advertised 231, suppressed 0, withdrawn 2
  Outbound path policy configured
  Route map for outgoing advertisements is filter
  Connections established 49; dropped 48
  Last reset 00:04:58, due to User reset
  0 accepted prefixes consume 0 bytes
  0 history paths consume 0 bytes
Connection state is ESTAB, I/O status: 1, unread input bytes: 0
Local host: 10.1.1.2, Local port: 11068
Foreign host: 10.1.1.1, Foreign port: 179
```

3 Verify that the correct neighbor address is being used with the **neighbor** *ip-address* **route-map** *route-map-name* **in** command.

4 Verify that you are using the correct route map name.

5 Verify the logic of your route map (see Appendix C).

6 You can view the route map using the command **show route-map** *route-map-name*:

```
rtrB#show route-map filter
route-map filter, permit, sequence 10
  Match clauses:
    ip address (access-lists): 1
  Set clauses:
    community 1
  Policy routing matches: 0 packets, 0 bytes
route-map filter, permit, sequence 20
  Match clauses:
    ip address (access-lists): 2
  Set clauses:
    community 2
  Policy routing matches: 0 packets, 0 bytes
route-map filter, permit, sequence 30
  Match clauses:
    ip address (access-lists): 3
  Set clauses:
    community 3
  Policy routing matches: 0 packets, 0 bytes
route-map filter, permit, sequence 40
  Match clauses:
    ip address (access-lists): 4
  Set clauses:
    community 4
  Policy routing matches: 0 packets, 0 bytes
route-map filtert, permit, sequence 50
  Match clauses:

  Set clauses:
  Policy routing matches: 0 packets, 0 bytes
```

8-27: neighbor {*ip-address* | *peer-group-name*} route-reflector-client

Syntax Description:

- *ip-address*—Neighbor's IP address.

- *peer-group-name*—Name of the peer group. See section 8-19.

Purpose: IBGP neighbors do not propagate routing information learned from one IBGP neighbor to another IBGP neighbor. Therefore, if you are running IBGP, every IBGP speaker must have a connection to every other IBGP speaker in the AS. This becomes a scaling problem as the number of IBGP speakers increases. The number of IBGP connections for n speakers is $(n(n-1))/2$. Table 8-1 lists the number of connections needed for 2 to 10 IBGP speakers.

Table 8-1 *IBGP Connections Needed for a Full Mesh*

Number of IBGP Speakers	Number of Connections
2	1
3	3
4	6
5	10
6	15
7	21
8	28
9	36
10	45

A route reflector is one technique to overcome the scaling issue with IBGP. One or more routers serve as a route reflector, and other routers are clients to the route reflector. Route reflectors reflect routes learned from a route reflector client to the other clients. With one route reflector, the number of logical connections needed for n IBGP speakers is $n-1$.

Cisco IOS Software Release: 10.0. Peer group support was added in Release 11.0.

Configuration Example 1: Single Route Reflector

Assume that the network in Figure 8-27 requires IBGP for the exchange of routing information. Without a route reflector, we would need three BGP neighbor connections. We can reduce the number of BGP connections to two by using a single route reflector.

Figure 8-27 *Route Reflector*

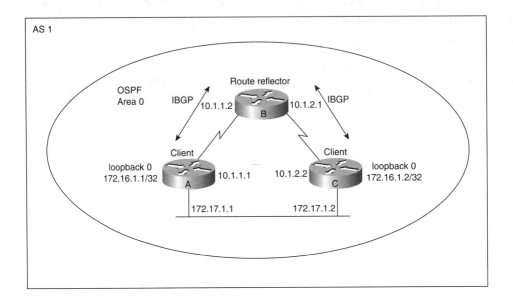

```
Router A
interface Loopback0
 ip address 172.16.1.1 255.255.255.255
!
interface Ethernet0
 ip address 172.17.1.1 255.255.255.0
!
interface Serial0
 ip address 10.1.1.1 255.255.255.252
!
router ospf 1
 network 10.0.0.0 0.255.255.255 area 0
 network 172.16.0.0 0.0.255.255 area 0
 network 172.17.0.0 0.0.255.255 area 0
!
router bgp 1
 neighbor 172.16.1.3 remote-as 1
 neighbor 172.16.1.3 update-source Loopback0
Router B
interface Loopback0
 ip address 172.16.1.3 255.255.255.0
!
interface Serial0
 ip address 10.1.1.2 255.255.255.252
 clockrate 64000
!
```

(Continued)
```
interface Serial1
 ip address 10.1.2.1 255.255.255.252
clockrate 64000
!
router ospf 1
 network 10.0.0.0 0.255.255.255 area 0
 network 172.16.0.0 0.0.255.255 area 0
!
router bgp 1
 neighbor 172.16.1.1 remote-as 1
 neighbor 172.16.1.1 update-source Loopback0
 neighbor 172.16.1.1 route-reflector-client
 neighbor 172.16.1.2 remote-as 1
 neighbor 172.16.1.2 update-source Loopback0
 neighbor 172.16.1.2 route-reflector-client
Router C
interface Loopback0
 ip address 172.16.1.2 255.255.255.255
!
interface Ethernet0
 ip address 172.17.1.2 255.255.255.0
!
interface Serial0
 ip address 10.1.2.2 255.255.255.252
!
router ospf 1
 network 10.0.0.0 0.255.255.255 area 0
 network 172.16.0.0 0.0.255.255 area 0
 network 172.17.0.0 0.0.255.255 area 0
!
router bgp 1
 neighbor 172.16.1.3 remote-as 1
 neighbor 172.16.1.3 update-source Loopback0
```

Notice that only the route reflector needs additional configuration. Loopback addresses were used in this configuration. See section 8-33 for a discussion of IBGP and loopback addresses.

Verification

Verify that the IBGP sessions are being established with the route reflector by examining the IBGP neighbors on Router B:

```
rtrB#
BGP neighbor is 172.16.1.1,  remote AS 1, internal link
 Index 1, Offset 0, Mask 0x2
 Route-Reflector Client
 BGP version 4, remote router ID 172.16.1.1
 BGP state = Established, table version = 3, up for 00:28:24
 Last read 00:00:26, hold time is 180, keepalive interval is 60 seconds
```

continues

(Continued)
```
  Minimum time between advertisement runs is 5 seconds
  Received 31 messages, 0 notifications, 0 in queue
  Sent 31 messages, 0 notifications, 0 in queue
  Prefix advertised 0, suppressed 0, withdrawn 0
  Connections established 1; dropped 0
  Last reset 00:28:34, due to RR client config change
  0 accepted prefixes consume 0 bytes
  0 history paths consume 0 bytes
Connection state is ESTAB, I/O status: 1, unread input bytes: 0
Local host: 172.16.1.3, Local port: 11026
Foreign host: 172.16.1.1, Foreign port: 179


BGP neighbor is 172.16.1.2,  remote AS 1, internal link
 Index 2, Offset 0, Mask 0x4
 Route-Reflector Client
  BGP version 4, remote router ID 172.16.1.2
  BGP state = Established, table version = 3, up for 00:28:21
  Last read 00:00:22, hold time is 180, keepalive interval is 60 seconds
  Minimum time between advertisement runs is 5 seconds
  Received 31 messages, 0 notifications, 0 in queue
  Sent 31 messages, 0 notifications, 0 in queue
  Prefix advertised 0, suppressed 0, withdrawn 0
  Connections established 1; dropped 0
  Last reset 00:28:33, due to RR client config change
  0 accepted prefixes consume 0 bytes
  0 history paths consume 0 bytes
Connection state is ESTAB, I/O status: 1, unread input bytes: 0
Local host: 172.16.1.3, Local port: 11027
Foreign host: 172.16.1.2, Foreign port: 179
```

Configuration Example 2: Multiple Route Reflectors

Multiple route reflectors can be used in an AS to further scale the network. Figure 8-28 has nine routers. Three of them—Routers A, D, and H—are acting as route reflectors. Router A has route reflector clients B and C, Router D has route reflector clients E and F, and Router H has route reflector clients I and J. A full IBGP mesh is required between Routers A, D, and H, as shown in the following configurations.

Figure 8-28 *Multiple Route Reflectors*

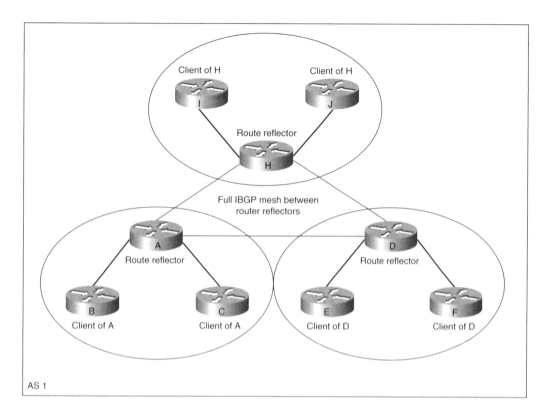

```
Router A
router bgp 1
 neighbor (IP address for Router B) remote-as 1
 neighbor (IP address for Router B) route-reflector-client
 neighbor (IP address for Router C) remote-as 1
 neighbor (IP address for Router C) route-reflector-client
 neighbor (IP address for Router D) remote-as 1
 neighbor (IP address for Router H) remote-as 1
Router B
router bgp 1
 neighbor (IP address for Router A) remote-as 1
Router C
router bgp 1
 neighbor (IP address for Router A) remote-as 1
Router D
router bgp 1
 neighbor (IP address for Router E) remote-as 1
 neighbor (IP address for Router E) route-reflector-client
```

continues

(Continued)

```
 neighbor (IP address for Router F) remote-as 1
 neighbor (IP address for Router F) route-reflector-client
 neighbor (IP address for Router A) remote-as 1
 neighbor (IP address for Router H) remote-as 1
Router E
router bgp 1
 neighbor (IP address for Router D) remote-as 1
Router F
router bgp 1
 neighbor (IP address for Router D) remote-as 1
Router H
router bgp 1
 neighbor (IP address for Router I) remote-as 1
 neighbor (IP address for Router I) route-reflector-client
 neighbor (IP address for Router J) remote-as 1
 neighbor (IP address for Router J) route-reflector-client
 neighbor (IP address for Router A) remote-as 1
 neighbor (IP address for Router D) remote-as 1
Router I
router bgp 1
 neighbor (IP address for Router H) remote-as 1
Router J
router bgp 1
 neighbor (IP address for Router H) remote-as 1
```

There are three clusters of routers. The first cluster contains Routers A, B, and C. The second cluster contains Routers D, E, and F. The third cluster contains Routers H, I, and J. Each cluster is configured with one route reflector and two clients in the same fashion as Configuration Example 1. The route reflectors need to be configured using a full IBGP mesh using normal IBGP connections or a nonclient peer connection. Route reflectors advertise routes based on the following rules:

- Advertisements received from nonclient peers are reflected to the route reflector's clients.

- Advertisements received from client peers then reflect to all nonclient and client peers (except the one from which the advertisement was received).

- Advertisements received from EBGP neighbors are reflected to all client and nonclient peers.

Troubleshooting

1 Verify that the BGP neighbors are in the Established state using the **show ip bgp neighbors** command.

   If the neighbor relationship is not in the Established state, see section 8-23. For IBGP and loopbacks, see section 8-33.

2 Verify that clients are actually clients and that nonclients are nonclients using the **show ip bgp neighbors** command.

8-28: neighbor {*ip-address* | *peer-group-name*} send-community

Syntax Description:

- *ip-address*—Neighbor's IP address.

- *peer-group-name*—Name of the peer group. See section 8-19.

Purpose: By default, BGP community attributes are not advertised to peers. The **neighbor send-community** command enables the sending of BGP community attributes to BGP peers. Routing policies can be based on a neighbor address, a peer group name, or AS path information. Situations might arise in which you need to apply policies to routes that do not have any of the previously mentioned attributes in common. A community value is a numerical value or set of values that can be attached to a BGP route. Routing policies can then be applied to routes that contain a particular community value or attribute.

Cisco IOS Software Release: 10.3. The *peer-group-name* option was added in Release 11.0.

Configuration Example: NO-EXPORT Community Value

Two well-known community values are NO-EXPORT and NO-ADVERTISE. If a route carries the NO-EXPORT community value, the route is not advertised outside the AS. The behavior of the NO-EXPORT community value is illustrated in Figure 8-29. The NO-ADVERTISE community value prevents a router from advertising the route to any peer, as shown in Figure 8-30. To configure a COMMUNITY attribute, we will use an outbound route map on Router A, as shown in the following configuration. For a complete discussion of route maps, see Appendix C.

Figure 8-29 *NO-EXPORT Community*

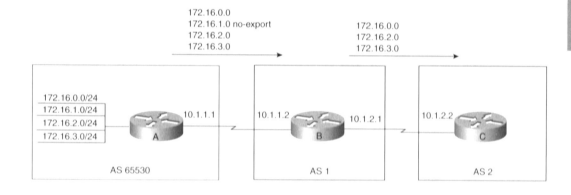

Figure 8-30 *NO-ADVERTISE Community*

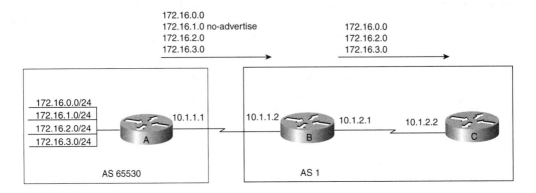

```
Router A
router bgp 65530
 network 172.16.0.0 mask 255.255.255.0
 network 172.16.1.0 mask 255.255.255.0
 network 172.16.2.0 mask 255.255.255.0
 network 172.16.3.0 mask 255.255.255.0
 neighbor 10.1.1.2 remote-as 1
 neighbor 10.1.1.2 send-community
 neighbor 10.1.1.2 route-map setnoexport out
 !
 access-list 1 permit 172.16.1.0 0.0.0.255
 !
 route-map setnoexport permit 10
  match ip address 1
 set community no-export
 route-map setnoexport permit 20
Router B
router bgp 1
 neighbor 10.1.1.1 remote-as 65530
 neighbor 10.1.2.2 remote-as 2
Router C
router bgp 2
 neighbor 10.1.2.1 remote-as 1
```

For this configuration, Router B should receive the four 172.16 prefixes from Router A. Because the 172.16.1.0 prefix has the NO_EXPORT community value, Router B should not advertise this route to Router C.

Verify the effect of the NO_EXPORT community value by checking the BGP tables on Routers B and C:

```
rtrB#show ip bgp
BGP table version is 41, local router ID is 10.1.1.2
Status codes: s suppressed, d damped, h history, * valid, > best, i - internal
Origin codes: i - IGP, e - EGP, ? - incomplete

   Network          Next Hop          Metric LocPrf Weight Path
*> 172.16.0.0/24    10.1.1.1               0              0 65530 i
*> 172.16.1.0/24    10.1.1.1               0              0 65530 i
*> 172.16.2.0/24    10.1.1.1               0              0 65530 i
*> 172.16.3.0/24    10.1.1.1               0              0 65530 i
```
```
rtrC#show ip bgp
BGP table version is 41, local router ID is 10.1.2.2
Status codes: s suppressed, d damped, h history, * valid, > best, i - internal
Origin codes: i - IGP, e - EGP, ? - incomplete

   Network          Next Hop          Metric LocPrf Weight Path
*> 172.16.0.0/24    10.1.2.1               0            0 1 65530 i
*> 172.16.2.0/24    10.1.2.1               0            0 1 65530 i
*> 172.16.3.0/24    10.1.2.1               0            0 1 65530 i
```

The community values of routes can be checked using the **show ip bgp community** command:

```
rtrB#show ip bgp community no-export
BGP table version is 41, local router ID is 10.1.1.2
Status codes: s suppressed, d damped, h history, * valid, > best, i - internal
Origin codes: i - IGP, e - EGP, ? - incomplete

   Network          Next Hop          Metric LocPrf Weight Path
*> 172.16.1.0/24    10.1.1.1               0              0 65530 i
```

Troubleshooting

1 Verify that the BGP neighbors are in the Established state using the **show ip bgp neighbors** command.

   If the neighbor relationship is not in the Established state, see section 8-23.

2 Verify that you have configured the **neighbor send-community** command.

3 Check the syntax of the route map used to set the community attribute.

4 Use the command **show ip bgp community** *community-value* in order to verify that the community value has been set and received.

8-29: neighbor {*ip-address* | *peer-group-name*} **shutdown**

Syntax Description:

- *ip-address*—Neighbor's IP address.

- *peer-group-name*—Name of the peer group. See section 8-19.

Section 8-29

Purpose: Prior to Cisco IOS Software Release 12.0, the only way you could shut down a BGP neighbor was to remove the neighbor configuration using **no neighbor** *ip-address* **remote-as** *as-number*. This was an inconvenience, because all configuration statements associated with the neighbor were also deleted. The **shutdown** form of the **neighbor** command terminates the BGP session without deleting the **neighbor** configuration commands.

Cisco IOS Software Release: 12.0

Configuration Example: Administratively Shutting Down a BGP Session

The following configuration administratively shuts down the BGP session. To reenable the session, use the **no** form of the command:

```
router bgp 1
 neighbor 10.1.1.2 remote-as 1
 neighbor 10.1.1.2 shutdown
```

Verification

Use the **show ip bgp neighbors** command to verify that the neighbor has been shut down:

```
rtrA#show ip bgp neighbors
BGP neighbor is 10.1.1.2,  remote AS 1, internal link
 Administratively shut down
 Index 1, Offset 0, Mask 0x2
  BGP version 4, remote router ID 0.0.0.0
  BGP state = Idle, table version = 0
  Last read 00:00:15, hold time is 180, keepalive interval is 60 seconds
  Minimum time between advertisement runs is 5 seconds
  Received 259 messages, 0 notifications, 0 in queue
  Sent 257 messages, 0 notifications, 0 in queue
  Prefix advertised 0, suppressed 0, withdrawn 0
  Connections established 5; dropped 5
  Last reset 00:00:16, due to Admin. shutdown
```

Troubleshooting

This is the one time that the neighbors should not be in the Established state. If they are, the only error can be in the IP address used with the **shutdown** command.

8-30: neighbor {*ip-address* | *peer-group-name*} soft-reconfiguration inbound

Syntax Description:

- *ip-address*—Neighbor's IP address.

- *peer-group-name*—Name of the peer group. See section 8-19.

Purpose: If you have a policy configured with a BGP neighbor, such as a route map or distribute list, and you change the policy, the BGP session needs to be cleared in order for the new policy to take effect. When a BGP session is cleared, the cache is invalidated. This has a momentary impact on your routing. The **soft-reconfiguration** option allows you to change policies without clearing the BGP session. The two forms of soft reconfiguration are inbound and outbound. When you use inbound, soft reconfiguration updates from a neighbor are stored in memory, regardless of the inbound policy. Be aware that using inbound soft reconfiguration uses more memory than not using inbound soft reconfiguration. Outbound soft reconfiguration does not require additional memory and is always enabled.

Cisco IOS Software Release: 11.2

Configuration Example: Setting Inbound Soft Reconfiguration with a Specific Neighbor

To configure inbound soft reconfiguration with a specific neighbor, use the following configuration as a guide:

```
router bgp 2
 neighbor 10.1.1.2 remote-as 1
 neighbor 10.1.1.2 soft-reconfiguration inbound
```

Verification

Use the **show ip bgp neighbors** command to verify that soft reconfiguration has been enabled:

```
router#
BGP neighbor is 10.1.1.2,  remote AS 1, external link
 Index 1, Offset 0, Mask 0x2
   Inbound soft reconfiguration allowed
   BGP version 4, remote router ID 172.16.1.1
   BGP state = Established, table version = 6, up for 00:00:33
   Last read 00:00:33, hold time is 180, keepalive interval is 60 seconds
   Minimum time between advertisement runs is 30 seconds
   Received 52 messages, 0 notifications, 0 in queue
   Sent 58 messages, 0 notifications, 0 in queue
   Connections established 5; dropped 4
Connection state is ESTAB, I/O status: 1, unread input bytes: 0
Local host: 10.1.1.1, Local port: 11456
Foreign host: 10.1.1.2, Foreign port: 179
```

Troubleshooting

1 Verify that the BGP neighbors are in the Established state using the **show ip bgp neighbors** command.

If the neighbor relationship is not in the Established state, see section 8-23.

2 Verify that soft reconfiguration inbound has been enabled by using **show ip bgp neighbors**.

3 If the session is established and soft reconfiguration has not been enabled, check the neighbor's IP address in the **neighbor** *ip-address* **soft-reconfiguration inbound** command.

8-31: neighbor {*ip-address* | *peer-group-name*} timers *keepalive holdtime*

Syntax Description:

- *ip-address*—Neighbor's IP address.
- *peer-group-name*—Name of the peer group. See section 8-19.
- *keepalive*—1 to 4,294,967,295 seconds.
- *holdtime*—1 to 4,294,967,295 seconds.

Purpose: Keepalive and holdtime are common among IP routing protocols. The keepalive time indicates how often a router sends a keepalive message to a neighbor to inform the neighbor that the router is still alive and well. The holdtime is used as a deathwatch. If a keepalive message is not received within the holdtime, the neighbor is declared dead, and the session is terminated. The default value for the keepalive time is 60 seconds. The holdtime is 3 times the keepalive time, or 180 seconds. Generally, these values do not need to be changed. If you do change them, it is a good rule to make the holdtime equal to 3 times whatever keepalive value you use. Of course, the holdtime should always be greater than the keepalive time. A good practice to follow is to configure the same keepalive and holdtimes on both sides of the link.

Cisco IOS Software Release: 12.0

Configuration Example: Changing the Keepalive and Holdtime Values

Change the default settings for keepalive and holdtime to 50 and 150 seconds, respectively:

```
Router A
router bgp 1
 neighbor 10.1.1.2 remote-as 2
 neighbor 10.1.1.2 timers 50 150
 no auto-summary
```

Verification

Verify the new keepalive and holdtime values by using the **show ip bgp neighbors** command:

```
rtrA#show ip bgp neighbors
BGP neighbor is 10.1.1.2,  remote AS 2, external link
  Index 1, Offset 0, Mask 0x2
  BGP version 4, remote router ID 10.1.1.2
  BGP state = Established, table version = 7, up for 00:53:07
  Last read 00:00:08, hold time is 150, keepalive interval is 50 seconds
  Minimum time between advertisement runs is 30 seconds
  Received 375 messages, 0 notifications, 0 in queue
  Sent 343 messages, 0 notifications, 0 in queue
  Prefix advertised 0, suppressed 0, withdrawn 0
 Connections established 20; dropped 19
  Last reset 00:53:28, due to User reset
  6 accepted prefixes consume 192 bytes, maximum limit 8
  Threshold for warning message 75%
  0 history paths consume 0 bytes
 Connection state is ESTAB, I/O status: 1, unread input bytes: 0
Local host: 10.1.1.1, Local port: 11015
Foreign host: 10.1.1.2, Foreign port: 179
```

Troubleshooting

1 Verify that the BGP neighbors are in the Established state using the **show ip bgp neighbors** command.

If the neighbor relationship is not in the Established state, see section 8-23.

2 Verify the keepalive and holdtime values using **show ip bgp neighbors**.

8-32: neighbor {*ip-address* | *peer-group-name*} unsuppress-map *route-map-name*

Syntax Description:

- *ip-address*—Neighbor's IP address.

- *peer-group-name*—Name of the peer group. See section 8-19.

- *route-map-name*—Name of the route map used to select routes to be unsuppressed.

Purpose: When the **aggregate-address** command is used with the **summary-only** option, the more-specific routes of the aggregate are suppressed (see section 1-7). The **aggregate-address summary-only** command suppresses the more-specific routes to all neighbors. You can use an unsuppress map to selectively leak more-specific routes to a particular neighbor.

Cisco IOS Software Release: 10.0. Peer group support was added in Release 11.0.

Configuration Example: Selectively Advertising Routes with an Unsuppress Map

In Figure 8-31, Router A is advertising four prefixes to Router B. Router B aggregates these prefixes and advertises only the summary while suppressing the four specific routes. This will be used as the initial configuration so that we can inspect the BGP tables for Routers B and C. The unsuppress map is then added to Router B's configuration.

Figure 8-31 *Globally Suppressed Routes Can Be Selectively Unsuppressed on a Per-Neighbor Basis*

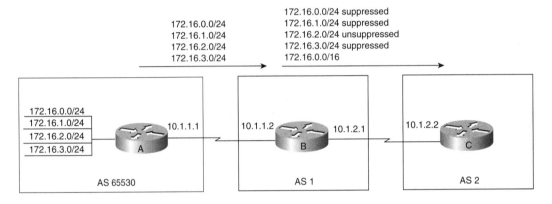

```
Router A
interface Loopback0
 ip address 172.16.0.1 255.255.255.0
!
interface Loopback1
 ip address 172.16.1.1 255.255.255.0
!
interface Loopback2
 ip address 172.16.2.1 255.255.255.0
!
interface Loopback3
 ip address 172.16.3.1 255.255.255.0
!
router bgp 65530
 network 172.16.0.0 mask 255.255.255.0
 network 172.16.1.0 mask 255.255.255.0
 network 172.16.2.0 mask 255.255.255.0
 network 172.16.3.0 mask 255.255.255.0
 neighbor 10.1.1.2 remote-as 1
```

(Continued)

```
Router B
router bgp 1
 aggregate-address 172.16.0.0 255.255.0.0 summary-only
 neighbor 10.1.1.1 remote-as 65530
 neighbor 10.1.2.2 remote-as 2
Router C
router bgp 2
 neighbor 10.1.2.1 remote-as 1
```

Before proceeding to the unsuppress map, check the BGP tables on Routers B and C:

```
rtrB#show ip bgp
BGP table version is 42, local router ID is 172.16.1.1
Status codes: s suppressed, d damped, h history, * valid, > best, i - internal
Origin codes: i - IGP, e - EGP, ? - incomplete

   Network          Next Hop          Metric LocPrf Weight Path
s> 172.16.0.0/24    10.1.1.1               0            0 65530 i
*> 172.16.0.0       0.0.0.0                         32768 i
s> 172.16.1.0/24    10.1.1.1               0            0 65530 i
s> 172.16.2.0/24    10.1.1.1               0            0 65530 i
s> 172.16.3.0/24    10.1.1.1               0            0 65530 i
rtrC#show ip bgp
BGP table version is 10, local router ID is 156.26.32.1
Status codes: s suppressed, d damped, h history, * valid, > best, i - internal
Origin codes: i - IGP, e - EGP, ? - incomplete

   Network          Next Hop          Metric LocPrf Weight Path
*> 172.16.0.0       10.1.2.1                         0 1 i
```

As you can see, Router B is suppressing the more-specific routes. Next, we want to unsuppress prefix 172.16.2.0 on Router B and allow this route to be advertised to Router C:

```
Router B
router bgp 1
 aggregate-address 172.16.0.0 255.255.0.0 summary-only
 neighbor 10.1.1.1 remote-as 65530
 neighbor 10.1.2.2 remote-as 2
 neighbor 10.1.2.2 unsuppress-map allow
!
access-list 1 permit 172.16.2.0 0.0.0.255
route-map allow permit 10
 match ip address 1
```

Verification

There should be no change to Router B's BGP table:

```
rtrB#sh ip bgp
BGP table version is 10, local router ID is 172.16.1.1
Status codes: s suppressed, d damped, h history, * valid, > best, i - internal
Origin codes: i - IGP, e - EGP, ? - incomplete

   Network          Next Hop         Metric LocPrf Weight Path
s> 172.16.0.0/24    10.1.1.1              0           0 65530 i
*> 172.16.0.0       0.0.0.0                        32768 i
s> 172.16.1.0/24    10.1.1.1              0           0 65530 i
s> 172.16.2.0/24    10.1.1.1              0           0 65530 i
s> 172.16.3.0/24    10.1.1.1              0           0 65530 i
```

However, Router C should not be receiving the unsuppressed route:

```
RtrC#sh ip bgp
BGP table version is 14, local router ID is 156.26.32.1
Status codes: s suppressed, d damped, h history, * valid, > best, i - internal
Origin codes: i - IGP, e - EGP, ? - incomplete

   Network          Next Hop         Metric LocPrf Weight Path
*> 172.16.0.0       10.1.2.1                         0 1 i
*> 172.16.2.0/24    10.1.2.1                         0 1 65530 i
```

Troubleshooting

1   Verify that the BGP neighbors are in the Established state using the **show ip bgp neighbors** command.

    If the neighbor relationship is not in the Established state, see section 8-23.

2   Check to see that the route you want to unsuppress is actually being suppressed by executing the **show ip bgp** command.

3   The route map should permit only routes that are to be unsuppressed. Check your syntax.

4   Check the syntax of your access list.

8-33: neighbor {*ip-address | peer-group-name*} update-source *interface-name*

Syntax Description:

*   *ip-address*—Neighbor's IP address.

*   *peer-group-name*—Name of the peer group. See section 8-19.

- *interface-name*—Any physical or logical router interface. Usually, a loopback interface is used.

Purpose: An IBGP connection can occur as long as there is a TCP/IP path between the routers. If multiple paths exist between the IBGP routers, using a loopback interface as the neighbor's address can add stability to the network. Using loopback interfaces with EBGP speakers is not necessary, because EBGP neighbors are usually directly connected.

Cisco IOS Software Release: 10.0. Peer group support was added in Release 11.0.

Configuration Example: Using a Loopback Interface for Network Stability

In Figure 8-32, we want to establish an IBGP session between Routers A and C. From Router A's point of view, we can use one of two addresses in the **neighbor** command, 172.17.1.2 or 10.1.2.2. From Router C's perspective, either address 172.17.1.1 or 10.1.1.1 can be used to form a neighbor relationship with Router A. The following configurations show these options:

```
Router A
router bgp 1
 neighbor 172.17.1.2 remote-as 1
 or
 neighbor 10.1.2.2 remote-as 1
Router C
 neighbor 172.17.1.1 remote-as 1
 or
 neighbor 10.1.1.1 remote-as 1
```

These configurations assume that Routers A and C have routes to these addresses through either an IGP or static routes. If the physical interface addresses that are used in the **neighbor** commands are functional, the IBGP session remains active. If one of the physical interfaces used in the **neighbor** command goes down, the IBGP session is terminated. If loopback addresses are used and we are running an IGP that advertises the loopback addresses, the IBGP session remains established even if one of the paths goes down. Because we are using OSPF, the Ethernet network is the shortest path between Routers A and C. The IP routing table on Router A contains a route to the loopback on Router C via the Ethernet network. If the Ethernet network goes down, OSPF converges and installs the path through Router B into the routing table. IBGP packets now take this route, and the IBGP session is maintained. The **update-source** option uses the address of the indicated interface as the source IP address in the IBGP packets. When configured on both neighbors, the session remains established as long as a path between the loopback addresses exists. If only one path exists between the IBGP speakers, using loopback addresses does not provide additional stability.

Figure 8-32 *When Multiple Paths Exist Between IBGP Peers, Using a Loopback Interface as the Source Adds Stability to the Design*

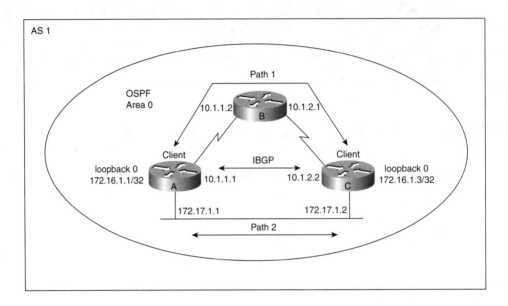

```
Router A
interface Loopback0
 ip address 172.16.1.1 255.255.255.255
!
interface Ethernet0
 ip address 172.17.1.1 255.255.255.0
!
interface Serial0
 ip address 10.1.1.1 255.255.255.252
!
router ospf 1
 network 10.0.0.0 0.255.255.255 area 0
 network 172.16.0.0 0.0.255.255 area 0
 network 172.17.0.0 0.0.255.255 area 0
!
router bgp 1
 neighbor 172.16.1.3 remote-as 1
 neighbor 172.16.1.3 update-source Loopback0
Router B
interface Loopback0
 ip address 172.16.1.2 255.255.255.0
!
interface Serial0
 ip address 10.1.1.2 255.255.255.252
 clockrate 64000
!
```

(Continued)
```
interface Serial1
 ip address 10.1.2.1 255.255.255.252
 clockrate 64000
!
router ospf 1
 network 10.0.0.0 0.255.255.255 area 0
 network 172.16.0.0 0.0.255.255 area 0
!
```
```
Router C
interface Loopback0
 ip address 172.16.1.3 255.255.255.255
!
interface Ethernet0
 ip address 172.17.1.2 255.255.255.0
!
interface Serial0
 ip address 10.1.2.2 255.255.255.252
!
router ospf 1
 network 10.0.0.0 0.255.255.255 area 0
 network 172.16.0.0 0.0.255.255 area 0
 network 172.17.0.0 0.0.255.255 area 0
!
router bgp 1
 neighbor 172.16.1.1 remote-as 1
 neighbor 172.16.1.1 update-source Loopback0
```

Verification

Verify that the IBGP session is being established by examining the IBGP neighbors on Router A:

```
rtrA#
BGP neighbor is 172.16.1.3,  remote AS 1, internal link
 Index 1, Offset 0, Mask 0x2
BGP version 4, remote router ID 172.16.1.1
 BGP state = Established, table version = 3, up for 00:28:24
 Last read 00:00:26, hold time is 180, keepalive interval is 60 seconds
 Minimum time between advertisement runs is 5 seconds
 Received 31 messages, 0 notifications, 0 in queue
 Sent 31 messages, 0 notifications, 0 in queue
 Prefix advertised 0, suppressed 0, withdrawn 0
 Connections established 1; dropped 0
 Last reset 00:28:34, due to RR client config change
 0 accepted prefixes consume 0 bytes
 0 history paths consume 0 bytes
Connection state is ESTAB, I/O status: 1, unread input bytes: 0
Local host: 172.16.1.3, Local port: 11026
Foreign host: 172.16.1.1, Foreign port: 179
```

Troubleshooting

1 Ensure that the loopback address for the neighbor is in the IP routing table.

2 Each neighbor should be able to ping the other neighbor's loopback address. If the pings are successful, the routers can form an IBGP connection using the loopback interface.

3 Verify the neighbor's IP address and remote AS number in the BGP configuration.

8-34: neighbor {*ip-address* | *peer-group-name*} version *version-number*

Syntax Description:

- *ip-address*—Neighbor's IP address.

- *peer-group-name*—Name of the peer group. See section 8-19.

- *version-number*—2, 3, or 4.

Purpose: Currently, the default BGP version number is 4. Cisco's implementation of BGP begins using version 4 and negotiates down to version 2. If you do not want to form a neighbor connection with a router that is not running version 4, you can lock down the version number using this command.

Cisco IOS Software Release: 10.0. Peer group support was added in Release 11.0.

Configuration Example: Locking Down the Neighbor BGP Version

The following configuration locks down the version number with one neighbor to 4 and leaves the version number in auto-negotiate for the other neighbors:

```
Router A
router bgp 1
 neighbor 10.1.1.2 remote-as 2
 neighbor 10.1.1.2 version 4
 neighbor 10.2.1.2 remote-as 3
 neighbor 10.3.1.2 remote-as 4
```

Verification

Verify the version number by using the **show ip bgp neighbors** command:

```
rtrA#show ip bgp neighbors
BGP neighbor is 10.1.1.2,  remote AS 2, external link
  Index 1, Offset 0, Mask 0x2
  BGP version 4, remote router ID 10.1.1.2
  BGP state = Established, table version = 7, up for 00:53:07
```

(Continued)

```
  Last read 00:00:08, hold time is 180, keepalive interval is 60 seconds
  Minimum time between advertisement runs is 30 seconds
  Received 375 messages, 0 notifications, 0 in queue
  Sent 343 messages, 0 notifications, 0 in queue
  Prefix advertised 0, suppressed 0, withdrawn 0
 Connections established 20; dropped 19
  Last reset 00:53:28, due to User reset
  6 accepted prefixes consume 192 bytes, maximum limit 8
  Threshold for warning message 75%
  0 history paths consume 0 bytes
Connection state is ESTAB, I/O status: 1, unread input bytes: 0
Local host: 10.1.1.1, Local port: 11015
Foreign host: 10.1.1.2, Foreign port: 179
```

Troubleshooting

Verify that the BGP neighbors are in the Established state using the **show ip bgp neighbors** command. If the neighbor relationship is not in the Established state, check for a version number mismatch between neighbors.

8-35: neighbor *{ip-address | peer-group-name}* **weight** *default-weight*

Syntax Description:

- *ip-address*—Neighbor's IP address.

- *peer-group-name*—Name of the peer group. See section 8-19.

- *default-weight*—1 to 65535.

Purpose: The **weight** attribute has meaning only to the local router. By default, advertisements received from BGP neighbors have their **weight** attribute set to 0. This command sets all routes learned from a particular neighbor to the default weight used in the command.

Cisco IOS Software Release: 10.0. Peer group support was added in Release 11.0.

Configuration Example: Setting the Route Weight for the Local Router

The following configuration sets the weight of all routes learned from neighbor 10.1.1.2 to 451:

```
Router A
interface Serial0
 ip address 10.1.1.1 255.255.255.252
 !
```

continues

```
(Continued)
router bgp 1
 neighbor 10.1.1.2 remote-as 2
 neighbor 10.1.1.2 weight 451
Router B
interface Loopback0
 ip address 172.16.0.1 255.255.255.0
!
interface Loopback1
 ip address 172.16.1.1 255.255.255.0
!
interface Loopback2
 ip address 172.16.2.1 255.255.255.0
!
interface Loopback3
 ip address 172.16.3.1 255.255.255.0
!
interface Serial0
 ip address 10.1.1.2 255.255.255.252
 clockrate 64000
!
router bgp 2
 network 172.16.0.0 mask 255.255.255.0
 network 172.16.1.0 mask 255.255.255.0
 network 172.16.2.0 mask 255.255.255.0
 network 172.16.3.0 mask 255.255.255.0
 neighbor 10.1.1.1 remote-as 1
```

Verification

Verify the setting of the **weight** attribute by examining the BGP table on Router A:

```
rtrA#show ip bgp
BGP table version is 6, local router ID is 172.17.1.1
Status codes: s suppressed, d damped, h history, * valid, > best, i - internal
Origin codes: i - IGP, e - EGP, ? - incomplete

   Network          Next Hop          Metric LocPrf Weight Path
*> 172.16.0.0/24    10.1.1.2               0           451 2 i
*> 172.16.1.0/24    10.1.1.2               0           451 2 i
*> 172.16.2.0/24    10.1.1.2               0           451 2 i
*> 172.16.3.0/24    10.1.1.2               0           451 2 i
```

Troubleshooting

1 Verify that the BGP neighbors are in the Established state using the **show ip bgp neighbors** command. If the neighbor relationship is not in the Established state, see section 8-23.

2 If the neighbors are in the Established state, the only error would be an incorrect IP address in the configuration statement **neighbor** *ip-address* **weight** *default-weight*.

CHAPTER 9

Route Advertisement

9-1: network *ip-address*

9-2: network *ip-address* mask *network-mask*

Syntax Description:

- *ip-address*—Network to advertise to BGP peers.
- *network-mask*—Optional parameter used to advertise nonclassful network prefixes.

Defaults: None

Limitations: Up to 200 instances of the **network** command may be used in the configuration. For Cisco IOS Software Release 12.0 and later, this restriction has been removed.

Purpose: Interior Gateway Protocols such as RIP and OSPF use the **network** command to determine on which interfaces the protocol will be active. The BGP **neighbor** command is used to determine which interfaces will run BGP. The BGP **network** command is used to determine the networks that will be advertised to BGP neighbors. In order for a network to be advertised by BGP, it must be known to the originating router. Routes learned via EBGP are automatically advertised to other EBGP neighbors. A known network is one that is directly connected, static, or learned through a dynamic routing protocol. The first form of the **network** command requires a classful IP address. A classful address is either Class A with an 8-bit subnet mask, Class B with a 16-bit subnet mask, or Class C with a 24-bit subnet mask. The second form can be used with either a classful or classless prefix.

Cisco IOS Software Release: 10.0

Configuration Example 1: Directly Connected Networks

Figure 9-1 illustrates a basic scenario for the use of the **network** command. Router A has two directly connected networks that are advertised to router B via BGP.

Figure 9-1 *Basic Use of the* **network** *Command*

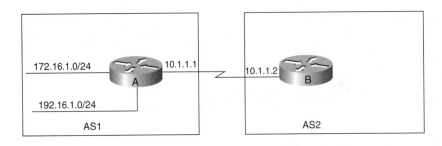

```
Router A
interface loopback 0
 ip address 172.16.1.1 255.255.255.0
 !
interface loopback 1
 ip address 192.16.1.1 255.255.255.0
 !
router bgp 1
 neighbor 10.1.1.2 remote-as 2
 network 172.16.1.0 mask 255.255.255.0
 network 192.16.1.0
Router B
router bgp 2
 neighbor 10.1.1.1 remote-as 1
```

Notice that the *mask* option was used with network 172.16.1.0. The classful address for this
network is 172.16.0.0. Because we want to advertise a subnet of 172.16.0.0, the mask
option is required.

Verification

Before using the **network** command, verify that the networks are in the IP routing table
using the **show ip route** command:

```
rtrA#show ip route
Codes: C - connected, S - static, I - IGRP, R - RIP, M - mobile, B - BGP
       D - EIGRP, EX - EIGRP external, O - OSPF, IA - OSPF inter area
       N1 - OSPF NSSA external type 1, N2 - OSPF NSSA external type 2
       E1 - OSPF external type 1, E2 - OSPF external type 2, E - EGP
       i - IS-IS, L1 - IS-IS level-1, L2 - IS-IS level-2, * - candidate default
       U - per-user static route, o - ODR, P - periodic downloaded static route
       T - traffic engineered route

Gateway of last resort is not set
```

(Continued)
```
        172.16.0.0/24 is subnetted, 1 subnets
C          172.16.1.0 is directly connected, Loopback0
        10.0.0.0/30 is subnetted, 1 subnets
C          10.1.1.0 is directly connected, Serial0
C       192.16.1.0/24 is directly connected, Loopback1
```

The networks to be advertised are in the IP routing table. The next step is to add the **network** commands to the BGP router configuration and to verify that the networks are in the BGP routing table using the **show ip bgp** command:

```
rtrA#show ip bgp
BGP table version is 538, local router ID is 10.1.1.1
Status codes: s suppressed, d damped, h history, * valid, > best, i - internal
Origin codes: i - IGP, e - EGP, ? - incomplete

   Network          Next Hop            Metric LocPrf Weight Path
*> 192.16.1.0       0.0.0.0                  0         32768 i
*> 172.16.1.0       0.0.0.0                  0         32768 i
```

Configuration Example 2: Aggregation Using Static Routes

A static route can be used to allow BGP to advertise any network prefix. Configuring a static route installs the static network in the local IP routing table. Any route in the IP routing table can be advertised by BGP using the **network** command. Of course, the router should advertise only networks that it can actually reach. The main use of static routes with BGP is to allow the advertisement of an aggregate address. Figure 9-2 shows an ISP that owns the range of Class C addresses from 192.16.0.x through 192.16.255.x. The **network** command could be used 256 times—once for each Class C prefix—or we could use a static route to create an aggregate prefix.

Figure 9-2 *Using a Static Route and the **network** Command to Advertise an Aggregate Prefix*

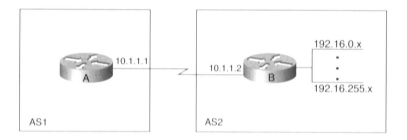

```
Router A
router bgp 1
 neighbor 10.1.1.2 remote-as 2
```
```
Router B
router bgp 2
 neighbor 10.1.1.1 remote-as 1
 network 192.16.0.0 mask 255.255.0.0
 !
 ip route 192.16.0.0 255.255.0.0 null 0
```

The optional *mask* parameter is needed because 192.16.0.0/16 is a supernet of the Class C
address 192.16.0.0/24. The static route has the next hop as the interface null 0. Router B
has more specific routes to networks contained in the range 192.16.0.x to 192.16.255.x.
Assume that network 192.16.8.0 is down. Router A thinks that 192.16.8.0 is reachable
because it is receiving the advertisement to 192.16.x.x from Router B. When Router B
receives a packet destined for network 192.16.8.0, the route is looked up in the IP routing
table. A specific match is not found, because the network is down. Router B tries to find a
shorter match. It finds 192.16.x.x and instructs Router B to send the packet to null 0 or
simply discard the packet. Prefixes can also be aggregated using the **aggregate-address**
command, covered in Chapter 1, "Route Aggregation."

Verification

BGP won't advertise the aggregate route unless it is in the IP routing table. As before, verify
that the route is in the IP routing table and the BGP table:

```
rtrB#show ip route
Codes: C - connected, S - static, I - IGRP, R - RIP, M - mobile, B - BGP
       D - EIGRP, EX - EIGRP external, O - OSPF, IA - OSPF inter area
       N1 - OSPF NSSA external type 1, N2 - OSPF NSSA external type 2
       E1 - OSPF external type 1, E2 - OSPF external type 2, E - EGP
       i - IS-IS, L1 - IS-IS level-1, L2 - IS-IS level-2, * - candidate default
       U - per-user static route, o - ODR, P - periodic downloaded static route
       T - traffic engineered route

Gateway of last resort is not set

10.0.0.0/30 is subnetted, 2 subnets
C       10.1.1.0 is directly connected, Serial0
S       192.16.0.0/16 is directly connected, Null0
rtrB#show ip bgp
BGP table version is 44, local router ID is 192.16.1.1
Status codes: s suppressed, d damped, h history, * valid, > best, i - internal
Origin codes: i - IGP, e - EGP, ? - incomplete

   Network          Next Hop          Metric LocPrf Weight Path
*> 192.16.0.0/16    0.0.0.0                0         32768 i
```

Troubleshooting

Step 1   Verify that the BGP neighbors are in the Established state using the **show ip bgp neighbors** command.

If the neighbor relationship is not in the Established state, see section 8-23.

Step 2   Verify that the network you are attempting to advertise is in the IP routing table. There must be an exact match between prefix and mask.

9-3: network *ip-address* backdoor

9-4: network *ip-address* mask *network-mask* backdoor

Syntax Description:

- *ip-address*—Network to advertise to BGP peers.

- *network-mask*—Optional parameter used to advertise nonclassful network prefixes.

Defaults: None

Limitations: Up to 200 instances of the **network** command may be used in the configuration. For Cisco IOS Software Release 12.0 and later, this restriction has been removed.

Purpose: When a router is running more than one IP routing protocol, the possibility exists that a particular route might be learned by two or more protocols. Because different IP routing protocols calculate the cost to a route using different metrics, the protocol cost cannot be used to select the best path. When a route is known by more than one IP routing protocol, Cisco routers use the administrative distance to select the best path, with the lowest administrative distance being preferred. EBGP routes have an administrative distance of 20, and IGPs have a higher administrative distance:

- EBGP—20

- EIGRP—90

- IGRP—100

- OSPF—110

- RIP—120

- IBGP—200

EBGP routes are preferred over IGP routes. The **backdoor** option instructs BGP to set the administrative distance for the network specified to 200, allowing the IGP route to be preferred.

Cisco IOS Software Release: 10.0

Configuration Example: Finding the Best Route Through Administrative Distance

In Figure 9-3, Router A is learning about network 172.17.2.0 via EBGP and EIGRP.

Figure 9-3 *EBGP Route to 172.17.2.0 Is Preferred Over the EIGRP Route*

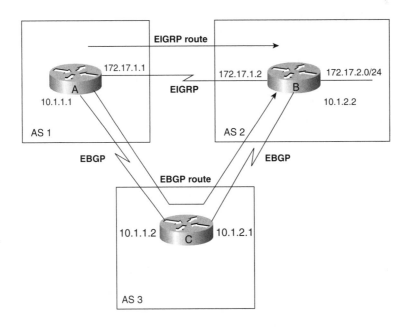

```
Router A
router eigrp 1
 network 172.17.0.0
 !
router bgp 1
 neighbor 10.1.1.2 remote-as 3
Router B
router eigrp 1
network 172.17.0.0
 !
router bgp 2
 network 172.17.2.0 mask 255.255.255.0
 neighbor 10.1.2.1 remote-as 3
Router C
router bgp 3
 network 10.1.1.0 mask 255.255.255.252
 network 10.1.2.0 mask 255.255.255.252
 neighbor 10.1.1.1 remote-as 1
 neighbor 10.1.2.2 remote-as 2
```

Because EBGP has a lower administrative distance than EIGRP, the EBGP route is installed in Router A's IP routing table.

```
rtrA#show ip route
Codes: C - connected, S - static, I - IGRP, R - RIP, M - mobile, B - BGP
       D - EIGRP, EX - EIGRP external, O - OSPF, IA - OSPF inter area
       N1 - OSPF NSSA external type 1, N2 - OSPF NSSA external type 2
       E1 - OSPF external type 1, E2 - OSPF external type 2, E - EGP
       i - IS-IS, L1 - IS-IS level-1, L2 - IS-IS level-2, * - candidate default
       U - per-user static route, o - ODR, P - periodic downloaded static route
       T - traffic engineered route

Gateway of last resort is not set


     172.17.0.0/24 is subnetted, 2 subnets
C       172.17.1.0 is directly connected, Ethernet0
B       172.17.2.0 [20/0] via 10.1.1.2
     10.0.0.0/30 is subnetted, 2 subnets
B       10.1.2.0 [20/0] via 10.1.1.2
C       10.1.1.0 is directly connected, Serial0
```

The preferred path from Router A to network 172.17.2.0 is through Router C. The shortest path to network 172.17.2.0 is through the direct connection to Router B. A number of methods can be used to modify routing table entries so that Router A prefers the direct path to network 172.17.2.0. Using the **backdoor** option is relatively easy, as shown in the following modified listing for Router A:

```
Router A
router bgp 1
 network 172.17.2.0 mask 255.255.255.0 backdoor
 neighbor 10.1.1.2 remote-as 3
```

The **backdoor** option causes the network learned via EBGP to have an administrative distance of 200. The EIGRP route for network 172.17.2.0 has an administrative distance of 90, causing it to be installed in the IP routing table.

Verification

By inspecting the IP routing table on Router A, we can see that the route to 172.17.2.0 learned via EIGRP has been installed in the IP routing table, replacing the EBGP route:

```
rtrA#show ip route
Codes: C - connected, S - static, I - IGRP, R - RIP, M - mobile, B - BGP
       D - EIGRP, EX - EIGRP external, O - OSPF, IA - OSPF inter area
       N1 - OSPF NSSA external type 1, N2 - OSPF NSSA external type 2
       E1 - OSPF external type 1, E2 - OSPF external type 2, E - EGP
       i - IS-IS, L1 - IS-IS level-1, L2 - IS-IS level-2, * - candidate default
       U - per-user static route, o - ODR, P - periodic downloaded static route
       T - traffic engineered route
```

continues

(Continued)

```
Gateway of last resort is not set

     172.17.0.0/24 is subnetted, 2 subnets
C       172.17.1.0 is directly connected, Ethernet0
D       172.17.2.0 [90/409600] via 172.17.1.2, Ethernet0
     10.0.0.0/30 is subnetted, 2 subnets
B       10.1.2.0 [20/0] via 10.1.1.2
C       10.1.1.0 is directly connected, Serial0
```

Troubleshooting

Step 1   Verify that the BGP neighbors are in the Established state using the **show ip bgp neighbors** command.

   If the neighbor relationship is not in the Established state, see section 8-23.

Step 2   Before using the **backdoor** option, use the **show ip bgp** command to ensure that the route you intend to modify is in the BGP table. For example, on Router A, verify a BGP entry for network 172.17.2.0:

```
rtrA#show ip bgp
BGP table version is 43, local router ID is 192.16.1.1
Status codes: s suppressed, d damped, h history, * valid, > best, i - internal
Origin codes: i - IGP, e - EGP, ? - incomplete

   Network          Next Hop          Metric LocPrf Weight Path
*> 10.1.1.0/30      10.1.1.2               0           0 3 i
*> 10.1.2.0/30      10.1.1.2               0           0 3 i
*> 172.17.2.0/24    10.1.1.2                           0 3 2 I
```

Step 3   If the network is in the BGP table, the **backdoor** option will work as described.

9-5: network *ip-address* route-map *route-map-name*

9-6: network *ip-address* mask *network-mask* route-map *route-map-name*

Purpose: In theory, these commands allow you to modify a network's BGP attributes. In our experience, they are too buggy and should not be used. See sections 8-25 and 8-26 if you need to modify the BGP attributes of received or transmitted network advertisements.

9-7: network *ip-address* **weight** *weight*

9-8: network *ip-address* **mask** *network-mask* **weight** *weight*

Obsolete: These commands don't work and are considered obsolete. They will be removed from future versions of Cisco IOS Software. They are included here because they exist in current Cisco IOS Software Releases, but they do nothing. See sections 8-25 or 8-35 if you need to modify the weight of received network advertisements.

CHAPTER **10**

Route Redistribution

10-1: redistribute *protocol*

Syntax Description:

- *protocol*—Routes learned via *protocol* will be redistributed into BGP.

Purpose: To redistribute routes into BGP that have been learned via a routing protocol other than BGP. The metric of the non-BGP-learned routes is transferred to the metric or multi-exit discriminator (MED) of the new BGP route. Routes can be redistributed from **connected, dvmrp, egp, eigrp, igrp, isis, iso-igrp, mobile, odr, ospf, rip,** and **static**.

Cisco IOS Software Release: 10.0

Configuration Example: Redistributing Connected, Static, and EIGRP Learned Routes into BGP

In Figure 10-1, Router C is advertising 172.16.2.0/24 and 172.16.3.0/24 to Router B via EIGRP. Routers A and B have an EBGP relationship. This example redistributes EIGRP and static into BGP on Router B and redistributes connected on Router A.

Figure 10-1 *Redistributing Routes into BGP*

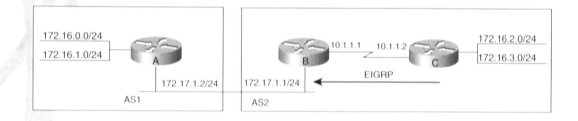

```
Router A
interface loopback 0
 ip address 172.16.0.1 255.255.255.0
!
interface loopback 1
 ip address 172.16.1.1 255.255.255.0
!
router bgp 1
 network 172.17.1.0 mask 255.255.255.0
 neighbor 172.17.1.1 remote-as 2
```
```
Router B
router eigrp 1
 network 10.0.0.0
 network 172.17.0.0
 no auto-summary
!
router bgp 2
 network 10.1.0.0 mask 255.255.255.252
 network 172.17.1.0 mask 255.255.255.0
 neighbor 172.17.1.2 remote-as 1
!
ip route 172.16.4.0 255.255.255.0 s2/0
```
```
Router C
interface loopback 0
 ip address 172.16.2.1 255.255.255.0
!
interface loopback 1
 ip address 172.16.3.1 255.255.255.0
!
router eigrp 1
 network 172.16.0.0
 network 10.0.0.0
 no auto-summary
```

Before proceeding with the redistribution of routes into BGP, inspect the IP and BGP routing tables on Routers A and B. Router B should be learning routes 172.16.2.0/24 and 172.16.3.0/24 from Router C via EIGRP. Because you are not redistributing routes on Router B, Router A should not be learning about the 172.16.2.0/24 or 172.16.3.0/24 routes.

```
rtrB#show ip route
Codes: C - connected, S - static, I - IGRP, R - RIP, M - mobile, B - BGP
       D - EIGRP, EX - EIGRP external, O - OSPF, IA - OSPF inter area
       N1 - OSPF NSSA external type 1, N2 - OSPF NSSA external type 2
       E1 - OSPF external type 1, E2 - OSPF external type 2, E - EGP
       i - IS-IS, L1 - IS-IS level-1, L2 - IS-IS level-2, ia - IS-IS inter area
       * - candidate default, U - per-user static route, o - ODR
       P - periodic downloaded static route

Gateway of last resort is not set
```

(Continued)

```
     172.17.0.0/24 is subnetted, 1 subnets
C       172.17.1.0 is directly connected, Ethernet0/0
     172.16.0.0/24 is subnetted, 3 subnets
S       172.16.4.0 is directly connected, Serial2/0
D       172.16.2.0 [90/1889792] via 10.1.1.2, 00:26:32, Serial2/0
D       172.16.3.0 [90/1889792] via 10.1.1.2, 00:26:32, Serial2/0
     10.0.0.0/30 is subnetted, 1 subnets
C       10.1.1.0 is directly connected, Serial2/0

rtrB#show ip bgp
BGP table version is 3, local router ID is 172.17.1.1
Status codes: s suppressed, d damped, h history, * valid, > best, i - internal
Origin codes: i - IGP, e - EGP, ? - incomplete

   Network          Next Hop          Metric LocPrf Weight Path
*> 10.1.1.0/30      0.0.0.0                0           32768 i
*  172.17.1.0/24    172.17.1.2             0               0 1 i
*>                  0.0.0.0                0           32768 i
```

```
rtrA#show ip route
Codes: C - connected, S - static, I - IGRP, R - RIP, M - mobile, B - BGP
       D - EIGRP, EX - EIGRP external, O - OSPF, IA - OSPF inter area
       N1 - OSPF NSSA external type 1, N2 - OSPF NSSA external type 2
       E1 - OSPF external type 1, E2 - OSPF external type 2, E - EGP
       i - IS-IS, L1 - IS-IS level-1, L2 - IS-IS level-2, ia - IS-IS inter area
       * - candidate default, U - per-user static route, o - ODR
       P - periodic downloaded static route

Gateway of last resort is not set

     172.17.0.0/24 is subnetted, 1 subnets
C       172.17.1.0 is directly connected, FastEthernet0
     172.16.0.0/24 is subnetted, 2 subnets
C       172.16.0.0 is directly connected, Loopback0
C       172.16.1.0 is directly connected, Loopback1
     10.0.0.0/30 is subnetted, 1 subnets
B       10.1.1.0 [20/0] via 172.17.1.1, 00:25:38

rtrA#show ip bgp
BGP table version is 4, local router ID is 172.16.1.1
Status codes: s suppressed, d damped, h history, * valid, > best, i - internal
Origin codes: i - IGP, e - EGP, ? - incomplete

   Network          Next Hop          Metric LocPrf Weight Path
*> 10.1.1.0/30      172.17.1.1             0               0 2 i
*> 172.17.1.0/24    0.0.0.0                0           32768 i
*                   172.17.1.1             0               0 2 i
```

Notice that the metric for the EIGRP learned routes on Router B is 1889792. Because the form of the **redistribute** command that you will use does not contain a metric, the router uses the EIGRP metric for the BGP MED for the redistributed EIGRP routes. Now modify the BGP configuration on Router B to enable the redistribution of the EIGRP and static routes into BGP. Also modify the configuration on Router A to enable the redistribution of connected routes:

```
Router A
router bgp 1
 network 172.17.1.0 mask 255.255.255.0
 redistribute connected
 neighbor 172.17.1.1 remote-as 2
Router B
router bgp 1
 network 10.1.0.0 mask 255.255.255.0
 network 172.17.1.0 mask 255.255.255.0
 redistribute static
 redistribute eigrp 1
 neighbor 172.17.1.2 remote-as 2
```

Verification

Verify that the connected routes are being redistributed in BGP on Router A and that the static and EIGRP routes are being redistributed on Router B:

```
rtrA#show ip bgp
BGP table version is 8, local router ID is 172.17.1.1
Status codes: s suppressed, d damped, h history, * valid, > best, i - internal
Origin codes: i - IGP, e - EGP, ? - incomplete

   Network          Next Hop          Metric LocPrf Weight Path
*> 10.0.0.0         0.0.0.0                0           32768 ?
*> 10.1.1.0/30      0.0.0.0                0           32768 i
*> 172.16.0.0       0.0.0.0                0           32768 ?
*                   172.17.1.2             0               0 1 ?
*> 172.17.0.0       172.17.1.2             0               0 1 ?
*> 172.17.1.0/24    0.0.0.0                0           32768 i
*                   172.17.1.2             0               0 1 i
rtrB#show ip bgp
BGP table version is 19, local router ID is 172.16.1.1
Status codes: s suppressed, d damped, h history, * valid, > best, i - internal
Origin codes: i - IGP, e - EGP, ? - incomplete

   Network          Next Hop          Metric LocPrf Weight Path
*> 10.0.0.0         172.17.1.1             0               0 2 ?
*> 10.1.1.0/30      172.17.1.1             0               0 2 i
*  172.16.0.0       172.17.1.1             0               0 2 ?
*>                  0.0.0.0                0           32768 ?
*> 172.17.0.0       0.0.0.0                0           32768 ?
*  172.17.1.0/24    172.17.1.1             0               0 2 i
*>                  0.0.0.0                0           32768 i
```

Why is the mask for the 172.16.x.x routes /16 (the entire Class B address 172.16.x.x)? By default, BGP summarizes redistributed routes on a classful boundary (see Chapter 2, "Auto-Summary"). Routers A and B now indicate that they can reach the entire Class B address block 172.16.x.x. Typically, this is not the behavior you want. When redistributing routes into BGP, it is a good idea to turn off auto-summarization. Modify the BGP configuration on Routers A and B to do this. Notice that Router A also summarizes the 10.0.0.0 and 172.17.0.0 networks because they are also directly connected.

```
Router A
router bgp 1
 network 172.17.1.0 mask 255.255.255.0
 redistribute connected 5
 neighbor 172.17.1.1 remote-as 2
 no auto-summary
Router B
router bgp 1
 network 10.1.0.0 mask 255.255.255.252
 network 172.17.1.0 mask 255.255.255.0
 redistribute static 10
 redistribute eigrp 15
 neighbor 172.17.1.2 remote-as 2
 no auto-summary
```

Reinspect the BGP tables on Routers A and B:

```
rtrA#show ip bgp
BGP table version is 8, local router ID is 172.16.1.1
Status codes: s suppressed, d damped, h history, * valid, > best, i - internal
Origin codes: i - IGP, e - EGP, ? - incomplete

   Network          Next Hop            Metric LocPrf Weight Path
*> 10.1.1.0/30      172.17.1.1               0             0 2 i
*> 172.16.0.0/24    0.0.0.0                  0         32768 ?
*> 172.16.1.0/24    0.0.0.0                  0         32768 ?
*> 172.16.2.0/24    172.17.1.1         1889792             0 2 ?
*> 172.16.3.0/24    172.17.1.1         1889792             0 2 ?
*> 172.16.4.0/24    172.17.1.1               0             0 2 ?
*  172.17.1.0/24    172.17.1.1               0             0 2 i
*>                  0.0.0.0                  0         32768 i
rtrB#show ip bgp
BGP table version is 19, local router ID is 172.17.1.1
Status codes: s suppressed, d damped, h history, * valid, > best, i - internal
Origin codes: i - IGP, e - EGP, ? - incomplete

   Network          Next Hop            Metric LocPrf Weight Path
*> 10.1.1.0/30      0.0.0.0                  0         32768 i
*> 172.16.0.0/24    172.17.1.2               0             0 1 ?
*> 172.16.1.0/24    172.17.1.2               0             0 1 ?
*> 172.16.2.0/24    10.1.1.2           1889792         32768 ?
*> 172.16.3.0/24    10.1.1.2           1889792         32768 ?
*> 172.16.4.0/24    0.0.0.0                  0         32768 ?
*  172.17.1.0/24    172.17.1.2               0             0 1 i
*>                  0.0.0.0                  0         32768 i
```

The metric or MED value for the redistributed EIGRP routes is equal to the EIGRP metric for those routes. The metric or MED value for the redistributed connected and static routes is 0.

Troubleshooting

Step 1 Verify that the BGP neighbors are in the Established state using the **show ip bgp neighbors** command.

If the neighbor relationship is not in the Established state, see section 8-23.

Step 2 Verify that the protocol you are redistributing routes from is active on the router.

Step 3 When redistributing from a protocol that requires a process ID, verify that you are using the proper process ID in the **redistribute** command.

Step 4 Use the **no auto-summary** command under router BGP when redistributing routes into BGP.

10-2: redistribute *protocol* **metric** *metric*

Syntax Description:

- *protocol*—Routes learned via *protocol* will be redistributed into BGP.

- *metric*—Metric to assign to the redistributed routes. The value is in the range of 0 to 4294967295.

Purpose: To redistribute routes into BGP that have been learned via a routing protocol other than BGP. The metric value is assigned to the metric or multi-exit discriminator (MED) of the new BGP route. Routes can be redistributed from **connected**, **dvmrp**, **egp**, **eigrp**, **igrp**, **isis**, **iso-igrp**, **mobile**, **odr**, **ospf**, **rip**, and **static**.

Cisco IOS Software Release: 10.0

Configuration Example: Redistributing Connected, Static, and EIGRP Learned Routes into BGP

In Figure 10-2, Router C is advertising 172.16.2.0/24 and 172.16.3.0/24 to Router B via EIGRP. Routers A and B have an EBGP relationship. This example redistributes EIGRP and static into BGP on Router B and redistributes connected on Router A. The static routes are assigned a metric of 10, the EIGRP routes a metric of 15, and the connected routes a metric of 5.

Figure 10-2 *Redistributing Routes into BGP*

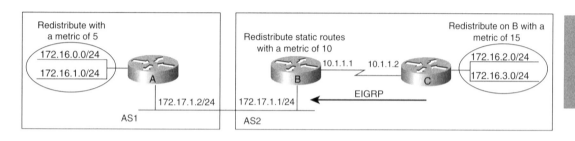

```
Router A
interface loopback 0
 ip address 172.16.0.1 255.255.255.0
 !
interface loopback 1
 ip address 172.16.1.1 255.255.255.0
 !
router bgp 1
 network 172.17.1.0 mask 255.255.255.0
 neighbor 172.17.1.1 remote-as 2
```
```
Router B
router eigrp 1
 network 10.0.0.0
 network 172.17.0.0
 no auto-summary
 !
router bgp 2
 network 10.1.0.0 mask 255.255.255.252
 network 172.17.1.0 mask 255.255.255.0
 neighbor 172.17.1.2 remote-as 1
 !
ip route 172.16.4.0 255.255.255.0 s2/0
```
```
Router C
interface loopback 0
 ip address 172.16.2.1 255.255.255.0
 !
interface loopback 1
 ip address 172.16.3.1 255.255.255.0
 !
router eigrp 1
 network 172.16.0.0
 network 10.0.0.0
 no auto-summary
```

Before proceeding with the redistribution of routes into BGP, inspect the IP and BGP routing tables on Routers A and B. Router B should be learning routes 172.16.2.0/24 and 172.16.3.0/24 from Router C via EIGRP. Because you are not redistributing routes on Router B, Router A should not be learning about the 172.16.2.0/24 or 172.16.3.0/24 routes.

```
rtrB#show ip route
Codes: C - connected, S - static, I - IGRP, R - RIP, M - mobile, B - BGP
       D - EIGRP, EX - EIGRP external, O - OSPF, IA - OSPF inter area
       N1 - OSPF NSSA external type 1, N2 - OSPF NSSA external type 2
       E1 - OSPF external type 1, E2 - OSPF external type 2, E - EGP
       i - IS-IS, L1 - IS-IS level-1, L2 - IS-IS level-2, ia - IS-IS inter area
       * - candidate default, U - per-user static route, o - ODR
       P - periodic downloaded static route

Gateway of last resort is not set

     172.17.0.0/24 is subnetted, 1 subnets
C       172.17.1.0 is directly connected, Ethernet0/0
     172.16.0.0/24 is subnetted, 3 subnets
S       172.16.4.0 is directly connected, Serial2/0
D       172.16.2.0 [90/1889792] via 10.1.1.2, 00:26:32, Serial2/0
D       172.16.3.0 [90/1889792] via 10.1.1.2, 00:26:32, Serial2/0
     10.0.0.0/30 is subnetted, 1 subnets
C       10.1.1.0 is directly connected, Serial2/0

rtrB#show ip bgp
BGP table version is 3, local router ID is 172.17.1.1
Status codes: s suppressed, d damped, h history, * valid, > best, i - internal
Origin codes: i - IGP, e - EGP, ? - incomplete

   Network          Next Hop          Metric LocPrf Weight Path
*> 10.1.1.0/30      0.0.0.0               0           32768 i
*  172.17.1.0/24    172.17.1.2            0               0 1 i
*>                  0.0.0.0               0           32768 i
```
```
rtrA#show ip route
Codes: C - connected, S - static, I - IGRP, R - RIP, M - mobile, B - BGP
       D - EIGRP, EX - EIGRP external, O - OSPF, IA - OSPF inter area
       N1 - OSPF NSSA external type 1, N2 - OSPF NSSA external type 2
       E1 - OSPF external type 1, E2 - OSPF external type 2, E - EGP
       i - IS-IS, L1 - IS-IS level-1, L2 - IS-IS level-2, ia - IS-IS inter area
       * - candidate default, U - per-user static route, o - ODR
       P - periodic downloaded static route

Gateway of last resort is not set

     172.17.0.0/24 is subnetted, 1 subnets
C       172.17.1.0 is directly connected, FastEthernet0
     172.16.0.0/24 is subnetted, 2 subnets
C       172.16.0.0 is directly connected, Loopback0
C       172.16.1.0 is directly connected, Loopback1
     10.0.0.0/30 is subnetted, 1 subnets
B       10.1.1.0 [20/0] via 172.17.1.1, 00:25:38

rtrA#show ip bgp
BGP table version is 4, local router ID is 172.16.1.1
Status codes: s suppressed, d damped, h history, * valid, > best, i - internal
Origin codes: i - IGP, e - EGP, ? - incomplete
```

(Continued)
```
    Network          Next Hop           Metric LocPrf Weight Path
*> 10.1.1.0/30      172.17.1.1              0            0 2 i
*> 172.17.1.0/24    0.0.0.0                 0        32768 i
*                   172.17.1.1             0            0 2 i
```

Notice that the metric for the EIGRP learned routes on Router B is 1889792. The form of the **redistribute** command that you will use does not use the metric of the route that is being redistributed but assigns one statically. Now modify the BGP configuration on Router B to enable the redistribution of the EIGRP and static routes into BGP. Also modify the configuration on Router A to enable the redistribution of connected routes.

```
Router A
router bgp 1
 network 172.17.1.0 mask 255.255.255.0
 redistribute connected metric 5
 neighbor 172.17.1.1 remote-as 2
Router B
router bgp 1
 network 10.1.0.0 mask 255.255.255.0
 network 172.17.1.0 mask 255.255.255.0
 redistribute static metric 10
 redistribute eigrp 1 metric 15
 neighbor 172.17.1.2 remote-as 2
```

Verification

Verify that the connected routes are being redistributed in BGP on Router A and that the static and EIGRP routes are being redistributed on Router B.

```
rtrA#show ip bgp
BGP table version is 15, local router ID is 172.16.1.1
Status codes: s suppressed, d damped, h history, * valid, > best, i - internal
Origin codes: i - IGP, e - EGP, ? - incomplete

    Network          Next Hop           Metric LocPrf Weight Path
*> 10.0.0.0         172.17.1.1              0            0 2 ?
*> 10.1.1.0/30      172.17.1.1              0            0 2 i
*  172.16.0.0       172.17.1.1             10            0 2 ?
*>                  0.0.0.0                 5        32768
*> 172.17.0.0       0.0.0.0                 5        32768 ?
*  172.17.1.0/24    172.17.1.1             0            0 2 i
*>                  0.0.0.0                 5        32768 i
rtrB#show ip bgp
BGP table version is 8, local router ID is 172.17.1.1
Status codes: s suppressed, d damped, h history, * valid, > best, i - internal
Origin codes: i - IGP, e - EGP, ? - incomplete
```

continues

(Continued)

Network	Next Hop	Metric	LocPrf	Weight	Path
*> 10.0.0.0	0.0.0.0	0		32768	?
*> 10.1.1.0/30	0.0.0.0	0		32768	i
*> 172.16.0.0	0.0.0.0	10		32768	?
*	172.17.1.2	5		0	1 ?
*> 172.17.0.0	172.17.1.2	5		0	1 ?
*> 172.17.1.0/24	0.0.0.0	0		32768	i
*	172.17.1.2	5		0	1 i

Why is the mask for the 172.16.x.x routes /16 (the entire Class B address 172.16.x.x)? By default, BGP summarizes redistributed routes on a classful boundary (see Chapter 2). Routers A and B now indicate that they can reach the entire Class B address block 172.16.x.x. Typically, this is not the behavior you want. When redistributing routes into BGP, it is a good idea to turn off auto-summarization. Modify the BGP configuration on Routers A and B to do this. Notice that Router A also summarizes the 10.0.0.0 and 172.17.0.0 networks because they are also directly connected.

```
Router A
router bgp 1
 network 172.17.1.0 mask 255.255.255.0
 redistribute connected 5
 neighbor 172.17.1.1 remote-as 2
 no auto-summary
Router B
router bgp 1
 network 10.1.0.0 mask 255.255.255.252
 network 172.17.1.0 mask 255.255.255.0
 redistribute static 10
 redistribute eigrp 1 15
 neighbor 172.17.1.2 remote-as 2
 no auto-summary
```

Reinspect the BGP tables on Routers A and B:

```
rtrA#show ip bgp
BGP table version is 9, local router ID is 172.16.1.1
Status codes: s suppressed, d damped, h history, * valid, > best, i - internal
Origin codes: i - IGP, e - EGP, ? - incomplete
```

Network	Next Hop	Metric	LocPrf	Weight	Path
*> 10.1.1.0/30	172.17.1.1	0		0	2 i
*> 172.16.0.0/24	0.0.0.0	5		32768	?
*> 172.16.1.0/24	0.0.0.0	5		32768	?
*> 172.16.2.0/24	172.17.1.1	15		0	2 ?
*> 172.16.3.0/24	172.17.1.1	15		0	2 ?
*> 172.16.4.0/24	172.17.1.1	10		0	2 ?
*> 172.17.1.0/24	0.0.0.0	5		32768	i
*	172.17.1.1	0		0	2 i

(Continued)

```
rtrB#show ip bgp
BGP table version is 20, local router ID is 172.17.1.1
Status codes: s suppressed, d damped, h history, * valid, > best, i - internal
Origin codes: i - IGP, e - EGP, ? - incomplete

   Network          Next Hop         Metric LocPrf Weight Path
*> 10.1.1.0/30      0.0.0.0               0         32768 i
*> 172.16.0.0/24    172.17.1.2            5             0 1 ?
*> 172.16.1.0/24    172.17.1.2            5             0 1 ?
*> 172.16.2.0/24    10.1.1.2             15         32768 ?
*> 172.16.3.0/24    10.1.1.2             15         32768 ?
*> 172.16.4.0/24    0.0.0.0              10         32768 ?
*  172.17.1.0/24    172.17.1.2            5             0 1 i
*>                  0.0.0.0               0         32768 i
```

Troubleshooting

Step 1   Verify that the BGP neighbors are in the Established state using the **show ip bgp neighbors** command.

If the neighbor relationship is not in the Established state, see section 8-23.

Step 2   Verify that the protocol you are redistributing routes from is active on the router.

Step 3   When redistributing from a protocol that requires a process ID, verify that you are using the proper process ID in the **redistribute** command.

Step 4   Use the **no auto-summary** command under router BGP when redistributing routes into BGP.

10-3: redistribute *protocol* **route-map** *route-map-name*

10-4: redistribute *protocol* **route-map** *route-map-name* **metric** *metric*

Syntax Description:

- *protocol*—Routes learned via *protocol* will be redistributed into BGP.

- *route-map-name*—Name of the route map used to control which routes will be redistributed into BGP. The route map can also be used to modify the BGP attributes of the redistributed routes.

- *metric*—Metric to assign to the redistributed routes. The value is in the range of 0 to 4294967295.

Purpose: To redistribute routes into BGP that have been learned via a routing protocol other than BGP. The metric of the non-BGP-learned routes is transferred to the metric or multi-exit discriminator (MED) of the new BGP route if the **metric** option is not used. If the **metric** option is used, the assigned metric will be applied to all routes redistributed from the protocol. A route map can be used for each redistributed protocol to control which routes are redistributed. A route map can also be used to modify the BGP attributes of the redistributed routes. Routes can be redistributed from **connected**, **dvmrp**, **egp**, **eigrp**, **igrp**, **isis**, **iso-igrp**, **mobile**, **odr**, **ospf**, **rip**, and **static**.

Cisco IOS Software Release: 10.0

Configuration Example: Selectively Redistributing Connected, Static, and EIGRP Learned Routes into BGP

In Figure 10-3, Router C is advertising 172.16.2.0/24 and 172.16.3.0/24 to Router B via EIGRP. Routers A and B have an EBGP relationship. This example redistributes EIGRP and static into BGP on Router B and redistributes connected on Router A. On Router B, you want to block the redistribution of the EIGRP route 172.16.2.0. On Router A, you want to allow only the redistribution of network 172.16.1.0/24. Another route map is used on Router B to set the weight of the redistributed static route to 88.

Figure 10-3 *Selectively Redistributing Routes into BGP*

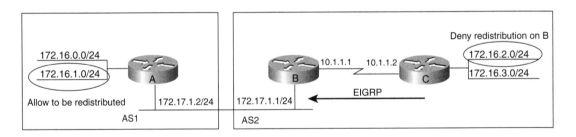

```
Router A
interface loopback 0
 ip address 172.16.0.1 255.255.255.0
!
interface loopback 1
 ip address 172.16.1.1 255.255.255.0
!
router bgp 1
 network 172.17.1.0 mask 255.255.255.0
 neighbor 172.17.1.1 remote-as 2
```

(Continued)

```
Router B
router eigrp 1
 network 10.0.0.0
 network 172.17.0.0
 no auto-summary
!
router bgp 2
 network 10.1.0.0 mask 255.255.255.252
 network 172.17.1.0 mask 255.255.255.0
 neighbor 172.17.1.2 remote-as 1
!
ip route 172.16.4.0 255.255.255.0 s2/0
```
```
Router C
interface loopback 0
 ip address 172.16.2.1 255.255.255.0
!
interface loopback 1
 ip address 172.16.3.1 255.255.255.0
!
router eigrp 1
 network 172.16.0.0
 network 10.0.0.0
 no auto-summary
```

Before proceeding with the redistribution and filtering of routes into BGP, inspect the IP and BGP routing tables on Routers A and B. Router B should be learning routes 172.16.2.0/24 and 172.16.3.0/24 from Router C via EIGRP. Because you are not redistributing routes on Router B, Router A should not be learning about the 172.16.2.0/24 or 172.16.3.0/24 routes.

```
rtrB#show ip route
Codes: C - connected, S - static, I - IGRP, R - RIP, M - mobile, B - BGP
       D - EIGRP, EX - EIGRP external, O - OSPF, IA - OSPF inter area
       N1 - OSPF NSSA external type 1, N2 - OSPF NSSA external type 2
       E1 - OSPF external type 1, E2 - OSPF external type 2, E - EGP
       i - IS-IS, L1 - IS-IS level-1, L2 - IS-IS level-2, ia - IS-IS inter area
       * - candidate default, U - per-user static route, o - ODR
       P - periodic downloaded static route

Gateway of last resort is not set

     172.17.0.0/24 is subnetted, 1 subnets
C       172.17.1.0 is directly connected, Ethernet0/0
     172.16.0.0/24 is subnetted, 3 subnets
S       172.16.4.0 is directly connected, Serial2/0
D       172.16.2.0 [90/1889792] via 10.1.1.2, 00:26:32, Serial2/0
D       172.16.3.0 [90/1889792] via 10.1.1.2, 00:26:32, Serial2/0
     10.0.0.0/30 is subnetted, 1 subnets
C       10.1.1.0 is directly connected, Serial2/0
```

continues

```
(Continued)
rtrB#show ip bgp
BGP table version is 3, local router ID is 172.17.1.1
Status codes: s suppressed, d damped, h history, * valid, > best, i - internal
Origin codes: i - IGP, e - EGP, ? - incomplete

   Network          Next Hop         Metric LocPrf Weight Path
*> 10.1.1.0/30      0.0.0.0               0         32768 i
*  172.17.1.0/24    172.17.1.2            0             0 1 i
*>                  0.0.0.0               0         32768 i
```

```
rtrA#show ip route
Codes: C - connected, S - static, I - IGRP, R - RIP, M - mobile, B - BGP
       D - EIGRP, EX - EIGRP external, O - OSPF, IA - OSPF inter area
       N1 - OSPF NSSA external type 1, N2 - OSPF NSSA external type 2
       E1 - OSPF external type 1, E2 - OSPF external type 2, E - EGP
       i - IS-IS, L1 - IS-IS level-1, L2 - IS-IS level-2, ia - IS-IS inter area
       * - candidate default, U - per-user static route, o - ODR
       P - periodic downloaded static route

Gateway of last resort is not set

     172.17.0.0/24 is subnetted, 1 subnets
C       172.17.1.0 is directly connected, FastEthernet0
     172.16.0.0/24 is subnetted, 2 subnets
C       172.16.0.0 is directly connected, Loopback0
C       172.16.1.0 is directly connected, Loopback1
     10.0.0.0/30 is subnetted, 1 subnets
B       10.1.1.0 [20/0] via 172.17.1.1, 00:25:38

rtrA#show ip bgp
BGP table version is 4, local router ID is 172.16.1.1
Status codes: s suppressed, d damped, h history, * valid, > best, i - internal
Origin codes: i - IGP, e - EGP, ? - incomplete

   Network          Next Hop         Metric LocPrf Weight Path
*> 10.1.1.0/30      172.17.1.1            0             0 2 i
*> 172.17.1.0/24    0.0.0.0              0         32768 i
*                   172.17.1.1            0             0 2 i
```

Notice that the metric for the EIGRP learned routes on Router B is 1889792. Because the form of the **redistribute** command that you will use does not contain a metric, the router will use the EIGRP metric for the BGP MED for the redistributed EIGRP routes. Now modify the BGP configuration on Router B to enable the redistribution of the EIGRP and static routes into BGP. Also modify the configuration on Router A to enable the redistribution of connected routes. On Router A, allow only the connected network 172.16.1.0/24 to be redistributed. On Router B, block the 172.16.2.0/24 route from being redistributed, and set the weight of the redistributed static route to 88.

```
Router A
router bgp 1
 network 172.17.1.0 mask 255.255.255.0
 redistribute connected route-map allow
 neighbor 172.17.1.1 remote-as 2
 no auto-summary
 !
access-list 1 permit 172.16.1.0 0.0.0.255
route-map allow permit 10
 match ip address 1
Router B
router bgp 1
 network 10.1.0.0 mask 255.255.255.0
 network 172.17.1.0 mask 255.255.255.0
 redistribute static route-map setwt
 redistribute eigrp 1 route-map block
 neighbor 172.17.1.2 remote-as 2
 no auto-summary
 !
access-list 1 deny 172.16.2.0 0.0.0.255
access-list 1 permit any
route-map block permit 10
 match ip add 1
route-map setwt permit 10
 set weight 88
```

Section2 10-3 — 10-4

Verification

Verify that the selected connected routes are being redistributed in BGP on Router A and that the static and selected EIGRP routes are being redistributed on Router B. Also verify that the weight of the static route is being set to 88:

```
rtrA#show ip bgp
BGP table version is 14, local router ID is 172.16.1.1
Status codes: s suppressed, d damped, h history, * valid, > best, i - internal
Origin codes: i - IGP, e - EGP, ? - incomplete

   Network          Next Hop            Metric LocPrf Weight Path
*> 10.1.1.0/30      172.17.1.1               0          0 2 i
*> 172.16.1.0/24    0.0.0.0                  0      32768 ?
*> 172.16.3.0/24    172.17.1.1         1889792          0 2 ?
*> 172.16.4.0/24    172.17.1.1               0          0 2 ?
*  172.17.1.0/24    172.17.1.1               0          0 2 i
*>                  0.0.0.0                  0      32768 I
rtrB#show ip bgp
BGP table version is 6, local router ID is 172.17.1.1
Status codes: s suppressed, d damped, h history, * valid, > best, i - internal
Origin codes: i - IGP, e - EGP, ? - incomplete
```

continues

```
(Continued)
     Network          Next Hop         Metric LocPrf Weight Path
 *> 10.1.1.0/30       0.0.0.0              0            32768 i
 *> 172.16.1.0/24     172.17.1.2           0                0 1 ?
 *> 172.16.3.0/24     10.1.1.2        1889792            32768 ?
 *> 172.16.4.0/24     0.0.0.0              0               88 ?
 *  172.17.1.0/24     172.17.1.2           0                0 1 i
 *>                   0.0.0.0              0            32768 i
```

Troubleshooting

Step 1   Verify that the BGP neighbors are in the Established state using the **show ip bgp neighbors** command.

If the neighbor relationship is not in the Established state, see section 8-23.

Step 2   Verify that the protocol you are redistributing routes from is active on the router.

Step 3   When redistributing from a protocol that requires a process ID, verify that you are using the proper process ID in the **redistribute** command.

Step 4   Use the **no auto-summary** command under router BGP when redistributing routes into BGP.

Step 5   Verify the syntax of any route maps and access lists. Remember that an IP access list has an implicit **deny all** as the last statement.

10-5: redistribute *protocol* **weight** *weight*

Syntax Description:

- *protocol*—Routes learned via *protocol* will be redistributed into BGP.

- *weight*—Weight assigned to the redistributed routes. The value is in the range of 0 to 65535.

Obsolete: This command is considered obsolete. It will be removed from future versions of the IOS. This command is included here because it exists in current IOS versions. Use a **route-map** (see section 10-4) if you need to set the weight of redistributed routes.

CHAPTER 11

Address Summarization

11-1: summary-address

Purpose: The **summary-address** command works only with OSPF and IS-IS. Even though this command appears as a BGP router configuration option, do not use this command when configuring BGP. Use the **aggregate-address** commands described in Chapter 1, "Route Aggregation."

CHAPTER 12

Synchronization

12-1: synchronization

Syntax Description:

This command has no arguments.

Purpose: IBGP learned routes are not installed in the IP routing table if the route has not been learned by an IGP or if the advertised next hop is inaccessible. This is called synchronization.

IOS Release: 10.0

Configuration Example: BGP Synchronization

In Figure 12-1, BGP synchronization is enabled by default. Router A is advertising network 199.172.1.0/24 to Router B via EBGP, and Router B is advertising 199.172.1.0/24 to Router C via IBGP.

Figure 12-1 *Synchronization Applies to IBGP Routes*

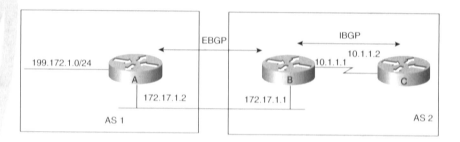

```
Router A
interface Loopback0
 ip address 199.172.1.1 255.255.255.0
 !
```

continues

(Continued)

```
router bgp 1
 neighbor 172.17.1.1 remote-as 2
 !
Router B
router bgp 2
 neighbor 172.17.1.2 remote-as 1
 neighbor 10.1.1.2 remote-as 2
Router C
router bgp 2
 neighbor 10.1.1.1 remote-as 2
```

Routers A and B have an EBGP connection, so there is no need for the BGP learned routes to be synchronized with an IGP. The 199.172.1.0/24 route will be installed in the IP routing table on Router B:

```
rtrB#show ip route
p2#show ip route
Codes: C - connected, S - static, I - IGRP, R - RIP, M - mobile, B - BGP
       D - EIGRP, EX - EIGRP external, O - OSPF, IA - OSPF inter area
       N1 - OSPF NSSA external type 1, N2 - OSPF NSSA external type 2
       E1 - OSPF external type 1, E2 - OSPF external type 2, E - EGP
       i - IS-IS, L1 - IS-IS level-1, L2 - IS-IS level-2, ia - IS-IS inter area
       * - candidate default, U - per-user static route, o - ODR
       P - periodic downloaded static route

Gateway of last resort is not set

     172.17.0.0/24 is subnetted, 1 subnets
C       172.17.1.0 is directly connected, Ethernet0/1
     10.0.0.0/30 is subnetted, 1 subnets
C       10.1.1.0 is directly connected, Serial2/1
B    199.172.1.0/24 [20/0] via 172.17.1.2, 00:22:24
```

The 199.172.1.0/24 route will not be installed in the IP routing table on Router C, because this route was not learned by an IGP. Also, Router C does not have an entry in the IP routing table for the next hop. IBGP preserves the EBGP next-hop information.

```
rtrC#show ip bgp 199.172.1.0
BGP routing table entry for 199.172.1.0/24, version 0
Paths: (1 available, no best path)
  Not advertised to any peer
  1
    172.17.1.2 (inaccessible) from 10.1.1.1 (132.1.1.1)
      Origin IGP, metric 0, localpref 100, valid, internal, not synchronized, ref 2

rtrC#show ip route
Codes: C - connected, S - static, I - IGRP, R - RIP, M - mobile, B - BGP
       D - EIGRP, EX - EIGRP external, O - OSPF, IA - OSPF inter area
       N1 - OSPF NSSA external type 1, N2 - OSPF NSSA external type 2
       E1 - OSPF external type 1, E2 - OSPF external type 2, E - EGP
```

(Continued)
```
        i - IS-IS, L1 - IS-IS level-1, L2 - IS-IS level-2, * - candidate default
        U - per-user static route, o - ODR

Gateway of last resort is not set


     10.0.0.0/30 is subnetted, 1 subnets
C        10.1.1.0 is directly connected, Serial1
```

Disable synchronization on router C and determine if the 199.172.1.0 route will be installed in the IP routing table.

```
Router C
router bgp 2
 no synchronization
 neighbor 10.1.1.1 remote-as 2

rtrC#show ip route
Codes: C - connected, S - static, I - IGRP, R - RIP, M - mobile, B - BGP
       D - EIGRP, EX - EIGRP external, O - OSPF, IA - OSPF inter area
       N1 - OSPF NSSA external type 1, N2 - OSPF NSSA external type 2
       E1 - OSPF external type 1, E2 - OSPF external type 2, E - EGP
       i - IS-IS, L1 - IS-IS level-1, L2 - IS-IS level-2, * - candidate default
       U - per-user static route, o - ODR

Gateway of last resort is not set


     10.0.0.0/30 is subnetted, 1 subnets
C        10.1.1.0 is directly connected, Serial1

rtrC#show ip bgp 199.172.1.0
BGP routing table entry for 199.172.1.0/24, version 0
Paths: (1 available, no best path)
  1
    172.17.1.2 (inaccessible) from 10.1.1.1 (132.1.1.1)
        Origin IGP, metric 0, localpref 100, valid, internal
```

Even with synchronization disabled, the route will not be installed in the IP routing table, because the next hop is inaccessible. There are three ways to correct this problem:

- Advertise the next hop via an IGP.

- Have router B advertise itself as the next hop for all advertised BGP routes.

- Advertise the BGP routes via an IGP.

The third method involves redistributing the BGP routes into your IGP. Redistribution is not recommended due to the possible size of the BGP routing table. Also, when you redistribute BGP into an IGP, the BGP attributes such as AS path, metric, weight, and local preference are lost. If an autonomous system is being used as a transit AS, it is important to preserve the BGP attributes. Modify the configurations on Routers B and C so that the EBGP next hop received from Router A is advertised to router C via an IGP:

```
Router B
router eigrp 1
 network 172.17.0.0
 network 10.0.0.0
Router C
router eigrp 1
 network 172.17.0.0
```

Verification

Verify that the BGP route 199.172.1.0/24 has been installed in the IP routing table on Router C:

```
rtrC#show ip route
Codes: C - connected, S - static, I - IGRP, R - RIP, M - mobile, B - BGP
       D - EIGRP, EX - EIGRP external, O - OSPF, IA - OSPF inter area
       N1 - OSPF NSSA external type 1, N2 - OSPF NSSA external type 2
       E1 - OSPF external type 1, E2 - OSPF external type 2, E - EGP
       i - IS-IS, L1 - IS-IS level-1, L2 - IS-IS level-2, * - candidate default
       U - per-user static route, o - ODR

Gateway of last resort is not set

     10.0.0.0/30 is subnetted, 1 subnets
C       10.1.1.0 is directly connected, Serial1
B    199.172.1.0/24 [200/0] via 172.17.1.2, 00:00:38
D    172.17.0.0/16 [90/2195456] via 10.1.1.1, 00:01:37, Serial1
```

Although we have managed to get the 199.172.1.0/24 network in the IP routing table, we do not have IP connectivity to this network. Router A does not have a route back to Router C. Router B would need to advertise the 10.0.0.0 network to Router A via EBGP. If we ping the 199.172.1.0 network from Router C, we will be unsuccessful. Advertise the 10.1.1.0 network to Router A.

```
Router B
router bgp 2
 network 10.1.1.0 mask 255.255.255.252
```

Verify IP connectivity to 199.172.1.0/24 by pinging the loopback on Router A:

```
rtrC#ping 199.172.1.1

Type escape sequence to abort.
Sending 5, 100-byte ICMP Echos to 199.172.1.1, timeout is 2 seconds:
!!!!!
Success rate is 100 percent (5/5), round-trip min/avg/max = 28/31/32 ms
```

Troubleshooting

Step 1 Verify that the BGP neighbors are in the Established state using the **show ip bgp neighbors** command.

If the neighbor relationship is not in the Established state, see section 8-23.

Step 2 If synchronization is enabled, routes learned via IBGP will not be installed in the IP routing table unless the next hop is accessible and the prefixes have been learned via an IGP.

CHAPTER 13

BGP Timers

13-1: timers bgp *keepalive holdtime*

Syntax Description:

*   *keepalive*—1 to 4294967295 seconds.
*   *holdtime*—1 to 4294967295 seconds.

Purpose: To globally set the keepalive and holdtime values for all neighbors. Keepalive and holdtime are common among IP routing protocols. The keepalive time indicates how often a router sends a keepalive message to a neighbor to inform the neighbor that the router is still alive and well. The holdtime is used as a deathwatch. If a keepalive message is not received within the holdtime, the neighbor is declared dead, and the session is terminated. The default value for the keepalive time is 60 seconds. The holdtime is three times the keepalive time, or 180 seconds. Generally, these values do not need to be changed. If you do change them, it is a good rule to make the holdtime equal to three times whatever keepalive value you use. Of course, the holdtime should always be greater than the keepalive time. When two BGP speakers establish a connection, the smaller of the advertised keepalive and holdtime values will be used. For example, if one neighbor advertises a keepalive value of 70 and a holdtime of 210 and the other neighbor advertises a keepalive value of 72 and a holdtime of 205, the keepalive value will be 70 and the holdtime will be 205. If the timer values are set using the **neighbor timers** command (see section 8-31), these values will override the global values only for that neighbor.

IOS Release: 10.0

Configuration Example: BGP Timers

In this example, we will examine the result of various settings of keepalive and holdtimers. Figure 13-1 illustrates the basic setup for these examples.

Figure 13-1 *Network Setup for BGP Timer Examples*

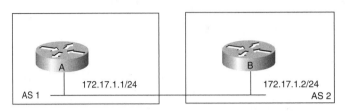

```
Router A
router bgp 1
neighbor 172.17.1.2 remote-as 2
Router B
router bgp 2
 neighbor 172.17.1.1 remote-as 1
```

The default values for the timers can be examined using the **show ip bgp neighbors** command:

```
rtrA#show ip bgp neighbors
BGP neighbor is 172.17.1.2,  remote AS 2, external link
  BGP version 4, remote router ID 172.17.1.2
  BGP state = Established, up for 00:01:50
  Last read 00:00:50, hold time is 180, keepalive interval is 60 seconds
```

Change the BGP timer values on Router A to 70 and 210:

```
Router A
router bgp 1
 timers bgp 70 210
 neighbor 172.17.1.2 remote-as 2
```

Clear the connection to force the timer values to take effect, and then inspect the new values:

```
rtrA#show ip bgp neighbors
BGP neighbor is 172.17.1.2,  remote AS 2, external link
  BGP version 4, remote router ID 172.17.1.2
  BGP state = Established, up for 00:00:14
  Last read 00:00:14, hold time is 180, keepalive interval is 60 seconds
```

The timer values did not change. Router B is advertising the defaults of 60 and 180. These values are smaller than the values configured on Router A, so the smaller values are used. Configure Router B with the same timer values as Router A:

```
Router B
router bgp 2
 timers bgp 70 210
 neighbor 172.17.1.1 remote-as 1
```

Clear the connection and view the timer values:

```
rtrA#show ip bgp neighbors
BGP neighbor is 172.17.1.2,  remote AS 2, external link
  BGP version 4, remote router ID 172.17.1.2
  BGP state = Established, up for 00:01:04
  Last read 00:01:03, hold time is 210, keepalive interval is 70 seconds
```

Finally, configure the timers and Routers A and B using the **neighbor timers** command, using values larger than 70 and 210.

```
Router A
router bgp 1
 timers bgp 70 210
 neighbor 172.17.1.2 timers 80 240
 neighbor 172.17.1.2 remote-as 2
Router B
router bgp 2
 timers bgp 70 210
 neighbor 172.17.1.1 timers 80 240
 neighbor 172.17.1.1 remote-as 1
```

Clear the connection and view the timers:

```
rtrA#show ip bgp neighbors
BGP neighbor is 172.17.1.2,  remote AS 2, external link
  BGP version 4, remote router ID 172.17.1.2
  BGP state = Established, up for 00:01:04
  Last read 00:01:04, hold time is 240, keepalive interval is 80 seconds
  Configured hold time is 240, keepalive interval is 80 seconds
```

The timer values used with the **neighbor** command override the values used with the **timers bgp** command, regardless of their value.

Verification

Use the **show ip bgp neighbors** command to verify timer values.

Troubleshooting

Step 1   Verify that the BGP neighbors are in the Established state using the **show ip bgp neighbors** command.

If the neighbor relationship is not in the Established state, see section 8-23.

Step 2   The holdtime should be three times the keepalive value. If neighbors are using different keepalive and holdtime values, the smaller value is used.

Step 3   Timer values set using the **neighbor** command override values set using the **timers bgp** command, but only for that neighbor.

CHAPTER 14

BGP show Commands

14-1: show ip bgp

14-2: show ip bgp | begin *line*

14-3: show ip bgp | exclude *line*

14-4: show ip bgp | include *line*

Syntax Description:

- *line*—Regular expression. See Appendix B, "Regular Expressions."

Purpose: To display the contents of the local BGP routing table.

Cisco IOS Software Release: 10.0

Example: Display the BGP Routing Table

The following is some sample output from the **show ip bgp** command:

```
rtrA#show ip bgp
BGP table version is 9, local router ID is 200.1.4.1
Status codes: s suppressed, d damped, h history, * valid, > best, i - internal
Origin codes: i - IGP, e - EGP, ? - incomplete

   Network          Next Hop          Metric LocPrf Weight Path
*> 199.172.1.0      172.17.1.2             0             0 1 i
*> 199.172.2.0      172.17.1.2             0             0 1 i
*> 199.172.3.0      172.17.1.2             0             0 1 i
*> 199.172.4.0      172.17.1.2             0             0 1 i
*> 200.1.1.0        0.0.0.0                0         32768 i
*s 200.1.2.0        0.0.0.0                0         32768 i
*> 200.1.2.0/23     0.0.0.0                          32768 i
*s 200.1.3.0        0.0.0.0                0         32768 i
*> 200.1.4.0        0.0.0.0                0         32768 i
*>i156.26.1.0       10.1.1.2               0             0 i
```

The following list describes the various fields displayed when using the **show ip bgp** command:

- **BGP table version**—Whenever the BGP table is changed, the version number is incremented.

- **local router ID**—The highest IP address assigned to an interface. If loopbacks are used, the router ID is the highest IP address assigned to a loopback interface. The router ID can be changed using the **bgp router-id** configuration command (see section 3-17).

- **Status codes**

  ⇒ **s**—The entry is suppressed (see Chapter 8, section 8-32).

  ⇒ *****—The entry is valid.

  ⇒ **h**—Dampening is enabled for the prefix (see sections 3-9 through 3-12).

  ⇒ **>**—If there are multiple entries for the prefix, this indicates the best route.

  ⇒ **i**—The prefix was learned via IBGP. This is the i to the left of the network entry.

- **Origin codes**

  ⇒ **i**—Routes installed using the **network** command.

  ⇒ **e**—Routes learned via EGP.

  ⇒ **?**—Routes learned via redistribution.

- **Network**—Prefix entry in the table. If a mask is not listed, the prefix is using the standard mask for the entry's class.

- **Next Hop**—Next-hop attribute advertised by the BGP neighbor. A value of 0.0.0.0 indicates that the prefix originated locally (see section 8-17).

- **Metric**—Value of the multi-exit discriminator advertised by the BGP neighbor.

- **LocPrf**—Local preference value. The default is 100.

- **Weight**—Weight assigned to the prefix. Local routes default to 32768. Unless set, the weight of received routes is set to 0.

- **Path**—A list of the autonomous system paths leading back to the prefix.

List the 199 prefixes in the BGP routing table:

```
rtrA#show ip bgp ¦ include 199
BGP table version is 90, local router ID is 199.172.15.1
*> 199.172.1.0      0.0.0.0                 0          32768 i
s> 199.172.2.0      0.0.0.0                 0          32768 i
*> 199.172.2.0/23   0.0.0.0                            32768 i
s> 199.172.3.0      0.0.0.0                 0          32768 i
*> 199.172.4.0 .    0.0.0.0                 0          32768 I
```

List everything but the 199 prefixes in the BGP routing table:

```
ce2red#show ip bgp ¦ exclude 199
Status codes: s suppressed, d damped, h history, * valid, > best, i - internal
Origin codes: i - IGP, e - EGP, ? - incomplete
Network          Next Hop           Metric LocPrf Weight Path
*> 200.1.1.0        172.17.1.1               0            0 2 i
*> 200.1.2.0        172.17.1.1               0            0 2 i
*> 200.1.3.0        172.17.1.1               0            0 2 i
*> 200.1.4.0        172.17.1.1               0            0 2 I
```

14-5: show ip bgp *prefix*

Syntax Description:

- *prefix*—IP address of the prefix to display.

Purpose: To display the contents of the local BGP routing table for a specific prefix.

Cisco IOS Software Release: 10.0

Example: Display a Specific Prefix from the BGP Routing Table

The following is some sample output from the **show ip bgp** *prefix* command:

```
rtrA#show ip bgp 199.172.1.0
BGP routing table entry for 199.172.1.0/24, version 6
Paths: (1 available, best #1)
  Advertised to non peer-group peers:
    172.17.1.1
  Local
    0.0.0.0 from 0.0.0.0 (199.172.15.1)
      Origin IGP, metric 0, localpref 100, weight 32768, valid, sourced, local,
best, ref 2
```

14-6: show ip bgp *prefix mask*

14-7: show ip bgp *prefix/mask-length*

Syntax Description:

- *prefix*—IP address of the prefix to display.
- *mask*—Display prefix with a specific network mask.
- *mask-length*—Bit length of the mask.

Purpose: To display the contents of the local BGP routing table for a specific prefix with a specific mask.

Cisco IOS Software Release: 10.0

Example: Display a Specific Prefix from the BGP Routing Table with the Specified Mask

The following is some sample output from the **show ip bgp** *prefix mask* command. First, list the entire contents of the BGP routing table:

```
rtrA#show ip bgp
BGP table version is 90, local router ID is 199.172.15.1
Status codes: s suppressed, d damped, h history, * valid, > best, i - internal
Origin codes: i - IGP, e - EGP, ? - incomplete

   Network          Next Hop          Metric LocPrf Weight Path
*> 199.172.1.0      0.0.0.0                0         32768 i
s> 199.172.2.0      0.0.0.0                0         32768 i
*> 199.172.2.0/23   0.0.0.0                          32768 i
s> 199.172.3.0      0.0.0.0                0         32768 i
*> 199.172.4.0      0.0.0.0                0         32768 i
*> 200.1.1.0        172.17.1.1             0             0 2 i
*> 200.1.2.0        172.17.1.1             0             0 2 i
*> 200.1.3.0        172.17.1.1             0             0 2 i
*> 200.1.4.0        172.17.1.1             0             0 2 i
```

Now list entries for the prefix 199.172.2.0 having a mask equal to 24 bits:

```
rtrA#show ip bgp 199.172.1.0 255.255.255.0
BGP routing table entry for 199.172.1.0/24, version 6
Paths: (1 available, best #1)
  Advertised to non peer-group peers:
    172.17.1.1
  Local
    0.0.0.0 from 0.0.0.0 (199.172.15.1)
      Origin IGP, metric 0, localpref 100, weight 32768, valid, sourced, local,
best, ref 2
```

14-8: show ip bgp *prefix mask* longer-prefixes

14-9: show ip bgp *prefix/mask-length* longer-prefixes

Syntax Description:

- *prefix*—IP address of the prefix to display.

- *mask*—Display prefix with a specific network mask.

- *mask-length*—Bit length of the mask.

Purpose: To display the contents of the local BGP routing table for a specific prefix with a specific mask and any prefixes having a longer mask than the one specified.

Cisco IOS Software Release: 10.0

Example: Display a Specific Prefix from the BGP Routing Table Having a Mask Greater Than or Equal to the Mask Specified in the Command

The following is some sample output from the **show ip bgp** *prefix mask* **longer-prefixes** command. First, list the entire BGP routing table:

```
rtrA#show ip bgp
BGP table version is 90, local router ID is 199.172.15.1
Status codes: s suppressed, d damped, h history, * valid, > best, i - internal
Origin codes: i - IGP, e - EGP, ? - incomplete

   Network          Next Hop            Metric LocPrf Weight Path
*> 199.172.1.0      0.0.0.0                  0         32768 i
s> 199.172.2.0      0.0.0.0                  0         32768 i
*> 199.172.2.0/23   0.0.0.0                            32768 i
s> 199.172.3.0      0.0.0.0                  0         32768 i
*> 199.172.4.0      0.0.0.0                  0         32768 i
*> 200.1.1.0        172.17.1.1               0             0 2 i
*> 200.1.2.0        172.17.1.1               0             0 2 i
*> 200.1.3.0        172.17.1.1               0             0 2 i
*> 200.1.4.0        172.17.1.1               0             0 2 i
```

Now list entries for the prefix 199.172.2.0 having a mask greater than or equal to 23 bits:

```
rtrA#show ip bgp 199.172.2.0 255.255.254.0 longer-prefixes
BGP table version is 90, local router ID is 199.172.15.1
Status codes: s suppressed, d damped, h history, * valid, > best, i - internal
Origin codes: i - IGP, e - EGP, ? - incomplete

   Network          Next Hop            Metric LocPrf Weight Path
s> 199.172.2.0      0.0.0.0                  0         32768 i
*> 199.172.2.0/23   0.0.0.0                            32768 i
s> 199.172.3.0      0.0.0.0                  0         32768 i
```

An alternative form is to use the mask length:

```
rtrA#show ip bgp 199.172.2.0/23 longer-prefixes
BGP table version is 90, local router ID is 199.172.15.1
Status codes: s suppressed, d damped, h history, * valid, > best, i - internal
Origin codes: i - IGP, e - EGP, ? - incomplete

   Network          Next Hop            Metric LocPrf Weight Path
s> 199.172.2.0      0.0.0.0                  0         32768 i
*> 199.172.2.0/23   0.0.0.0                            32768 i
s> 199.172.3.0      0.0.0.0                  0         32768 i
```

Sections 14-8 – 14-10

14-10: show ip bgp *prefix* | **begin** *line*

14-11: show ip bgp *prefix* | **exclude** *line*

14-12: show ip bgp *prefix* | **include** *line*

14-13: show ip bgp *prefix mask* | **begin** *line*

14-14: show ip bgp *prefix mask* | **exclude** *line*

14-15: show ip bgp *prefix mask* | **include** *line*

14-16: show ip bgp *prefix/mask-length* | **begin** *line*

14-17: show ip bgp *prefix/mask-length* | **exclude** *line*

14-18: show ip bgp *prefix/mask-length* | **include** *line*

14-19: show ip bgp *prefix mask* **longer-prefixes** | **begin** *line*

14-20: show ip bgp *prefix mask* **longer-prefixes** | **exclude** *line*

14-21: show ip bgp *prefix mask* **longer-prefixes** | **include** *line*

14-22: show ip bgp *prefix/mask-length* longer-prefixes | begin *line*

14-23: show ip bgp *prefix/mask-length* longer-prefixes | exclude *line*

14-24: show ip bgp *prefix/mask-length* longer-prefixes | include *line*

Syntax Description:

- *prefix*—IP address of the prefix to display.
- *mask*—Display prefix with a specific network mask.
- *line*—Regular expression. See Appendix B.
- *mask-length*—Bit length of the mask.

Purpose: To display the contents of the local BGP routing table for a specific prefix or a specific prefix/mask using output modifiers.

Cisco IOS Software Release: 10.0

Example: Display a Specific Prefix from the BGP Routing Table Using Output Modifiers

The following is some sample output from the **show ip bgp** *prefix mask* **longer-prefixes |
include** *line* command. First, list the entire BGP routing table:

```
rtrA#show ip bgp
BGP table version is 90, local router ID is 199.172.15.1
Status codes: s suppressed, d damped, h history, * valid, > best, i - internal
Origin codes: i - IGP, e - EGP, ? - incomplete

   Network          Next Hop         Metric LocPrf Weight Path
*> 199.172.1.0      0.0.0.0               0          32768 i
s> 199.172.2.0      0.0.0.0               0          32768 i
*> 199.172.2.0/23   0.0.0.0                          32768 i
s> 199.172.3.0      0.0.0.0               0          32768 i
*> 199.172.4.0      0.0.0.0               0          32768 i
*> 200.1.1.0        172.17.1.1            0              0 2 i
*> 200.1.2.0        172.17.1.1            0              0 2 i
*> 200.1.3.0        172.17.1.1            0              0 2 i
*> 200.1.4.0        172.17.1.1            0              0 2 i
```

Next, list all the entries for the prefix 199.172.2.0:

```
rtrA#show ip bgp 199.172.2.0 255.255.254.0 longer-prefixes
BGP table version is 90, local router ID is 199.172.15.1
Status codes: s suppressed, d damped, h history, * valid, > best, i - internal
Origin codes: i - IGP, e - EGP, ? - incomplete

   Network          Next Hop          Metric LocPrf Weight Path
s> 199.172.2.0      0.0.0.0                0         32768 i
*> 199.172.2.0/23   0.0.0.0                          32768 i
s> 199.172.3.0      0.0.0.0                0         32768 i
```

List only the suppressed entries for the 199.172.2.0 prefixes:

```
rtrA#show ip bgp 199.172.2.0 255.255.254.0 longer-prefixes ¦ include s
BGP table version is 90, local router ID is 199.172.15.1
Status codes: s suppressed, d damped, h history, * valid, > best, i - internal
Origin codes: i - IGP, e - EGP, ? - incomplete
s> 199.172.2.0      0.0.0.0                0         32768 i
s> 199.172.3.0      0.0.0.0                0         32768 I
```

Finally, list only the unsuppressed entries for the 199.172.2.0 prefixes:

```
rtrA#show ip bgp 199.172.2.0 255.255.254.0 longer-prefixes ¦ exclude s

   Network          Next Hop          Metric LocPrf Weight Path
*> 199.172.2.0/23   0.0.0.0                          32768 I
```

14-25: show ip bgp cidr-only

14-26: show ip bgp cidr-only | begin *line*

14-27: show ip bgp cidr-only | exclude *line*

14-28: show ip bgp cidr-only | include *line*

Syntax Description:

- *line*—Regular expression. See Appendix B.

Purpose: To display the contents of the local BGP routing table for prefixes having a nonnatural mask. A natural mask is 8 bits for a Class A network, 16 bits for Class B, and 24 bits for Class C.

Cisco IOS Software Release: 10.0

Example: Display BGP Prefixes Having a Nonnatural Mask

First, list the entire BGP routing table:

```
rtrA#show ip bgp
BGP table version is 90, local router ID is 199.172.15.1
Status codes: s suppressed, d damped, h history, * valid, > best, i - internal
Origin codes: i - IGP, e - EGP, ? - incomplete

   Network          Next Hop          Metric LocPrf Weight Path
*> 199.172.1.0      0.0.0.0                0          32768 i
s> 199.172.2.0      0.0.0.0                0          32768 i
*> 199.172.2.0/23   0.0.0.0                           32768 i
s> 199.172.3.0      0.0.0.0                0          32768 i
*> 199.172.4.0      0.0.0.0                0          32768 i
*> 200.1.1.0        172.17.1.1             0              0 2 i
*> 200.1.2.0        172.17.1.1             0              0 2 i
*> 200.1.3.0        172.17.1.1             0              0 2 i
*> 200.1.4.0        172.17.1.1             0              0 2 i
```

Next, list all the entries having a nonnatural mask:

```
rtrA#show ip bgp cidr-only
BGP table version is 90, local router ID is 199.172.15.1
Status codes: s suppressed, d damped, h history, * valid, > best, i - internal
Origin codes: i - IGP, e - EGP, ? - incomplete

   Network          Next Hop          Metric LocPrf Weight Path
*> 199.172.2.0/23   0.0.0.0                           32768 i
```

14-29: show ip bgp community *community-number(s)*

14-30: show ip bgp community *community-number(s)* exact-match

14-31: show ip bgp community *community-number(s)* | begin *line*

14-32: show ip bgp community *community-number(s)* | exclude *line*

14-33: show ip bgp community *community-number(s)* | include *line*

14-34: show ip bgp community *community-number(s)* | begin *line* exact-match

14-35: show ip bgp community *community-number(s)* | exclude *line* exact-match

14-36: show ip bgp community *community-number(s)* | include *line* exact-match

Syntax Description:

- *community-number(s)*—One or more BGP community numbers. Community numbers are in the range of 1 to 4294967295. Well-known community keywords that may be used are **local-as**, **no-advertise**, and **no-export** (see section 8-28).

- *line*—Regular expression. See Appendix B.

Purpose: To display the contents of the local BGP routing table for prefixes matching the supplied community number(s).

Cisco IOS Software Release: 10.3. The **local-as** keyword was added in Cisco IOS Software Release 12.0.

Example: Display BGP Prefixes Belonging to a Specific Community

Routes belonging to a specific community can be listed using the **show ip bgp community** command followed by the community value of interest.

```
rtrA#show ip bgp community no-export
BGP table version is 41, local router ID is 10.1.1.2
Status codes: s suppressed, d damped, h history, * valid, > best, i - internal
Origin codes: i - IGP, e - EGP, ? - incomplete

   Network          Next Hop          Metric LocPrf Weight Path
*> 172.16.1.0/24    10.1.1.1               0            0 65530 i
```

14-37: show ip bgp community-list *community-list-number*

14-38: show ip bgp community-list *community-list-number* | **begin** *line*

14-39: show ip bgp community-list *community-list-number* | **exclude** *line*

14-40: show ip bgp community-list *community-list-number* | **include** *line*

14-41: show ip bgp community-list *community-list-number* **exact-match**

14-42: show ip bgp community-list *community-list-number* **exact-match** | **begin** *line*

14-43: show ip bgp community-list *community-list-number* **exact-match** | **exclude** *line*

14-44: show ip bgp community-list *community-list-number* **exact-match** | **include** *line*

Syntax Description:

- *community-list-number*—IP community list number. Valid list numbers are 1 to 199.
- *line*—Regular expression. See Appendix B, "Regular Expressions."

Purpose: To display the contents of the local BGP routing table for prefixes matching the community listed in the community list.

Cisco IOS Software Release: 10.3

Example: Display BGP Prefixes Belonging to a Specific Community Using a Community List

An IP community list can be used to list routes belonging to a certain community or list of communities using the following configuration. This example lists only those routes with a community value of **no-export**.

```
ip community-list 1 permit no-export
rtrA#show ip bgp community 1
BGP table version is 41, local router ID is 10.1.1.2
Status codes: s suppressed, d damped, h history, * valid, > best, i - internal
Origin codes: i - IGP, e - EGP, ? - incomplete

   Network          Next Hop          Metric LocPrf Weight Path
*> 172.16.1.0/24    10.1.1.1               0             0 65530 I
```

14-45: show ip bgp dampened-paths

14-46: show ip bgp dampened-paths | begin *line*

14-47: show ip bgp dampened-paths | exclude *line*

14-48: show ip bgp dampened-paths | include *line*

Syntax Description:

- *line*—Regular expression. See Appendix B.

Purpose: To display the contents of the local BGP routing table for dampened prefixes (see sections 3-9 through 3-12).

Cisco IOS Software Release: 11.0

Example: Display BGP Dampened Prefixes

In order to display only those routes that have been dampened, use the **show ip bgp dampened-paths** command. BGP dampening must be enabled before the router will maintain this information in memory.

```
rtrA#show ip bgp dampened-paths
BGP table version is 7, local router ID is 10.1.1.2
Status codes: s suppressed, d damped, h history, * valid, > best, i - internal
Origin codes: i - IGP, e - EGP, ? - incomplete


    Network         From            Reuse   Path
*d 172.16.2.0/24   10.1.1.1        00:19:30 1 i
```

14-49: show ip bgp filter-list *as-path-access-list*

14-50: show ip bgp filter-list *as-path-access-list* | **begin** *line*

14-51: show ip bgp filter-list *as-path-access-list* | **exclude** *line*

14-52: show ip bgp filter-list *as-path-access-list* | **include** *line*

Syntax Description:

- *as-path-access-list*—AS path access list number. The range of valid numbers is 1 to 199.

- *line*—Regular expression. See Appendix B.

Purpose: To display the contents of the local BGP routing table for prefixes matching the specified AS path access list.

Cisco IOS Software Release: 10.0

Example: Displaying BGP Dampened Prefixes to Match Specified AS Path Access List

The AS path attribute of a BGP route can be used to determine the routes that are displayed when using the **show ip bgp command**. For this example, we want to use an access list to list only those routes that originated in AS 2. Only routes having the AS value(s) permitted in the access list will be displayed.

```
ip as-path access-list 1 permit ^2$

rtrA#show ip bgp filter-list 1
BGP table version is 90, local router ID is 199.172.15.1
Status codes: s suppressed, d damped, h history, * valid, > best, i - internal
Origin codes: i - IGP, e - EGP, ? - incomplete

    Network          Next Hop          Metric LocPrf Weight Path
*> 200.1.1.0         172.17.1.1             0             0 2 i
*> 200.1.2.0         172.17.1.1             0             0 2 i
*> 200.1.3.0         172.17.1.1             0             0 2 i
*> 200.1.4.0         172.17.1.1             0             0 2 I
```

14-53: show ip bgp flap-statistics

14-54: show ip bgp flap-statistics *prefix/mask-length*

14-55: show ip bgp flap-statistics *prefix/mask-length* longer-prefixes

14-56: show ip bgp flap-statistics *prefix/mask-length* longer-prefixes | begin *regular-expression*

14-57: show ip bgp flap-statistics *prefix/mask-length* longer-prefixes | exclude *regular-expression*

14-58: show ip bgp flap-statistics *prefix/mask-length* longer-prefixes | include *regular-expression*

14-59: show ip bgp flap-statistics *prefix/mask-length* | begin *regular-expression*

14-60: show ip bgp flap-statistics *prefix/mask-length* | exclude *regular-expression*

14-61: show ip bgp flap-statistics *prefix/mask-length* | include *regular-expression*

14-62: show ip bgp flap-statistics *prefix*

14-63: show ip bgp flap-statistics *prefix* | begin *regular-expression*

14-64: show ip bgp flap-statistics *prefix* | exclude *regular-expression*

14-65: show ip bgp flap-statistics *prefix* | include *regular-expression*

14-66: show ip bgp flap-statistics *prefix mask*

14-67: show ip bgp flap-statistics *prefix mask* | begin *regular-expression*

14-68: show ip bgp flap-statistics *prefix mask* | exclude *regular-expression*

Sections 14-53 – 14-68

14-69: show ip bgp flap-statistics *prefix mask* | **include** *regular-expression*

14-70: show ip bgp flap-statistics *prefix mask* **longer-prefixes**

14-71: show ip bgp flap-statistics *prefix mask* **longer-prefixes** | **begin** *regular-expression*

14-72: show ip bgp flap-statistics *prefix mask* **longer-prefixes** | **exclude** *regular-expression*

14-73: show ip bgp flap-statistics *prefix mask* **longer-prefixes** | **include** *regular-expression*

14-74: show ip bgp flap-statistics filter-list *list-number*

14-75: show ip bgp flap-statistics filter-list *list-number* | **begin** *regular-expression*

14-76: show ip bgp flap-statistics filter-list *list-number* | **exclude** *regular-expression*

14-77: show ip bgp flap-statistics filter-list *list-number* | **include** *regular-expression*

14-78: show ip bgp flap-statistics **quote-regexp** *quoted-line*

14-79: show ip bgp flap-statistics **quote-regexp** *quoted-line* | **begin** *regular-expression*

14-80: show ip bgp flap-statistics **quote-regexp** *quoted-line* | **exclude** *regular-expression*

14-81: show ip bgp flap-statistics **quote-regexp** *quoted-line* | **include** *regular-expression*

14-82: show ip bgp flap-statistics **regexp** *regular-expression*

14-83: show ip bgp flap-statistics | **begin** *regular-expression*

14-84: show ip bgp flap-statistics | **exclude** *regular-expression*

14-85: show ip bgp flap-statistics | **include** *regular-expression*

Syntax Description:

- *prefix*—IP address of the prefix to display.
- *mask*—Display prefix with a specific network mask.
- *mask-length*—Bit length of the mask.

- *line*—Regular expression. See Appendix B.
- *list-number*—Regular expression access list number. The range of values is 1 to 199.
- *quoted-line*—Regular expression in quotes.

Purpose: To display flap statistics for routes in the BGP table.

Cisco IOS Software Release: 11.0

Example: Display BGP Flap Statistics

A route flap occurs when a route is withdrawn and then later readvertised. This usually happens when an interface is going from the UP state to the DOWN state repeatedly. You can view the number of times a route has flapped using the **show ip bgp flap-statistics** command. This assumes that BGPP dampening has been enabled on the router.

```
rtrA#show ip bgp flap-statistics
BGP table version is 9, local router ID is 10.1.1.2
Status codes: s suppressed, d damped, h history, * valid, > best, i - internal
Origin codes: i - IGP, e - EGP, ? - incomplete

   Network         From          Flaps Duration Reuse    Path
*d 172.16.2.0/24   10.1.1.1        3    00:02:55 00:28:10 1
```

The following list explains some of the fields that appear in the preceding output from the **show ip bgp flap-statistics** command.

- **BGP table version**—Whenever the BGP table changes, the version number is incremented.

- **local router ID**—The highest IP address assigned to an interface. If loopbacks are used, the router ID is the highest IP address assigned to a loopback interface. The router ID can be changed using the **bgp router-id** configuration command (see section 3-17).

- **Status codes**

  ⇒ **s**—The entry is suppressed (see Chapter 8 and section 8-32).

  ⇒ *****—The entry is valid.

  ⇒ **d**—The prefix is dampened.

  ⇒ **h**—Dampening is enabled for the prefix (see sections 3-9 through 3-12).

  ⇒ **>**—If there are multiple entries for the prefix, this indicates the best route.

  ⇒ **i**—The prefix was learned via IBGP. This is the i to the left of the network entry.

- **Origin codes**

  ⇒ **i**—Routes installed using the **network** command.

  ⇒ **e**—Routes learned via EGP.

  ⇒ **?**—Routes learned via redistribution.

- **Network**—Prefix entry in the table. If a mask is not listed, the prefix is using the standard mask for the class of the entry.

- **From**—Next-hop attribute advertised by the BGP neighbor. A value of 0.0.0.0 indicates that the prefix was locally originated (see section 8-17).

- **Flaps**—The number of times the prefix has flapped.

- **Duration**—Time since the first flap.

- **Reuse**—Time until the prefix is undampened.

- **Path**—A list of the autonomous system paths leading back to the prefix.

14-86: show ip bgp inconsistent-as

14-87: show ip bgp inconsistent-as | begin *line*

14-88: show ip bgp inconsistent-as | exclude *line*

14-89: show ip bgp inconsistent-as | include *line*

Syntax Description:

- *line*—Regular expression. See Appendix B.

Purpose: To display routes with inconsistent originating autonomous systems.

Cisco IOS Software Release: 11.0

Example: Display BGP Routes Having an Inconsistent Originated AS

Routes that have the same next-hop address should come from the same AS. When this is not the case, inconsistent AS information exists. The inconsistent AS information can be displayed using the **show ip bgp inconsistent-as** command.

```
rtrA#show ip bgp inconsistent-as
BGP table version is 3, local router ID is 172.17.1.1
Status codes: s suppressed, * valid, > best, i - internal
Origin codes: i - IGP, e - EGP, ? - incomplete

   Network          Next Hop          Metric LocPrf Weight Path
*  199.1.1.0        172.17.1.2             0             0 1 2 ?
*>                  172.17.1.2             0             0 3 ?
```

14-90: show ip bgp neighbors

14-91: show ip bgp neighbors | begin *line*

14-92: show ip bgp neighbors | exclude *line*

14-93: show ip bgp neighbors | include *line*

14-94: show ip bgp neighbors *ip-address* **advertised-routes**

14-95: show ip bgp neighbors *ip-address* **dampened-routes**

14-96: show ip bgp neighbors *ip-address* **flap-statistics**

14-97: show ip bgp neighbors *ip-address* **paths**

14-98: show ip bgp neighbors *ip-address* **paths** *line*

14-99: show ip bgp neighbors *ip-address* **received-routes**

14-100: show ip bgp neighbors *ip-address* **routes**

Syntax Description:

- *ip-address*—IP address of the BGP neighbor.
- *line*—Regular expression. See Appendix B.

Purpose: To display routes with inconsistent originating autonomous systems. Soft inbound reconfiguration needs to be enabled before you use the **received-routes** form of this command.

Cisco IOS Software Release: 10.0. The **received-routes** keyword was added in Cisco IOS Software Release 11.2.

Example: Display Information for a Specific BGP Neighbor

The state of a BGP neighbor can be examined by using the **show ip bgp neighbors** command. This is usually the first command to use when debugging a BGP connection.

```
rtrA#show ip bgp neighbors 172.17.1.2
BGP neighbor is 172.17.1.2,  remote AS 1, external link
  BGP version 4, remote router ID 199.172.15.1
  BGP state = Established, up for 1w1d
  Last read 00:00:43, hold time is 180, keepalive interval is 60 seconds
  Neighbor capabilities:
    Route refresh: advertised
    Address family IPv4 Unicast: advertised and received
  Received 13174 messages, 0 notifications, 0 in queue
  Sent 13168 messages, 0 notifications, 0 in queue
  Route refresh request: received 0, sent 0
  Minimum time between advertisement runs is 30 seconds

 For address family: IPv4 Unicast
  BGP table version 14, neighbor version 14
  Index 1, Offset 0, Mask 0x2
  3 accepted prefixes consume 108 bytes
  Prefix advertised 40, suppressed 0, withdrawn 0

  Connections established 10; dropped 9
  Last reset 1w1d, due to User reset
Connection state is ESTAB, I/O status: 1, unread input bytes: 0
Local host: 172.17.1.1, Local port: 11106
Foreign host: 172.17.1.2, Foreign port: 179

Enqueued packets for retransmit: 0, input: 0  mis-ordered: 0 (0 bytes)

Event Timers (current time is 0x357A31F8):
Timer          Starts      Wakeups          Next
Retrans        11859          0             0x0
TimeWait         0            0             0x0
AckHold        11862        11505           0x0
SendWnd          0            0             0x0
KeepAlive        0            0             0x0
```

continues

```
(Continued)
GiveUp              0         0         0x0
PmtuAger            0         0         0x0
DeadWait            0         0         0x0

iss: 2220955579  snduna: 2221180949  sndnxt: 2221180949    sndwnd:  16327
irs: 1147082461  rcvnxt: 1147307991  rcvwnd:       16156  delrcvwnd:   228

SRTT: 300 ms, RTTO: 607 ms, RTV: 3 ms, KRTT: 0 ms
minRTT: 0 ms, maxRTT: 376 ms, ACK hold: 200 ms
Flags: higher precedence, nagle

Datagrams (max data segment is 1460 bytes):
Rcvd: 23247 (out of order: 0), with data: 11862, total data bytes: 225529
Sent: 23520 (retransmit: 0), with data: 11859, total data bytes: 225388
```

The following list explains some of the fields that appear in the preceding output from the
show ip bgp neighbors 172.17.1.2 command.

- **BGP neighbor**—IP address and autonomous system number of the BGP neighbor. If the link is internal, the neighbors are in the same autonomous system. If the link is external, the neighbors are in different autonomous systems.

- **remote AS**—BGP neighbor's autonomous system number.

- **external link**—Indicates that this peer is an Exterior Border Gateway Protocol (EBGP) peer.

- **BGP version**—BGP version that the neighbors are using.

- **remote router ID**—The ID of the remote neighbor. The ID is the highest IP address assigned to a physical interface or the highest loopback address.

- **BGP state**—Internal state of this BGP connection. If the state does not reach the Established state, there is a problem forming the BGP connection.

- **up for**—Amount of time that the TCP connection has been established.

- **Last read**—Time that BGP last read a message from this neighbor.

- **hold time**—Maximum amount of time that can elapse between messages from the peer before the neighbor is declared down.

- **keepalive interval**—Time period between sending keepalive packets. The keepalive interval is generally three times the hold time.

- **Neighbor capabilities**—BGP capabilities advertised and received from this neighbor. If you are running code earlier than 12.0, you do not see this field.

- **Route refresh**—Indicates that the neighbor supports dynamic soft reset using the route refresh capability. If you are running code earlier than 12.0, you do not see this field.

- **Address family IPv4 Unicast**—IPv4 unicast-specific properties of this neighbor. If you are running code earlier than 12.0, you do not see this field.

- **Address family IPv4 Multicast**—IPv4 multicast-specific properties of this neighbor. If you are running code earlier than 12.0, you do not see this field.
- **Received**—Number of total BGP messages received from this peer, including keepalives.
- **notifications**—Number of error messages received from this neighbor.
- **Sent**—Total number of BGP messages that have been sent to this neighbor, including keepalives.
- **notifications**—Number of error messages the router has sent to this neighbor.
- **Route refresh request**—Number of route refresh requests sent to and received from this neighbor.
- **advertisement runs**—Value of the minimum advertisement interval.
- **For address family**—Address family to which the following fields refer.
- **BGP table version**—Every time the BGP table changes, this number is incremented.
- **neighbor version**—Number used by the software to track the prefixes that have been sent and those that have to be sent to this neighbor.
- **Community attribute**—Appears if the neighbor **send-community** command is configured for this neighbor.
- **Inbound path policy**—Indicates if an inbound policy is configured.
- **Outbound path policy**—Indicates if an outbound policy is configured.
- **mul-in**—Name of the inbound route map for the multicast address family.
- **mul-out**—Name of outbound route map for the multicast address family.
- **accepted prefixes**—Number of prefixes accepted.
- **Prefix advertised**—Number of prefixes advertised.
- **suppressed**—Number of prefixes suppressed.
- **withdrawn**—Number of prefixes withdrawn.
- **Connections established**—Number of times the router has established a TCP connection and the two peers have agreed to speak BGP with each other.
- **dropped**—Number of times that a good connection has failed or been taken down.
- **Last reset**—Elapsed time since this peering session was last reset.
- **Connection state**—State of the BGP peer.
- **unread input bytes**—Number of bytes of packets still to be processed.
- **Local host, Local port**—Peering address of local router, plus port.
- **Foreign host, Foreign port**—Neighbor's peering address.

- **Event Timers Table**—Displays the number of starts and wakeups for each timer.
- **iss**—Initial send sequence number.
- **snduna**—Last send sequence number the local host sent but has not received an acknowledgment for.
- **sndnxt**—Sequence number the local host will send next.
- **sndwnd**—TCP window size of the remote host.
- **irs**—Initial receive sequence number.
- **rcvnxt**—Last receive sequence number the local host has acknowledged.
- **rcvwnd**—Local host's TCP window size.
- **delrecvwnd**—Delayed receive window. Data the local host has read from the connection but has not yet subtracted from the receive window the host has advertised to the remote host. The value in this field gradually increases until it is larger than a full-sized packet, at which point it is applied to the **rcvwnd** field.
- **SRTT**—A calculated smoothed round-trip time-out.
- **RTTO**—Round-trip time-out.
- **RTV**—Variance of the round-trip time.
- **KRTT**—New round-trip time-out (using the Karn algorithm). This field separately tracks the round-trip time of packets that have been retransmitted.
- **minRTT**—Smallest recorded round-trip time-out (hard-wire value used for calculation).
- **maxRTT**—Largest recorded round-trip time-out.
- **ACK hold**—Time the local host will delay an acknowledgment in order to piggyback data on it.
- **Flags**—IP precedence of the BGP packets.
- **Datagrams Rcvd**—Number of update packets received from this neighbor.
- **with data**—Number of update packets received with data.
- **total data bytes**—Total bytes of data.
- **Sent**—Number of update packets sent.
- **with data**—Number of update packets with data sent.
- **total data bytes**—Total number of data bytes.

14-101: show ip bgp paths

14-102: show ip bgp paths *line*

14-103: show ip bgp paths *line*

14-104: show ip bgp paths *line*

14-105: show ip bgp paths | begin *line*

14-106: show ip bgp paths | exclude *line*

14-107: show ip bgp paths | include *line*

Syntax Description:

- *ip-address*—IP address of the BGP neighbor.
- *line*—Regular expression. See Appendix B.

Purpose: To display all the BGP paths in the database.

Cisco IOS Software Release: 10.0

Example: Display BGP Path Information

The AS paths contained in the BGP database can be displayed using the **show ip bgp paths** command.

```
rtrA#show ip bgp paths
Address      Hash Refcount Metric Path
0x125E94       0        4      0 i
0x996F4        2        1      0 1 i
0x125D6C       2        2      0 1 i
```

The following list explains some of the fields that appear in the preceding output from the **show ip bgp paths** command.

- **Address**—Memory address of where the path is stored.
- **Hash**—Hash bucket where the path is stored.
- **Refcount**—Number of prefixes using that path.
- **Metric**—Multi-exit discriminator for the path.
- **Path**—The autonomous system path and origin code for the prefix.

14-108: show ip bgp peer-group

14-109: show ip bgp peer-group *peer-group-name*

14-110: show ip bgp peer-group *peer-group-name* summary

Syntax Description:

- *peer-group-name*—Name of the peer group.

Purpose: To display information regarding BGP peer groups.

Cisco IOS Software Release: 11.0

Example: Display BGP Peer Group Information

To view the parameters of a BGP peer group, use the **show ip bgp peer-group** command.

```
rtrA#show ip bgp peer-group
BGP neighbor is demo, peer-group leader
  BGP version 4
  Minimum time between advertisement runs is 5 seconds
  Incoming update AS path filter list is 30
  Outgoing update AS path filter list is 40
  Route map for outgoing advertisements is adjust-weight
```

14-111: show ip bgp summary

14-112: show ip bgp summary | begin *line*

14-113: show ip bgp summary | exclude *line*

14-114: show ip bgp summary | include *line*

Syntax Description:

- *line*—Regular expression. See Appendix B.

Purpose: To display the status of BGP connections.

Cisco IOS Software Release: 10.0. The PfxRcd and Admin fields were added in version 12.0.

Example: Display a Summary for All BGP Connections

Display the entire BGP table:

```
rtrA#show ip bgp summary
BGP router identifier 200.1.4.1, local AS number 2
BGP table version is 14, main routing table version 14
7 network entries and 7 paths using 931 bytes of memory
3 BGP path attribute entries using 156 bytes of memory
1 BGP AS-PATH entries using 24 bytes of memory
0 BGP route-map cache entries using 0 bytes of memory
0 BGP filter-list cache entries using 0 bytes of memory
BGP activity 193/657 prefixes, 193/186 paths, scan interval 15 secs

Neighbor        V    AS MsgRcvd MsgSent   TblVer  InQ OutQ Up/Down   State/PfxRcd

10.1.1.2        4     2    7584    7590       14    0    0 5d06h           0
172.17.1.2      4     1   13359   13353       14    0    0 1w1d            3
```

The following list explains some of the fields that appear in the preceding output from the **show ip bgp summary** command.

- **BGP router identifier**—ID of the neighbor router.

- **BGP table version**—Version number of the internal BGP database.

- **main routing table version**—Last version of the BGP database that was injected into the main routing table.

- **Neighbor**—BGP neighbor's IP address.

- **V**—BGP version number that the neighbors are using.

- **AS**—Neighbor's autonomous system number.

- **MsgRcvd**—Number of BGP messages received from the neighbor.

- **MsgSent**—Number of BGP messages sent to the neighbor.

- **TblVer**—Last version of the BGP database that was sent to that neighbor.

- **InQ**—Number of messages from that neighbor waiting to be processed.

- **OutQ**—Number of messages waiting to be sent to that neighbor.

- **Up/Down**—The length of time that the BGP session has been in the Established state, or the current state if it is not Established.

- **State/PfxRcd**—Current state of the BGP session/the number of prefixes the router has received from a neighbor or peer group. When the maximum number (as set by the **neighbor maximum-prefix** command; see sections 8-13 through 8-16) is reached, the string "PfxRcd" appears in the entry, the neighbor is shut down, and the connection is Idle. An (Admin) entry with Idle status indicates that the connection has been shut down using the **neighbor shutdown** command (see section 8-29).

CHAPTER 15

BGP clear Commands

15-1: clear ip bgp *

15-2: clear ip bgp * soft

15-3: clear ip bgp * soft in

15-4: clear ip bgp * soft out

15-5: clear ip bgp * soft in out

15-6: clear ip bgp *AS-number*

15-7: clear ip bgp *AS-number* **soft**

15-8: clear ip bgp *AS-number* **soft in**

15-9: clear ip bgp *AS-number* **soft out**

15-10: clear ip bgp *AS-number* **soft in out**

15-11: clear ip bgp *neighbor-ip-address*

15-12: clear ip bgp *neighbor-ip-address* soft

15-13: clear ip bgp *neighbor-ip-address* soft in

15-14: clear ip bgp *neighbor-ip-address* soft out

15-15: clear ip bgp *neighbor-ip-address* soft in out

15-16: clear ip bgp peer-group *peer-group-name*

15-17: clear ip bgp peer-group *peer-group-name* soft

15-18: clear ip bgp peer-group *peer-group-name* soft in

15-19: clear ip bgp peer-group *peer-group-name* soft out

15-20: clear ip bgp peer-group *peer-group-name* soft in out

Syntax Description:

- *AS-number*—Resets all neighbors in the specified autonomous system.
- *neighbor-ip-address*—Resets the specified BGP neighbor.
- *peer-group-name*—Resets all neighbors in the specified peer group.

Purpose: To reset a BGP connection. BGP neighbor connections can be reset based on the neighbor's IP address, the neighbor's autonomous system number, or the peer group name. You must reset a BGP connection when any of the following have been modified or added to:

- BGP access list
- BGP distribute list
- BGP route map
- BGP timers
- BGP weights
- BGP administrative distance

Clearing a BGP connection without the **soft** keyword causes the neighbor relationship to transition from Established to Idle. The neighbor relationship is then reestablished, and the new routing policies take effect. If the **soft** keyword is used, the session is not reset, and all routing updates are resent. When you use the **soft in** option, the local BGP configuration should include the **neighbor soft-reconfiguration** command (see section 8-30). Using the **soft in** option is memory-intensive. Using **soft out** for outbound reconfiguration does not incur additional memory overhead. Using **soft in out** is equivalent to using just **soft**.

Cisco IOS Software Release: 10.0

15-21: clear ip bgp dampening

15-22: clear ip bgp dampening *prefix mask*

Syntax Description:

- *prefix*—Prefix of the dampened route to clear.
- *mask*—Mask of the dampened route to clear.

Purpose: To clear dampening information for all dampened routes or for a specific dampened route. Suppressed routes will be unsuppressed.

Cisco IOS Software Release: 11.0

15-23: clear ip bgp flap-statistics

15-24: clear ip bgp flap-statistics *prefix mask*

15-25: clear ip bgp flap-statistics filter-list *list-number*

15-26: clear ip bgp flap-statistics regexp *regular-expression*

15-27: clear ip bgp *neighbor-ip-address* flap-statistics

Syntax Description:

- *prefix*—Prefix of the dampened route to clear.
- *mask*—Mask of the dampened route to clear.
- *list-number*—Number of the IP access list used to identify prefixes to be cleared.
- *regular-expression*—Clear statistics for routes matching the regular expression.
- *neighbor-ip-address*—Clear flap statistics of routes received from the neighbor.

Purpose: To clear the flap statistics for all routes or for specific routes. See sections 3-9 through 3-12 regarding the configuration of BGP dampening.

Cisco IOS Software Release: 11.0

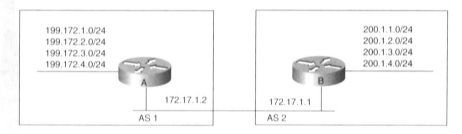

CHAPTER 16

BGP debug **Commands**

16-1: debug ip bgp

Syntax Description: This command has no arguments.

Purpose: Use to debug the formation of the BGP neighbor relationship.

Cisco IOS Software Release: 10.0

Configuration Example

In Figure 16-1, Router B has been configured with the wrong AS number for Router A.

Figure 16-1 *Use* **debug ip bgp** *to Determine Configuration Errors*

```
199.172.1.0/24                                        200.1.1.0/24
199.172.2.0/24                                        200.1.2.0/24
199.172.3.0/24                                        200.1.3.0/24
199.172.4.0/24                                        200.1.4.0/24


         A                                          B
                  172.17.1.2          172.17.1.1
         AS 1                            AS 2
```

```
Router A
router bgp 1
 neighbor 172.17.1.1 remote-as 2
Router B
router bgp 2
 neighbor 172.17.1.2 remote-as 1
```

Use **debug ip bgp** to identify the problem with the formation of the neighbor relationship between Routers A and B:

```
rtrB#debug ip bgp
rtrB#clear ip bgp *
1d03h: BGP: 172.17.1.2 went from Idle to Active
1d03h: BGP: 172.17.1.2 open active, delay 5492ms
1d03h: BGP: 172.17.1.2 open active, local address 172.17.1.1
1d03h: BGP: 172.17.1.2 went from Active to OpenSent
1d03h: BGP: 172.17.1.2 sending OPEN, version 4, my as: 2
1d03h: BGP: 172.17.1.2 send message type 1, length (incl. header) 41
1d03h: BGP: 172.17.1.2 rcv message type 1, length (excl. header) 10
1d03h: BGP: 172.17.1.2 rcv OPEN, version 4
1d03h: BGP: 172.17.1.2 rcv OPEN w/ OPTION parameter len: 0
1d03h: BGP: 172.17.1.2 bad OPEN, remote AS is 1, expected 2
1d03h: BGP: 172.17.1.2 went from OpenSent to Closing
1d03h: BGP: 172.17.1.2 sending NOTIFICATION 2/2 (peer in wrong AS) 2 bytes 0001
1d03h: BGP: 172.17.1.2 local error close, erroneous BGP update received
1d03h: BGP: 172.17.1.2 went from Closing to Idle
1d03h: BGP: 172.17.1.2 closing
```

Correct the remote AS number in the neighbor statement on Router B, but use an incorrect IP address for Router A:

```
Router B
router bgp 2
 neighbor 172.17.1.3 remote-as 1
```

Clear the connection and observe the debug output:

```
rtrB#debug ip bgp
rtrB#clear ip bgp *

1d04h: BGP: 172.17.1.3 open active, local address 172.17.1.1
1d04h: BGP: 172.17.1.3 open failed: Connection timed out; remote host not responding
```

16-2: debug ip bgp *neighbor-ip-address* updates

16-3: debug ip bgp *neighbor-ip-address* updates *access-list-number*

Syntax Description:

- *neighbor-ip-address*—BGP neighbor's IP address.
- *access-list-number*—IP access list number.

Purpose: To debug BGP updates from a particular neighbor. The first form debugs all updates from the neighbor. The second form can be used to debug specific updates from the neighbor. The IP access list number can be in the range 1 to 199 or 1300 to 2699.

Cisco IOS Software Release: 10.0

Example 1: Debug All Updates to and from a Particular Neighbor

In Figure 16-2, Router A is advertising four prefixes to Router B, and Router B is advertising four prefixes to Router A. Debug all the updates received from and sent to Router A.

Figure 16-2 *Debug All Updates from a Neighbor*

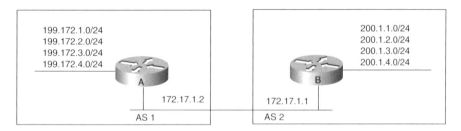

```
Router A
interface loopback 1
 ip address 199.172.1.1 255.255.255.0
 !
interface loopback 2
 ip address 199.172.2.1 255.255.255.0
 !
interface loopback 3
 ip address 199.172.3.1 255.255.255.0
 !
interface loopback 4
 ip address 199.172.4.1 255.255.255.0
 !
router bgp 1
network 199.172.1.0
network 199.172.2.0
network 199.172.3.0
network 199.172.4.0
neighbor 172.17.1.1 remote-as 2
```
```
Router B
interface loopback 1
 ip address 200.1.1.1 255.255.255.0
 !
interface loopback 2
 ip address 200.1.2.1 255.255.255.0
 !
interface loopback 3
 ip address 200.1.3.1 255.255.255.0
 !
interface loopback 4
 ip address 200.1.4.1 255.255.255.0
 !
```

continues

```
(Continued)
router bgp 2
network 200.1.1.0
network 200.1.2.0
network 200.1.3.0
network 200.1.4.0
neighbor 172.17.1.2 remote-as 1
```

Verify that Routers A and B have formed a BGP neighbor relationship, and then debug BGP updates on Router B:

```
rtrB#debug ip bgp 172.17.1.2 updates
BGP updates debugging is on for neighbor 172.17.1.2
clear ip bgp 172.17.1.2

rtrB#
01:58:38: BGP(0): 172.17.1.2 computing updates, afi 0, neighbor version 0, table
  version 1, starting at 0.0.0.0
01:58:38: BGP(0): 172.17.1.2 update run completed, afi 0, ran for 0ms, neighbor
  version 0, start version 1, throttled to 1
01:58:39: BGP(0): 172.17.1.2 rcvd UPDATE w/ attr: nexthop 172.17.1.2, origin i,
  metric 0, path 1
01:58:39: BGP(0): 172.17.1.2 rcvd 199.172.1.0/24
01:58:39: BGP(0): 172.17.1.2 rcvd 199.172.2.0/24
01:58:39: BGP(0): 172.17.1.2 rcvd 199.172.3.0/24
01:58:39: BGP(0): 172.17.1.2 rcvd 199.172.4.0/24
01:59:09: BGP(0): 172.17.1.2 computing updates, afi 0, neighbor version 1, table
  version 9, starting at 0.0.0.0
01:59:09: BGP(0): 172.17.1.2 send UPDATE (format) 200.1.1.0/24, next 172.17.1.1,
  metric 0, path
01:59:09: BGP(0): 172.17.1.2 send UPDATE (prepend, chgflags: 0x208) 200.1.2.0/24,
  next 172.17.1.1, metric 0, path
01:59:09: BGP(0): 172.17.1.2 send UPDATE (prepend, chgflags: 0x208) 200.1.3.0/24,
  next 172.17.1.1, metric 0, path
01:59:09: BGP(0): 172.17.1.2 send UPDATE (prepend, chgflags: 0x208) 200.1.4.0/24,
  next 172.17.1.1, metric 0, path
01:59:09: BGP(0): 172.17.1.2 1 updates enqueued (average=64, maximum=64)
01:59:09: BGP(0): 172.17.1.2 update run completed, afi 0, ran for 0ms, neighbor
  version 1, start version 9, throttled to 9
```

Example 2: Debug Specific Updates to and/or from a Particular Neighbor

For this example, debug only updates from Router A regarding network 199.172.3.0. Also debug the prefix 200.1.2.0 from Router B to Router A:

```
Router B
access-list 1300 permit 199.172.3.0 0.0.0.255
access-list 1300 permit 200.1.2.0 0.0.0.255
```

(Continued)

```
rtrB#debug ip bgp 172.17.1.2 updates 1300
BGP updates debugging is on for access list 1300 for neighbor 172.17.1.2

rtrB#clear ip bgp *
02:08:59: BGP(0): 172.17.1.2 rcvd UPDATE w/ attr: nexthop 172.17.1.2, origin i,
 metric 0, path 1
02:08:59: BGP(0): 172.17.1.2 rcvd 199.172.2.0/24
02:09:25: BGP(0): 172.17.1.2 send UPDATE (prepend, chgflags: 0x208) 200.1.2.0/24,
 next 172.17.1.1, metric 0, path
```

16-4: debug ip bgp dampening

16-5: debug ip bgp dampening *access-list-number*

Syntax Description:

* *access-list-number*—IP access list number.

Purpose: To debug BGP events associated with dampening. The first form debugs all dampening events. The second form debugs only dampening events associated with routes identified by the IP access list. The IP access list number can be in the range from 1 to 199 or 1300 to 2699. Although it isn't necessary, use logging to store the results so that you can review them later.

Cisco IOS Software Release: 10.0

Example: Debug All BGP Dampening Events

In Figure 16-3, Router A is advertising network 199.172.2.0/24 via BGP to Router B. Dampening is enabled on Router B, and the 199.172.2.0/24 network on Router A is flapped by alternately bringing the interface up and down.

Figure 16-3 *Scenario for Debugging BGP Dampening*

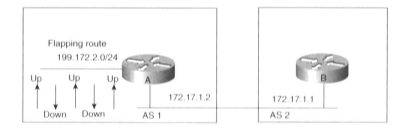

Sections 16-4 – 16-5

```
Router A
interface loopback 1
 ip address 199.172.2.0 255.255.255.0

router bgp 1
 neighbor 172.17.1.1 remote-as 2
```

```
Router B
router bgp 2
 bgp dampening
 neighbor 172.17.1.2 remote-as 1
```

After Routers A and B have established a neighbor relationship, enable BGP dampening debugging on Router B, and flap the loopback interface on Router A:

```
Router B
logging buffered

rtrB#debug ip bgp dampening
rtrB#show logging
Syslog logging: enabled (0 messages dropped, 0 flushes, 0 overruns)
    Console logging: level debugging, 297 messages logged
    Monitor logging: level debugging, 0 messages logged
    Buffer logging: level debugging, 63 messages logged
    Trap logging: level informational, 52 message lines logged

Log Buffer (4096 bytes):
03:26:07: BGP(0): Created dampening structures with halflife time 15,
 reuse/suppress 750/2000
03:26:43: BGP(0): charge penalty for 199.172.2.0/24 path 1 with halflife-time 15
 reuse/suppress 750/2000
03:26:43: BGP(0): flapped 1 times since 00:00:00. New penalty is 1000
03:27:39: BGP(0): charge penalty for 199.172.2.0/24 path 1 with halflife-time 15
 reuse/suppress 750/2000
03:27:39: BGP(0): flapped 2 times since 00:00:56. New penalty is 1961
03:28:32: BGP(0): charge penalty for 199.172.2.0/24 path 1 with halflife-time 15
 reuse/suppress 750/2000
03:28:32: BGP(0): flapped 3 times since 00:01:49. New penalty is 2886
03:29:05: BGP(0): suppress 199.172.2.0/24 path 1 for 00:28:40 (penalty 2819)
03:29:05: halflife-time 15, reuse/suppress 750/2000
03:57:52: BGP(0): Unsuppressed 199.172.2.0/24, path 1
```

If you want debugging information for a particular prefix, use the second form of this command. For example, to debug dampening for prefix 199.172.2.0/24, use the following configuration:

```
Router B
access-list 1 permit 199.172.2.0 0.0.0.255

rtrB#debug ip bgp dampening 1
```

16-6: debug ip bgp events

Syntax Description: This command has no arguments.

Purpose: To debug events relating to the BGP neighbor relationship.

Cisco IOS Software Release: 10.0

Example: Debug the Formation of the Neighbor Relationship

Enable BGP event debugging, and then clear the connection between the BGP neighbors:

```
rtrA#debug ip bgp events
BGP events debugging is on
rtrA#clear ip bgp *
rtrA#
1w3d: BGP: reset all neighbors due to User reset
1w3d: BGP: 172.17.1.1 went from Active to Idle
1w3d: BGP: 172.17.1.1 went from Idle to Active
1w3d: BGP: scanning routing tables
1w3d: BGP: 172.17.1.1 went from Active to Idle
1w3d: BGP: 172.17.1.1 went from Idle to Connect
1w3d: BGP: 172.17.1.1 went from Connect to OpenSent
1w3d: BGP: 172.17.1.1 went from OpenSent to OpenConfirm
1w3d: BGP: 172.17.1.1 went from OpenConfirm to Established
1w3d: BGP: 172.17.1.1 computing updates, neighbor version 0, table version 5,
  starting at 0.0.0.0
1w3d: BGP: 172.17.1.1 update run completed, ran for 0ms, neighbor version 0,
  start version 5, throttled to 5, check point net 0.0.0.0
```

16-7: debug ip bgp keepalives

Syntax Description: This command has no arguments.

Purpose: To debug keepalive messages sent between BGP neighbors. To configure the keepalive internal, see sections 8-31 and 13-1.

Cisco IOS Software Release: 10.0

Example: Debug BGP Keepalive Messages

Enable BGP keepalive message debugging between any two BGP neighbors:

```
rtrB#debug ip bgp keepalives
BGP keepalives debugging is on

rtrB#
1d06h: BGP: 172.17.1.2 sending KEEPALIVE
1d06h: BGP: 172.17.1.2 KEEPALIVE rcvd
```

Sections 16-6– 16-7

16-8: debug ip bgp in *neighbor-ip-address* updates

16-9: debug ip bgp in *neighbor-ip-address* updates *access-list-number*

16-10: debug ip bgp out *neighbor-ip-address* updates

16-11: debug ip bgp out *neighbor-ip-address* updates *access-list-number*

16-12: debug ip bgp updates

16-13: debug ip bgp updates in

16-14: debug ip bgp updates out

16-15: debug ip bgp updates *access-list-number*

16-16: debug ip bgp updates *access-list-number* in

16-17: debug ip bgp updates *access-list-number* out

Syntax Description:

- *neighbor-ip-address*—BGP neighbor's IP address.
- *access-list-number*—IP access list number.

Purpose: To debug BGP updates. The IP access list number can be in the range 1 to 199 or 1300 to 2699.

Cisco IOS Software Release: 10.0

Example 1: Debug All BGP Updates

In Figure 16-4, Router A is advertising four prefixes to Router B, and Router B is advertising four prefixes to Router A. Debug all the updates on Router B.

Figure 16-4 *Debug All Updates from a Neighbor*

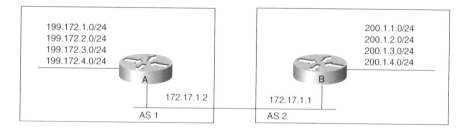

```
Router A
interface loopback 1
 ip address 199.172.1.1 255.255.255.0
!
interface loopback 2
 ip address 199.172.2.1 255.255.255.0
!
interface loopback 3
 ip address 199.172.3.1 255.255.255.0
!
interface loopback 4
 ip address 199.172.4.1 255.255.255.0
!
router bgp 1
network 199.172.1.0
network 199.172.2.0
network 199.172.3.0
network 199.172.4.0
neighbor 172.17.1.1 remote-as 2
```

```
Router B
interface loopback 1
 ip address 200.1.1.1 255.255.255.0
!
interface loopback 2
 ip address 200.1.2.1 255.255.255.0
!
interface loopback 3
 ip address 200.1.3.1 255.255.255.0
!
interface loopback 4
 ip address 200.1.4.1 255.255.255.0
!
```

continues

Sections 16-8 –16-17

(Continued)
```
router bgp 2
network 200.1.1.0
network 200.1.2.0
network 200.1.3.0
network 200.1.4.0
neighbor 172.17.1.2 remote-as 1

rtrB#debug ip bgp updates
BGP updates debugging is on
rtrB#clear ip bgp *
2d03h: BGP(0): 172.17.1.2 send UPDATE (format) 200.1.1.0/24, next 172.17.1.1,
 metric 0, path
2d03h: BGP(0): 172.17.1.2 send UPDATE (prepend, chgflags: 0x208) 200.1.2.0/24,
 next 172.17.1.1, metric 0, path
2d03h: BGP(0): 172.17.1.2 send UPDATE (prepend, chgflags: 0x208) 200.1.3.0/24,
 next 172.17.1.1, metric 0, path
2d03h: BGP(0): 172.17.1.2 send UPDATE (prepend, chgflags: 0x208) 200.1.4.0/24,
 next 172.17.1.1, metric 0, path
2d03h: BGP(0): 172.17.1.2 1 updates enqueued (average=64, maximum=64)
2d03h: BGP(0): 172.17.1.2 update run completed, afi 0, ran for 0ms, neighbor
 version 0, start version 5, throttled to 5
2d03h: BGP(0): 172.17.1.2 rcvd UPDATE w/ attr: nexthop 172.17.1.2, origin i,
 metric 0, path 1
2d03h: BGP(0): 172.17.1.2 rcvd 199.172.1.0/24
2d03h: BGP(0): 172.17.1.2 rcvd 199.172.2.0/24
2d03h: BGP(0): 172.17.1.2 rcvd 199.172.3.0/24
2d03h: BGP(0): 172.17.1.2 rcvd 199.172.4.0/24
```

Example 2: Debug Input Updates

Debug BGP updates on Router B for routes received from Router A.

```
rtrB#debug ip bgp updates in
BGP updates debugging is on (inbound)
rtrb#clear ip bgp *
2d03h: BGP(0): 172.17.1.2 rcvd UPDATE w/ attr: nexthop 172.17.1.2, origin i,
 metric 0, path 1
2d03h: BGP(0): 172.17.1.2 rcvd 199.172.1.0/24
2d03h: BGP(0): 172.17.1.2 rcvd 199.172.2.0/24
2d03h: BGP(0): 172.17.1.2 rcvd 199.172.3.0/24
2d03h: BGP(0): 172.17.1.2 rcvd 199.172.4.0/24
```

Example 3: Debug Output Updates for Specific Prefixes Sent to All BGP Neighbors

Debug BGP updates on Router B for local prefixes 200.1.2.0 and 200.1.3.2:

```
Router B
access-list 1 permit 200.1.2.0 0.0.1.255

rtrB#debug ip bgp updates 1 out
BGP updates debugging is on for access list 1 (outbound)
rtrB#clear ip bgp *
2d03h: BGP(0): nettable_walker 200.1.2.0/24 route sourced locally
2d03h: BGP(0): nettable_walker 200.1.3.0/24 route sourced locally
2d03h: BGP(0): 172.17.1.2 send UPDATE (prepend, chgflags: 0x208) 200.1.2.0/24,
 next 172.17.1.1, metric 0, path
2d03h: BGP(0): 172.17.1.2 send UPDATE (prepend, chgflags: 0x208) 200.1.3.0/24,
 next 172.17.1.1, metric 0, path
```

Example 4: Debug Input Updates for Specific Prefixes Received from a Specific BGP Neighbor

Debug updates for prefixes 199.172.2.0 and 199.172.3.0 received from Router A:

```
Router B
access-list 2 permit 199.172.2.0 0.0.1.255

rtrB#debug ip bgp in 172.17.1.2 updates 2
BGP updates debugging is on for access list 2 for neighbor 172.17.1.2 (inbound)
rtrB#clear ip bgp *
p2#
2d03h: BGP(0): 172.17.1.2 rcvd UPDATE w/ attr: nexthop 172.17.1.2, origin i,
 metric 0, path 1
2d03h: BGP(0): 172.17.1.2 rcvd 199.172.2.0/24
2d03h: BGP(0): 172.17.1.2 rcvd 199.172.3.0/24
```

Sections 16-8 –16-17

RFC 1771: Border Gateway Protocol 4

The objective of this appendix is to present the concepts and terminology contained in RFC 1771 in order to help you understand the operation of BGP. Many of the details have been omitted, such as packet format and contents. These topics are of interest to developers of the code that runs on a BGP-capable router. Border Gateway Protocol (BGP) is an interautonomous system routing protocol. An autonomous system (AS) is a network or group of networks that are under a common administration and that have common routing policies. BGP is used to exchange routing information for the Internet and is the protocol used between Internet service providers (ISPs). Customer networks, such as universities and corporations, usually employ an Interior Gateway Protocol (IGP) such as Routing Information Protocol (RIP) or Open Shortest Path First (OSPF) for the exchange of routing information within their networks. Customers connect to ISPs, and ISPs use BGP to exchange customer and ISP routes. When BGP is used between autonomous systems, the protocol is called External BGP (EBGP). If a service provider uses BGP to exchange routes within its AS, the protocol is called Interior BGP (IBGP). Figure A-1 illustrates this distinction.

BGP is a very robust and scalable routing protocol, as evidenced by the fact that BGP is the routing protocol employed on the Internet. Currently, the Internet BGP routing tables have more than 90,000 routes. In order to achieve scalability at this level, BGP uses many route parameters, called *attributes,* to define routing policies and maintain a stable routing environment.

In addition to BGP attributes, BGP uses Classless Interdomain Routing (CIDR) to reduce the size of the Internet routing tables. For example, assume that an ISP owns the IP address block 195.10.x.x from the traditional Class C address space. This block consists of 256 Class C address blocks, 195.10.0.x to 195.10.255.x. Assume that the ISP assigns a Class C block to each of its customers. Without CIDR, the ISP would advertise 256 Class C address blocks to its BGP peers. With CIDR, BGP can supernet the address space and advertise one block, 195.10.x.x. This block is the same size as a traditional Class B address block. The class distinctions are rendered obsolete by CIDR, allowing a significant reduction in the BGP routing tables.

BGP neighbors exchange full routing information when the TCP connection between neighbors is first established. When changes to the routing table are detected, the BGP routers send to their neighbors only those routes that have changed. BGP routers do not send periodic routing updates, and BGP routing updates advertise only the optimal path to a destination network.

Figure A-1   *External and Interior BGP*

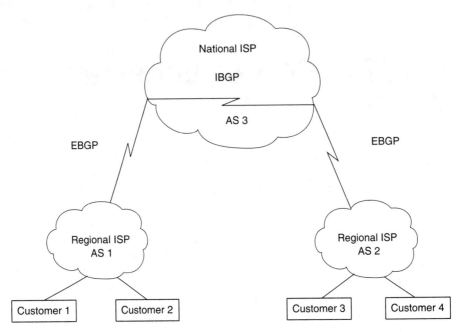

BGP Attributes

Routes learned via BGP have associated properties that are used to determine the best route to a destination when multiple paths exist. These properties are called BGP attributes. An understanding of how BGP attributes influence route selection is required for the design of robust networks. This section describes the attributes that BGP uses in the route selection process:

- Weight
- Local preference
- Multi-exit discriminator
- Origin
- AS_path
- Next-hop
- Community

Weight Attribute

Weight is a Cisco-defined attribute that is local to a router. The weight attribute is not advertised to neighboring routers. If the router learns about more than one route to the same destination, the route with the highest weight is preferred. In Figure A-2, Router A is receiving an advertisement for network 172.16.1.0 from Routers B and C. When Router A receives the advertisement from Router B, the associated weight is set to 50. When Router A receives the advertisement from Router C, the associated weight is set to 100. Both paths for network 172.16.1.0 will be in the BGP routing table with their respective weights. The route with the higher weight will be installed in the IP routing table.

Figure A-2 *BGP Weight Attribute*

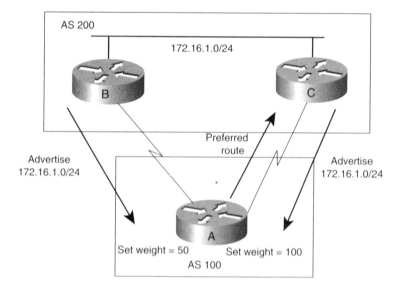

Local Preference Attribute

The local preference attribute is used to prefer an exit point from the local autonomous system. Unlike the weight attribute, the local preference attribute is propagated throughout the local AS. If there are multiple exit points from the AS, the local preference attribute is used to select the exit point for a specific route. In Figure A-3, AS 100 is receiving two advertisements for network 172.16.1.0 from AS 200. When router A receives the advertisement for network 172.16.1.0, the corresponding local preference is set to 50. When router B receives the advertisement for network 172.16.1.0, the corresponding local preference is set to 100. These local preference values are exchanged between routers A and B. Because router B has a higher local preference than router A, router B is used as the exit point from AS 100 to reach network 172.16.1.0 in AS 200.

Figure A-3 *BGP Local Preference Attribute*

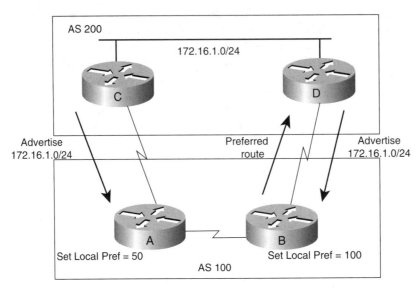

Multi-Exit Discriminator Attribute

The multi-exit discriminator (MED) or metric attribute is used as a suggestion to an external AS regarding the preferred route into the AS that is advertising the metric.

I say "suggestion" because the external AS that is receiving the MEDs might be using other BGP attributes for route selection. We will cover the rules of route selection in the next section. In Figure A-4, Router C is advertising the route 172.16.1.0 with a metric of 10, and Router D is advertising 172.16.1.0 with a metric of 5. The lower value of the metric is preferred, so AS 100 selects the route to router D for network 172.16.1.0 in AS 200. MEDs are advertised throughout the local AS.

Origin Attribute

The origin attribute indicates how BGP learned about a particular route. The origin attribute can have one of three possible values:

- **IGP**—The route is interior to the originating AS. This value is set when the network router configuration command is used to inject the route into BGP.
- **EGP**—The route is learned via the Exterior Gateway Protocol (EGP).
- **Incomplete**—The origin of the route is unknown or is learned some other way. An origin of Incomplete occurs when a route is redistributed into BGP.

The origin attribute is used for route selection. It is covered in the next section.

Figure A-4   *BGP Multi-Exit Discriminator Attribute*

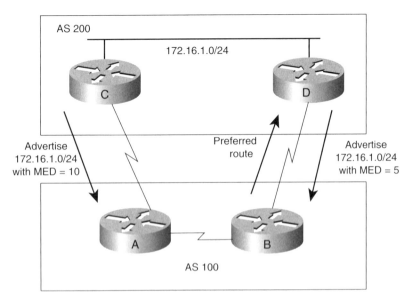

AS_path Attribute

When a route advertisement passes through an autonomous system, the AS number is added to an ordered list of AS numbers that the route advertisement has traversed. Figure A-5 shows a situation in which a route is passing through three autonomous systems.

AS1 originates the route to 172.16.1.0 and advertises this route to AS 2 and AS 3 with the AS_path attribute equal to {1}. AS 3 advertises back to AS 1 with AS_path attribute {3,1}, and AS 2 advertises back to AS 1 with AS_path attribute {2,1}. AS 1 rejects these routes when its own AS number is detected in the route advertisement. This is the mechanism that BGP uses to detect routing loops. AS 2 and AS 3 propagate the route to each other, with their AS number added to the AS_path attribute. These routes will not be installed in the IP routing table, because AS 2 and AS 3 are learning a route to 172.16.1.0 from AS 1 with a shorter AS-path list.

Next-Hop Attribute

The EBGP next-hop attribute is the IP address that is used to reach the advertising router. For EBGP peers, the next-hop address is the IP address of the connection between the peers. For IBGP, the EBGP next-hop address is carried into the local AS, as shown in Figure A-6.

Figure A-5   *BGP AS_Path Attribute*

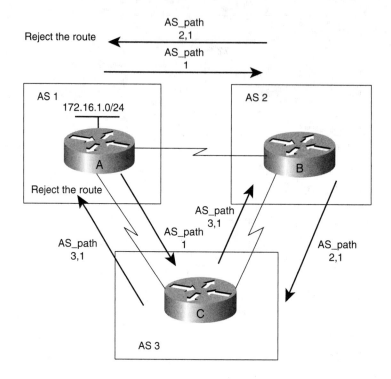

Figure A-6   *BGP Next-Hop Attribute*

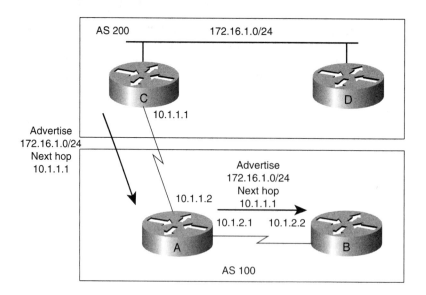

Router C advertises network 172.16.1.0 with a next hop of 10.1.1.1. When Router A propagates this route within its own AS, the EBGP next-hop information is preserved. If router B does not have routing information regarding the next hop, the route is discarded. Therefore, it is important to have an IGP running in the AS to propagate next-hop routing information.

Community Attribute

The community attribute provides a way of grouping destinations, called *communities,* to which routing decisions (such as acceptance, preference, and redistribution) can be applied. Route maps are used to set the community attribute. The predefined community attributes are as follows:

- **no-export**—Do not advertise this route to EBGP peers.

- **no-advertise**—Do not advertise this route to any peer.

- **internet**—Advertise this route to the Internet community; all routers in the network belong to it.

Figure A-7 illustrates the no-export community. AS 1 advertises 172.16.1.0 to AS 2 with the community attribute no-export. AS 2 propagates the route throughout AS 2 but does not send this route to AS 3 or to any other external AS.

Figure A-7 *BGP No-Export Community Attribute*

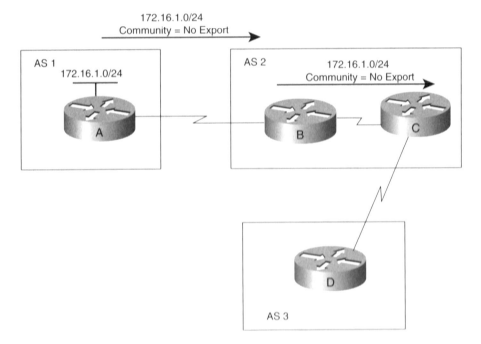

In Figure A-8, AS 1 advertises 172.16.1.0 to AS 2 with the community attribute no-advertise. Router B in AS 2 does not advertise this route to any other router.

Figure A-8   *BGP No-Advertise Community Attribute*

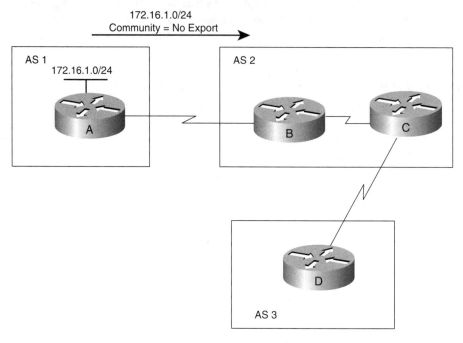

Figure A-9 demonstrates the internet community attribute. There are no limitations to the scope of the route advertisement from AS 1.

BGP attributes are classified as either well-known or optional. Well-known attributes are further classified as mandatory or discretionary. A well-known mandatory attribute must be present in the BGP UPDATE message. A well-known discretionary attribute must be recognized by all BGP speakers, but its presence in an UPDATE message is optional. Table A-1 lists the well-known BGP attributes.

Table A-1   *Well-Known BGP Attributes*

Attribute	Type
Origin	Mandatory
AS_path	Mandatory
Next-hop	Mandatory
Local-pref	Discretionary
Atomic-aggregate	Discretionary

Figure A-9 *BGP Internet Community Attribute*

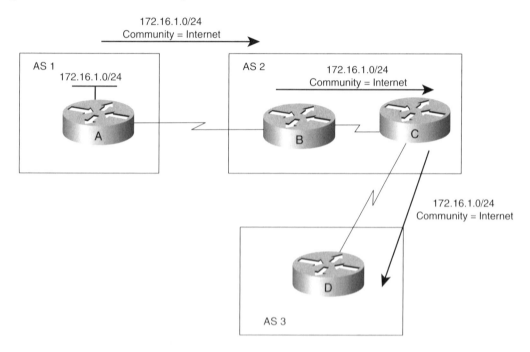

Optional attributes are either transitive or nontransitive. If an optional attribute is not known by the receiving BGP speaker, the BGP speaker determines whether the attribute is transitive or nontransitive by examining a bit in the UPDATE message. If the attribute is transitive, the BGP speaker passes the attribute to other BGP speakers. If the attribute is nontransitive, the attribute is discarded and is not advertised to other BGP speakers. Table A-2 lists the optional BGP attributes.

Table A-2 *Optional BGP Attributes*

Attribute	Type
MED	Nontransitive
Originator ID	Nontransitive
Cluster list	Nontransitive
Aggregator	Transitive
Community	Transitive

BGP Path Selection

BGP can receive multiple advertisements for the same route from multiple sources. BGP selects only one path as the best path. After the path is selected, BGP puts it in the IP routing table and propagates the path to its neighbors. BGP uses the following criteria, in the order listed, to select a path for a destination:

- Ignore a route if the next hop is not known.
- Ignore IBGP routes that are not synchronized.
- Prefer the route with the largest weight.
- Prefer the route with the largest local preference.
- Prefer the route that was locally originated.
- Prefer the route with the shortest AS path. If you're using **bgp bestpath as-path ignore**, skip this step. When you use the **as-set** option for aggregated routes, it counts as 1 regardless of the number of AS entries in the set. Confederation sub-AS numbers are not used to determine the AS-path length.
- Prefer the route with the lowest origin (IGP < EGP < Incomplete).
- Prefer the route with the lowest MED. This comparison is only between routes advertised by the same external AS.

    If you're using **bgp always-compare-med**, compare MEDs for all paths. If used, this command needs to be configured on every BGP router in the AS.

    If you're using **bgp bestpath med-confed**, the MEDs are compared only for routes that have an AS confederation sequence in their AS-path attribute.

    If a prefix is received with no MED value, it is assigned a MED value of 0. If you're using **bgp bestpath med missing-as-worst**, a prefix with a missing MED value is assigned a MED value of 4,294,967,294.

- Prefer EBGP routes to IBGP routes.
- Prefer the route with the nearest IGP neighbor.
- Prefer the oldest route.
- Prefer the path received from the router with the lowest router ID.

Forming a BGP Connection

BGP uses TCP/IP as its underlying transport and uses TCP port 179. BGP speakers transition through various states during the establishment of a neighbor relationship, as shown in Figure A-10.

Figure A-10 *States in the Formation of a BGP Neighbor Relationship*

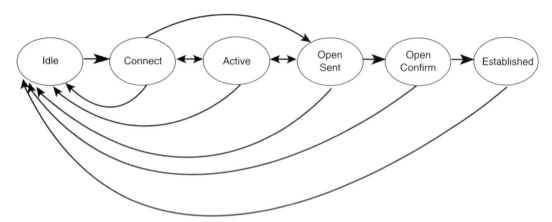

The Idle state usually represents the condition in which BGP has not been enabled on the router, or a particular neighbor relationship has been shut down. When a connection is initiated through either router configuration or the removal of the shut-down state for a particular neighbor, BGP moves to the Connect state.

In the Connect state, BGP waits for a TCP connection to be established with the remote neighbor. If the TCP connection is established, an Open message is sent, and the Open Sent state is entered. If the TCP connection is not established, the Active state is entered. While in the Active state, the router continues to listen for a connection.

In the Open Sent state, the router waits for an Open message from the remote neighbor. If there are errors in the Open message, a notification message is sent to the neighbor, and the local router enters the Idle state.

If the Open message contains no errors, a keepalive message is sent, and the holdtime is set to the negotiated value. The Open Confirm state is then entered. If the BGP neighbors are in the same AS, the BGP connection is internal. If the BGP neighbors are in different autonomous systems, the connection is external.

In the Open Confirm state, BGP waits for a keepalive or notification message. If a keepalive message is received, the connection moves to the Established state. If a keepalive message is not received before the hold timer expires, a notification message is sent, and the state transitions to Idle.

In the Established state, the BGP neighbors can exchange update, notification, and keepalive messages. Whenever BGP changes its state from Established to Idle, it closes the BGP and TCP connection, releases all resources associated with that connection, and deletes all routes derived from that connection.

Table A-3 lists additional references available from http://www.nexor.com/index-rfc.htm

Table A-3   *BGP-Related RFCs*

RFC Number	RFC Title
2918	Route Refresh Capability for BGP-4
2858	Multiprotocol Extensions for BGP-4
2842	Capabilities Advertisement with BGP-4
2796	BGP Route Reflection—An Alternative to Full-Mesh IBGP
2547	BGP/MPLS VPNs
2545	Use of BGP-4 Multiprotocol Extensions for IPv6 Inter-Domain Routing
2439	BGP Route Flap Damping
2385	Protection of BGP Sessions via the TCP MD5 Signature Option
2283	Multiprotocol Extensions for BGP-4
2042	Registering New BGP Attribute Types
1998	An Application of the BGP Community Attribute in Multi-Home Routing
1997	BGP Communities Attribute
1966	BGP Route Reflection—An Alternative to Full-Mesh IBGP
1965	Autonomous System Confederations for BGP
1863	A BGP/IDRP Route Server Alternative to a Full-Mesh Routing
1774	BGP-4 Protocol Analysis
1773	Experience with the BGP-4 Protocol

Regular Expressions

A regular expression is a sequence of one or more characters that can be used for two general purposes. The first purpose is to reduce the output from various **show** commands. For example, if you wanted to view the routing protocols that are active on a router, you could use **show running-config** and scroll through the output until you came to the section of the configuration that contained the routing configurations. Or, you could use an output modifier with a regular expression to display only those lines containing a **router** configuration command:

```
rtrA#show running-config | include router
router eigrp 1
router bgp 2
```

This code uses the output modifier **include** and the regular expression **router** to reduce the amount of output from the **show running-config** command. Each line of output from this command is examined, and if the pattern **router** is contained in the line, the line is displayed. You could use the same regular expression with a different output modifier to display the configuration, starting with the router configurations and everything that follows:

```
p2#show running-config | begin router
router eigrp 1
 network 10.0.0.0
 network 172.17.0.0
 !
router bgp 2
 network 200.1.1.0
 network 200.1.2.0
 neighbor 10.1.1.2 remote-as 2
 neighbor 172.17.1.2 remote-as 1
 !
line con 0
 exec-timeout 0 0
 transport input none
line aux 0
line vty 0 4
 login
 !
end
```

Having the capability to reduce the output of **show** commands is very useful with BGP. If your BGP routers contain the entire Internet routing table, using the **show ip bgp** command displays tens of thousands of routes. If you are interested in only a particular prefix, the use of a regular expression greatly reduces the amount of output:

```
rtrA#show ip bgp | include 200.1
BGP table version is 8, local router ID is 200.1.4.1
*> 200.1.1.0    0.0.0.0    0    32768    i
*> 200.1.2.0    0.0.0.0    0    32768    i
*> 200.1.3.0    0.0.0.0    0    32768    i
*> 200.1.4.0    0.0.0.0    0    32768    I
```

These regular expressions are simple character strings. Complex regular expressions can be constructed by using the characters A to Z, a to z, 0 to 9, and the special characters listed in Table B-1.

Table B-1   *Regular Expressions: Special Characters*

Character	Meaning
.	Matches any single character, including white space.
*	Matches zero or more sequences of the pattern.
+	Matches one or more sequences of the pattern.
?	Matches zero or one occurrence of the pattern.
^	Matches the beginning of the string.
$	Matches the end of the string.
_ (underscore)	Matches a comma (,), left brace ({), right brace (}), left parenthesis ((), right parenthesis ()), the beginning of the string, the end of the string, or a space.

Here are some examples:

- **c*** matches any occurrence of the letter c in the line, including no occurrences of the letter c.
- **c+** matches one or more occurrences of the letter c in the line.
- **ca?B** matches cb or caB.

If you want to use one of the special characters in Table B-1 as a regular character, precede it with a backslash (\). For example, \$ matches the dollar sign character, \+ matches the plus sign character, and _ matches the underscore character.

Square brackets are used to specify a range of single characters. Here are some examples:

- **[Aa]** matches either the single character A or a.
- **[1-35-7]** matches a single character with the value 1, 2, 3, 5, 6, or 7.

- **^[bB]** Matches a line that begins with b or B.
- **[2-5]$** Matches a line that ends with 2, 3, 4, or 5. The caret (^) is used to reverse the meaning of the characters within the bracket.
- **[^1-3]** Matches any occurrence of the characters 0 and 4 through 9.

Obviously, you can get carried away with the complexity of a regular expression.

The second general purpose of the regular expression is in an autonomous system path filter. BGP can filter incoming or outgoing updates based on the AS path information. A BGP router prepends its own AS number on the AS path list for every prefix that is advertised. Table B-2 lists common regular expressions for use in AS path filters.

Table B-2   *Common Regular Expressions for AS Path Filters*

Regular Expression	Routes Targeted
^$	Routes originating from this AS.
^2_	All routes from a directly connected neighbor in AS 2.
^2$	Routes originated by a neighbor in AS 2.
_3_	Routes containing AS 3.
{1 2}	Aggregate route using the **as-set** option. Routes from AS 1 and AS 2 form the aggregate.
(65530)	Confederation peer. The peer is in AS 65530.

The format of an AS path filter is

```
ip as-path access-list list_number permit regular_expression
```

or

```
ip as-path access-list list_number deny regular_expression
```

The AS path filter can be used to filter incoming or outgoing routes based on AS path information. An AS path filter can also be used in a route map to selectively modify BGP attributes based on the prefix's AS path.

Route Map Logic

A route map is an extremely powerful and versatile tool for route filtering and attribute manipulation. In regards to BGP, route maps are used in the following commands:

```
aggregate-address address mask advertise-map route-map-name
aggregate-address address mask as-set route-map-name
aggregate-address address mask attribute-map route-map-name
aggregate-address address mask route-map route-map-name
aggregate-address address mask suppress-map route-map-name
bgp dampening route-map route-map-name
neighbor ip-address advertise-map route-map-name non-exist-map route-map-name
neighbor ip-address default-originate route-map route-map-name
neighbor ip-address route-map route-map-name in
neighbor ip-address route-map route-map-name out
neighbor ip-address unsuppress-map route-map-name
redistribute protocol route-map route-map-name
```

These commands allow you to filter routes, manipulate BGP attributes, or both. The logic of route maps is demonstrated in Figure C-1.

Figure C-1 *Scenario for Illustrating Route Map Logic*

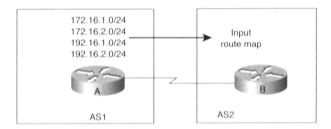

```
Router A
interface loopback 0
 ip address 172.16.1.0 255.255.255.0
!
interface loopback 1
 ip address 172.16.2.0 255.255.255.0
!
```

continues

```
(Continued)
interface loopback 2
 ip address 192.16.1.0 255.255.255.0
!
interface loopback 3
 ip address 192.16.2.0 255.255.255.0
!
router bgp 1
 network 172.16.1.0 mask 255.255.255.0
 network 172.16.2.0 mask 255.255.255.0
 network 192.16.1.0
 network 192.16.2.0
 neighbor 172.17.1.2 remote-as 2
```
```
Router B
router bgp 2
 neighbor 172.17.1.1 remote-as 1
```

Before continuing, verify that Router B is receiving the four network advertisements from Router A.

```
rtrB#show ip bgp
BGP table version is 5, local router ID is 172.17.1.2
Status codes: s suppressed, d damped, h history, * valid, > best, i - internal
Origin codes: i - IGP, e - EGP, ? - incomplete

   Network          Next Hop           Metric LocPrf Weight Path
*> 172.16.1.0/24    172.17.1.1              0          0 1 i
*> 172.16.2.0/24    172.17.1.1              0          0 1 i
*> 192.16.1.0       172.17.1.1              0          0 1 i
*> 192.16.2.0       172.17.1.1              0          0 1 i
```

Now modify the BGP configuration on router B to use an empty **route-map permit** statement.

```
Router B
router bgp 2
 neighbor 172.17.1.1 remote-as 1
 neighbor 172.17.1.1 route-map demo in
!
route-map demo permit 10
```

The BGP **neighbor** configuration command references the route map by name and indicates whether the route map is an input or output route map. **route-map** statements are numerically ordered and are executed in numerical order. Because we are using only one **route-map** statement, the number of the **route-map** statement really has no effect. Each **route-map** statement consists of a line referencing the name of the route map, the sequence number associated with the **route-map** statement, and the keyword **permit** or **deny**. The form used here might seem a bit strange, but we want to investigate the effect of using an empty **route-map** statement. List the BGP table on router B to determine the effect of the empty route map.

```
rtrB#show ip bgp
BGP table version is 5, local router ID is 172.17.1.2
Status codes: s suppressed, d damped, h history, * valid, > best, i - internal
Origin codes: i - IGP, e - EGP, ? - incomplete

   Network            Next Hop          Metric LocPrf Weight Path
*> 172.16.1.0/24      172.17.1.1             0            0 1 i
*> 172.16.2.0/24      172.17.1.1             0            0 1 i
*> 192.16.1.0         172.17.1.1             0            0 1 i
*> 192.16.2.0         172.17.1.1             0            0 1 I
```

The empty form of the **route-map permit** statement allows all routes. This is handy in certain situations. This form is equivalent to **permit any** in an IP access list. Now change the route map from **permit** to **deny**.

```
Router B
router bgp 2
 neighbor 172.17.1.1 remote-as 1
 neighbor 172.17.1.1 route-map demo in
 !
route-map demo deny 10
```

Does this have the opposite effect as the permit form? List the BGP table on Router B to find out.

```
rtrB#show ip bgp
```

The deny form of the empty route map denies all routes.

A route map has four basic forms. The numbered **route-map** statement can contain either a **permit** or **deny**. The **match** clause, if used, can also be either a **permit** or **deny**. Therefore, there are four permutations that we want to investigate:

- **route-map permit/match permit**
- **route-map permit/match deny**
- **route-map deny/match permit**
- **route-map deny/match deny**

For each of these forms, we need to determine under which conditions the routes are accepted, and if the execution of the route map is terminated or if the next **route-map** statement is executed.

The first and second forms are probably the most familiar. We want a route map to permit selected routes to be accepted from Router A while denying all others. For this example, permit only the 172.16.1.0/24 network.

```
router bgp 2
 neighbor 172.17.1.1 remote-as 1
 neighbor 172.17.1.1 route-map demo in
!
access-list 1 permit 172.16.1.0 0.0.0.255
route-map demo permit 10
 match ip address 1
```

When routing updates are received from Router A, each prefix is processed by the input route map. Because we are using the permit form of the route map, only those prefixes that are permitted by the access list are allowed. Remember that an IP access list has an implicit **deny all** as the last statement. This implicit **deny all** blocks all routes that are not permitted by the access list.

```
rtrB#show ip bgp
BGP table version is 2, local router ID is 172.17.1.2
Status codes: s suppressed, d damped, h history, * valid, > best, i - internal
Origin codes: i - IGP, e - EGP, ? - incomplete

   Network          Next Hop          Metric LocPrf Weight Path
*> 172.16.1.0/24    172.17.1.1             0            0 1 I
```

In order to determine if the route map terminates execution when a match is made, add another **route-map** statement to the route map on Router B:

```
router bgp 2
 neighbor 172.17.1.1 remote-as 1
 neighbor 172.17.1.1 route-map demo in
!
access-list 1 permit 172.16.1.0 0.0.0.255
route-map demo permit 10
 match ip address 1
route-map demo permit 20
 set metric 77
```

Using **set metric 77** allows us to determine if the route map terminates for either permitted or denied routes. List the BGP table on Router B to determine the result:

```
rtrB#show ip bgp
BGP table version is 5, local router ID is 172.17.1.2
Status codes: s suppressed, d damped, h history, * valid, > best, i - internal
Origin codes: i - IGP, e - EGP, ? - incomplete

   Network          Next Hop          Metric LocPrf Weight Path
*> 172.16.1.0/24    172.17.1.1             0            0 1 i
*> 172.16.2.0/24    172.17.1.1            77            0 1 i
*> 192.16.1.0       172.17.1.1            77            0 1 i
*> 192.16.2.0       172.17.1.1            77            0 1 i
```

When there is a match using the **permit** statement, the route is accepted and the route map is terminated—at least for that route. When there is a match using a **deny** statement, the route is not accepted, but execution continues to the next **route-map** statement. If there is no other **route-map** statement, all remaining routes are rejected. The 172.17.1.1 route is permitted in the IP access list, so the route is permitted, and the execution of the route map is terminated. This is evident because the metric for this route is unchanged. The other routes are denied by the IP access list, so the routes are not accepted by the first **route-map** statement. But because the routes are denied, the execution of the route map continues to the second statement. We have proven this because the remaining routes have a metric of 77.

The third and fourth forms of a route map contain a **deny** in the **route-map** statement. Change the **route-map** statement to a **deny**, but do not change the IP access list:

```
router bgp 2
  neighbor 172.17.1.1 remote-as 1
  neighbor 172.17.1.1 route-map demo in
 !
access-list 1 permit 172.16.1.0 0.0.0.255
route-map demo deny 10
  match ip address 1
```

This will permit 172.16.1.0/24 to be denied by the route map. What happens to the other prefixes? Are they rejected to be denied?

```
rtrB#show ip bgp
```

Yes, all routes are denied. The important question is, when do the other routes get denied? Are all routes being denied by the **route-map** statement? We can find out by modifying the route map.

```
router bgp 2
  neighbor 172.17.1.1 remote-as 1
  neighbor 172.17.1.1 route-map demo in
 !
access-list 1 permit 172.16.1.0 0.0.0.255
route-map demo deny 10
  match ip address 1
 !
route-map permit 20
```

List the BGP table for Router B to determine the answer to the preceding question.

```
rtrB#show ip bgp
BGP table version is 4, local router ID is 172.17.1.2
Status codes: s suppressed, d damped, h history, * valid, > best, i - internal
Origin codes: i - IGP, e - EGP, ? - incomplete

   Network            Next Hop            Metric LocPrf Weight Path
*> 172.16.2.0/24      172.17.1.1               0             0 1 i
*> 192.16.1.0         172.17.1.1               0             0 1 i
*> 192.16.2.0         172.17.1.1               0             0 1 I
```

The first statement in the route map denies only the 172.16.1.0/24 route. Because there were no more statements in the route map, however, the effect was to deny all routes. With an empty **route-map** statement, which we have seen acts like a **permit any**, the routes not specifically denied by **route-map** statement 10 are now permitted by statement 20. We can now formalize the logic associated with route maps.

Form 1: permit/permit

With form 1, the recommended form, if a match is made, accept the route, set the attribute (if you're using a set clause), and exit the route map. Otherwise, continue to the next **route-map** statement:

```
access-list 1 permit ip-address/mask
```

or

```
ip as-path access-list number permit regular-expression
```

or

```
ip prefix-list name permit prefix/length
```

or

```
ip community-list number permit community-number

route-map name permit sequence-number
  match ip address access-list-number
```

or

```
match as-path access-list-number
```

or

```
match ip address prefix-list list-name
```

or

```
match community community-list-number
```

Form 2: permit/deny

If a match is made, deny the route and exit the route map.

```
access-list 1 permit ip-address/mask
```

or

```
ip as-path access-list number permit regular-expression
```

or

```
  ip prefix-list name permit prefix/length
```

or

```
  ip community-list number permit community-number

route-map name deny sequence-number
  match ip address access-list-number
```

or

```
  match as-path access-list-number
```

or

```
  match ip address prefix-list list-name
```

or

```
  match community community-list-number
```

Form 3: deny/permit

If a match is made, deny the route and exit the route map:

```
  access-list 1 deny ip-address/mask
```

or

```
  ip as-path access-list number deny regular-expression
```

or

```
  ip prefix-list name deny prefix/length
```

or

```
  ip community-list number deny community-number

route-map name permit sequence-number
  match ip address access-list-number
```

or

```
  match as-path access-list-number
```

or

```
  match ip address prefix-list list-name
```

or

```
  match community community-list-number
```

Form 4: deny/deny

If a match is made, accept the route and continue to the next **route-map** statement:

```
access-list 1 deny ip-address/mask
```

or

```
ip as-path access-list number deny regular-expression
```

or

```
ip prefix-list name deny prefix/length
```

or

```
ip community-list number deny community-number

route-map name permit sequence-number
  match ip address access-list-number
```

or

```
match as-path access-list-number
```

or

```
match ip address prefix-list list-name
```

or

```
match community community-list-number
```

The recommended form is form 1. Use a **permit** in the **route-map** statement, and then permit or deny as needed in the IP access list, as-path list, prefix list, or community list.

COMMAND INDEX

INDEX

A

accepted prefixes field (show ip bgp neighbors command), 307

access lists
    corresponding dampened prefixes, displaying, 297
    extended, route filtering, 207
    standard
        configuring, 212–213
        route filtering, 205–206

ACK hold field (show ip bgp neighbors command), 308

adding
    aggregate entries to BGP table, 3–11
    descriptions to BGP configurations, 136–137
    learned paths to routing table, 113–116

Address family IPv4 Multicast field (show ip bgp neighbors command), 307

Address family IPv4 Unicast field (show ip bgp neighbors command), 306

addresses, classful, 243

administrative distance
    best path, selecting, 248–250
    modifying, 103–106
    verifying, 106

advertisement runs field (show ip bgp neighbors command), 307

advertising, 243
    conditional default routes, 133–135
    default routes, 95–97
    directly connected networks, 243–245
    primary route while suppressing secondary route, 119–124

aggregate-address command, 3–36
    as-set advertise-map option, 17–24
    as-set option, 12–17
    attribute-map option, 24
    route-map option, 24–29
    summary-only option, 29–32
    suppress-map option, 33–36

aggregation
    atomic-aggregate attribute, 6
    attributes, modifying, 24–29

based on subset of prefixes from different ASs, 18–24
    learned routes, 8–10
    locally-sourced routes, 3–8
    prefixes from different ASs, 12–17
    redistributed routes, 8
    static routes, 11–12, 245–246
    suppressing more-specific routes, 29–32
    suppressing subset of more-specific routes, 33–36
    verifying configuration, 10

appending AS path information to routes, 215

applying route dampening to flapping routes, 78–79

AS field (show ip bgp summary command), 311

AS MED values, comparing, 46–50, 60

AS numbers, prepending, 214

AS_path attribute, 335
    access lists, displaying corresponding dampened prefixes, 297
    appending to routes, 215
    as route filtering criteria, 210–211
    filtering with regular expressions, 347

as-set advertise-map option (aggregate-address command), 17–24

as-set option (aggregate-address command), 12–17

assigning
    BGP router IDs, 91–93
    metrics to redistributed routes, 98–100

atomic-aggregate attribute, 6

attribute-map option (aggregate-address command), 24

attributes, 331
    as best path selection criteria, 50–62
    AS path, appending to routes, 215
    AS_path, 335
    atomic-aggregate, 6
    community, 337–339
        NO-EXPORT community value, configuring, 225–227
    local preference, 333
        modifying, 84–86
    manipulating, 208
        with route maps, 212–218
    MED
        comparing from different ASs, 60
        deterministic best path selection, 86

N

W–Z

Cisco Press Fundamentals

Internet Routing Architectures, Second Edition

Bassam Halabi, Danny McPherson

1-57870-233-X • AVAILABLE NOW

The BGP bible! Updated from the best-selling first edition. Explore the ins and outs of interdomain routing network designs and discover current perspectives on internetworking routing architectures. Includes detailed, updated coverage of the defacto interdomain routing protocol BGP and provides numerous, comprehensive configurations of BGP's attributes and various routing policies. A great resource for any organization that needs to build an efficient, reliable enterprise network accessing the Internet.

Cisco Router Configuration

Allan Leinwand, Bruce Pinsky, Mark Culpepper

1-57870-022-1 • AVAILABLE NOW

An example-oriented and chronological approach helps you implement and administer your internetworking devices. Starting with the configuration devices "out of the box;" this book moves to configuring Cisco IOS for the three most popular networking protocols today: TCP/IP, AppleTalk, and Novell Interwork Packet Exchange (IPX). You also learn basic administrative and management configuration, including access control with TACACS+ and RADIUS, network management with SNMP, logging of messages, and time control with NTP.

IP Routing Fundamentals

Mark A. Sportack

1-57870-071-x • AVAILABLE NOW

This comprehensive guide provides essential background information on routing in IP networks for network professionals who are deploying and maintaining LANs and WANs daily. Explore the mechanics of routers, routing protocols, network interfaces, and operating systems.

Hey, you've got enough worries.

Don't let IT training be one of them.

Get on the fast track to IT training at InformIT,
your total Information Technology training network.

 | **www.informit.com** |

■ Hundreds of timely articles on dozens of topics ■ Discounts on IT books from all our publishing partners, including Cisco Press ■ Free, unabridged books from the InformIT Free Library ■ "Expert Q&A"—our live, online chat with IT experts ■ Faster, easier certification and training from our Web- or classroom-based training programs ■ Current IT news ■ Software downloads ■ Career-enhancing resources

Cisco Press

Committed to being your long-term learning resource while you grow as a Cisco Networking Professional

Help Cisco Press **stay connected** to the issues and challenges you face on a daily basis by registering your product and filling out our brief survey. Complete and mail this form, or better yet ...

Register online and enter to win a **FREE** book!

Jump to **www.ciscopress.com/register** and register your product online. Each complete entry will be eligible for our monthly drawing to win a FREE book of the winner's choice from the Cisco Press library.

May we contact you via e-mail with information about **new releases, special promotions**, and **customer benefits**?

❐ Yes   ❐ No

E-mail address _____

Name _____

Address _____

City _____   State/Province _____

Country_____   Zip/Post code _____

Where did you buy this product?

❐ Bookstore   ❐ Computer store/Electronics store   ❐ Direct from Cisco Systems
❐ Online retailer   ❐ Direct from Cisco Press   ❐ Office supply store
❐ Mail order   ❐ Class/Seminar   ❐ Discount store
❐ Other_____

When did you buy this product? _____ **Month** _____ **Year**

What price did you pay for this product?

❐ Full retail price   ❐ Discounted price   ❐ Gift

Was this purchase reimbursed as a company expense?

❐ Yes   ❐ No

How did you learn about this product?

❐ Friend   ❐ Store personnel   ❐ In-store ad   ❐ cisco.com
❐ Cisco Press catalog   ❐ Postcard in the mail   ❐ Saw it on the shelf   ❐ ciscopress.com
❐ Other catalog   ❐ Magazine ad   ❐ Article or review
❐ School   ❐ Professional organization ❐ Used other products
❐ Other_____

What will this product be used for?

❐ Business use   ❐ School/Education
❐ Certification training   ❐ Professional development/Career growth
❐ Other_____

How many years have you been employed in a computer-related industry?

❐ less than 2 years   ❐ 2–5 years   ❐ more than 5 years

Have you purchased a Cisco Press product before?

❐ Yes   ❐ No

Cisco Press

How many computer technology books do you own?
❑ 1 ❑ 2–7 ❑ more than 7

Which best describes your job function? (check all that apply)
❑ Corporate Management ❑ Systems Engineering ❑ IS Management ❑ Cisco Networking
❑ Network Design ❑ Network Support ❑ Webmaster Academy Program
❑ Marketing/Sales ❑ Consultant ❑ Student Instuctor
❑ Professor/Teacher ❑ Other _____

Do you hold any computer certifications? (check all that apply)
❑ MCSE ❑ CCNA ❑ CCDA
❑ CCNP ❑ CCDP ❑ CCIE ❑ Other _____

Are you currently pursuing a certification? (check all that apply)
❑ MCSE ❑ CCNA ❑ CCDA
❑ CCNP ❑ CCDP ❑ CCIE ❑ Other _____

On what topics would you like to see more coverage?
_____
_____

Do you have any additional comments or suggestions?
_____
_____

Thank you for completing this survey and registration. Please fold here, seal, and mail to Cisco Press.

Cisco BGP-4 Command and Configuration Handbook (1-58705-017-X)

Cisco Press
Customer Registration—CP050227
P.O. Box #781046
Indianapolis, IN 46278-8046

ciscopress.com
Indianapolis, IN 46290
201 West 103rd Street
Cisco Press

CISCO SYSTEMS

CISCO SYSTEMS/PACKET MAGAZINE
ATTN: C. Glover
170 West Tasman, Mailstop SJ8-2
San Jose, CA 95134-1706

Place
Stamp
Here

☐ YES! I'm requesting a **free** subscription to *Packet*™ magazine.

☐ No. I'm not interested at this time.

☐ Mr.
☐ Ms.

First Name (Please Print) _____ Last Name _____

Title/Position (Required) _____

Company (Required) _____

Address _____

City _____ State/Province _____

Zip/Postal Code _____ Country _____

Telephone (Include country and area codes) _____ Fax _____

E-mail _____

Signature (Required) _____ Date _____

☐ I would like to receive additional information on Cisco's services and products by e-mail.

1. Do you or your company:
   - A ☐ Use Cisco products
   - B ☐ Resell Cisco products
   - C ☐ Both
   - D ☐ Neither

2. Your organization's relationship to Cisco Systems:
   - A ☐ Customer/End User
   - B ☐ Prospective Customer
   - C ☐ Cisco Reseller
   - D ☐ Cisco Distributor
   - E ☐ Integrator
   - F ☐ Non-Authorized Reseller
   - G ☐ Cisco Training Partner
   - I ☐ Cisco OEM
   - J ☐ Consultant
   - K ☐ Other (specify): _____

3. How many people does your entire company employ?
   - A ☐ More than 10,000
   - B ☐ 5,000 to 9,999
   - C ☐ 1,000 to 4,999
   - D ☐ 500 to 999
   - E ☐ 250 to 499
   - F ☐ 100 to 249
   - G ☐ Fewer than 100

4. Is your company a Service Provider?
   - A ☐ Yes
   - B ☐ No

5. Your involvement in network equipment purchases:
   - A ☐ Recommend
   - B ☐ Approve
   - C ☐ Neither

6. Your personal involvement in networking:
   - A ☐ Entire enterprise at all sites
   - B ☐ Departments or network segments at more than one site
   - C ☐ Single department or network segment
   - F ☐ Public network
   - D ☐ No involvement
   - E ☐ Other (specify): _____

7. Your Industry:
   - A ☐ Aerospace
   - B ☐ Agriculture/Mining/Construction
   - C ☐ Banking/Finance
   - D ☐ Chemical/Pharmaceutical
   - E ☐ Consultant
   - F ☐ Computer/Systems/Electronics
   - G ☐ Education (K–12)
   - U ☐ Education (College/Univ.)
   - H ☐ Government—Federal
   - I ☐ Government—State
   - J ☐ Government—Local
   - K ☐ Health Care
   - L ☐ Telecommunications
   - M ☐ Utilities/Transportation
   - N ☐ Other (specify): _____

CPRESS

PACKET

PACKET

Packet magazine serves as the premier publication linking customers to Cisco Systems, Inc. Delivering complete coverage of cutting-edge networking trends and innovations, *Packet* is a magazine for technical, hands-on users. It delivers industry-specific information for enterprise, service provider, and small and midsized business market segments. A toolchest for planners and decision makers, *Packet* contains a vast array of practical information, boasting sample configurations, real-life customer examples, and tips on getting the most from your Cisco Systems' investments. Simply put, *Packet* magazine is straight talk straight from the worldwide leader in networking for the Internet, Cisco Systems, Inc.

We hope you'll take advantage of this useful resource. I look forward to hearing from you!

Cecelia Glover
Packet Circulation Manager
packet@external.cisco.com
www.cisco.com/go/packet